D1599121

# The Odyssey of A Southerner

## The Life and Times of Gustavus Woodson Smith

Gustavus Woodson Smith, USMA West Point
*Special Collections Division, United States Military
Academy at West Point*

# The Odyssey of A Southerner

## The Life and Times of
## Gustavus Woodson Smith

Leonne M. Hudson

Mercer University Press
Macon, Georgia
1998

ISBN 0-86554-589-5
MUP/H442


© 1998
All rights reserved
Mercer University Press
6316 Peake Road
Macon, Georgia 31210-3960


10 9 8 7 6 5 4 3 2 1

Book Design by Marc A. Jolley
Jacket design by Mary Frances Burt

*Library of Congress Cataloging-in-Publication Data*
Hudson, Leonne M.
The odyssey of a southerner: the life and times of Gustavus Woodson
Smith / Leonne M. Hudson
p. cm.
Includes bibliographical references and index.
ISBN 0-86554-589-5 (alk. paper)
1. Smith, Gustavus Woodson, 1822-1896. 2. Generals — Confederate
States of America — Biography. 3. Confederate States of America.
Army — Biography. 4. United States — History — Civil War, 1861-1865.
Army — Biography. 5. Military engineers — Southern States — Biography.
6. Georgetown (Ky) — Biography. 7. New York (N.Y.) — Biography. I.
Title.
E467.1S7H83 1998
973.7′13′092 — dc21
98-12686
[B] CIP

# Table of Contents

To Cassandra

# Acknowledgments

In the process of recreating the life of Gustavus Woodson Smith, I have incurred many debts of gratitude. The writing of a book is a major undertaking which requires the help of many individuals. I am grateful for the assistance of archivists, librarians, and researchers in various parts of the United States. This project would not have been possible without the help and cooperation of the following institutions:

The National Archives, Washington, D.C.; Courtesy of the New-York Historical Society, New York City; Virginia Historical Society, Richmond, Virginia; Special Collections Division, United States Military Academy, West Point, New York; William L. Clements Library, the University of Michigan, Ann Arbor, Michigan; Georgia Department of Archives and History, Atlanta, Georgia; Rare Book and Manuscript Library, Columbia University, New York City; Mississippi Department of Archives and History, Jackson, Mississippi; South Caroliniana Library, University of South Carolina, Columbia, South Carolina; Courtesy of the Jefferson Davis Papers, Louisiana Historical Association Collection, Manuscripts Department, Tulane University, New Orleans, Louisiana; Hargrett Rare Book and Manuscript Library, University of Georgia Libraries, Athens, Georgia; Southern Historical Collection, University of North Carolina, Chapel Hill, North Carolina; Special Collections and Archives, Margaret I. King Library, University of Kentucky, Lexington, Kentucky; William R. Perkins Library, Duke University, Durham, North Carolina; Kent State University Libraries, Kent, Ohio; Permission of the Haughton Library, Harvard University, Cambridge, Massachusetts; Surrogate's Court, County of New York, New York City; The Western Reserve Historical Society, Cleveland, Ohio; United States Army Military History Institute, Carlisle Barracks, Pennsylvania; South Carolina Historical Society, Charleston, South Carolina; North Carolina Department of Archives and History, Raleigh, North Carolina; and the Kentucky Department for Libraries and Archives, Frankfort, Kentucky.

I would like to thank the *South Carolina Historical Magazine* and the *Confederate Veteran Magazine* for permission to use portions of my articles that appeared in these journals. I thank the Western Reserve Historical Society and the United States Military Academy for permission to reproduce photographs of Gustavus Woodson Smith. I wish to extend thanks to my colleagues Professors Frank L. Byrne (emeritus) and John T. Hubbell of Kent State University for their advice and particularly their insightful criticism of the manuscript at various stages of its completion. I owe a debt of gratitude to Nancy Birk, University Archivist of Kent State University for preparing the index. A word of appreciation to Judith Bosau-Allen, a doctoral student in history at the University of Akron for proofreading the manuscript. I am indebted to Noel A. Simms, University Graphic Designer of Kent State University for assisting me in the preparation of the maps. I would also like to thank my family and friends, and especially my wife Cassandra E. August and my son Evan John Hudson for their faithful support, inspiration, and understanding as I labored on this project day after day.

# Illustrations

Frontispiece: Gustavus Woodson Smith (*Special Collections Division, United States Military Academy at West Point*).

p. x: Gustavus Woodson Smith (*Western Reserve Historical Society*).

p. xi: Map 1. The route of General Scott's army in 1846 and 1847 during the Mexican War.

p. 82: Map 2. Positions between Norfolk and Richmond including the location of Seven Pines.

p. 130: Map 3. General Foster's march from New Bern to Goldsboro in 1862.

p. 160: Map 4. Positions on the Western and Atlantic Railroad from Dalton to Atlanta.

p. 172: Map 5. Positions on the Charleston and Savannah Railroad including the location of Honey Hill.

Gustavus W. Smith
*Western Reserve Historical Society*
Cleveland, Ohio

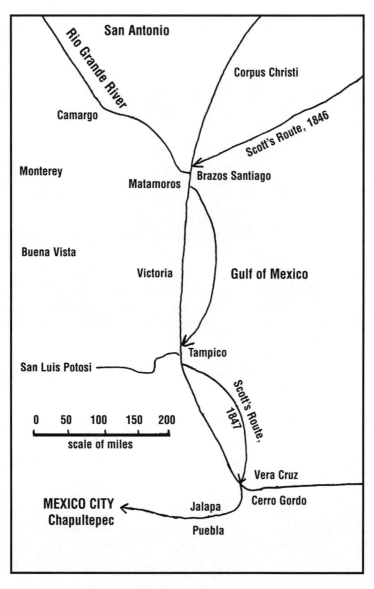

Map 1. The route of General Scott's army in 1846 and 1847 during the Mexican War.

# CHAPTER ONE

# From Elkhorn Stream to the Hudson River

The seventy-four years that Gustavus Woodson Smith lived from 1822-1896, was a time of change in America. The nation was expanding in size, increasing in population, and growing in strength. Each decade presented not only hope and optimism but difficulties as well. Although, Smith's life intersected several important events during the nineteenth century, he is best known for his participation in the Civil War. A turning point in Smith's life was his enrollment in the United States Military Academy in 1838. There he established an exemplary academic record which earned him a commission in the elite Engineer Corps upon graduation. The value of Smith's West Point education was evident during the siege of Vera Cruz. He reconnoitered the enemy's works and constructed the batteries that reduced that seaport town on the Gulf. The Military Academy had given Smith a chance to become an engineer; and the Mexican War an opportunity to prove his mettle under fire. Smith's admirable war record combined with his personal contacts with friends and associates were significant factors in advancing his career. Smith's experience in military engineering would serve him well in civilian businesses during the antebellum and post Civil War years.

Smith possessed an indomitable will and held tenaciously to his beliefs as illustrated by his profound commitment to the filibustering movement during the pre-Civil War years. Smith believed that Cuba should be under the hegemony of Southern planters. During the mid-1850s, he served as the construction engineer for the extension of the treasury building in Washington. And later as the superintendent for the construction of the new marine hospital at New Orleans. While employed at the Cooper and Hewitt Company an ironworks in Trenton,

New Jersey, Smith met prominent politicians who nurtured his growth in the Democratic party. His political connections resulted in his appointment as the New York City Street Commissioner in 1858 where he established an outstanding record of curbing corruption. The portentous question of the territorial expansion of slavery did not escape Smith's attention during his stay in New York.

The focal point of this biography is a critical analysis of Smith's wartime career. He joined the Confederacy at the rank of Major General in September 1861, and was made second in command of the Confederate Army of the Potomac.* His elevation from private life to such a prestigious rank and position seemed paradoxical. Doubtless, Smith's fine record in the Mexican War had won him high rank in the Rebel army in which he was unable to satisfy his superiors in Richmond. Because of frequent illness and an inability to handle large armies, Smith's performance did not match his reputation. The outcome of Smith's appointment showed the fallacy of the frequent claim that the Confederate government gained a significant advantage by attracting so many West Pointers and experienced officers.

General Smith's internecine squabbles with Jefferson Davis over rank and other issues contributed to his becoming one of the more controversial of Confederate officers. Nonetheless, he was briefly Acting Secretary of War in 1862. Smith was involved in several significant operations including Seven Pines, a lost opportunity for a Confederate victory. He also saw action at the battles of Atlanta, Goldsboro, Honey Hill, and Savannah. Davis' refusal to promote Smith to the rank of Lieutenant General caused the Kentuckian to resign his military commission in the winter of 1863. Upon leaving the Confederate army Smith traveled to Charleston, and then to Georgia where Governor Joseph E. Brown appointed him to command the state militia. The Georgia militia provided valuable service to the Army of Tennessee, confirming that Smith was more effective at handling small units.

The postwar years found Smith in the familiar setting of industrial management in Tennessee. After his tenure as general manager of the Southwestern Iron Works at Chattanooga, he became the Insurance

---

* Later, this army is renamed the Army of Northern Virginia when Jefferson Davis asks Robert E. Lee to take over after Seven Pines, where Joseph Johnston is wounded and Gustavus Woodson Smith, next in command, fails to gain Davis's confidence.

Commissioner of Kentucky in 1870. Spending his last twenty years in New York City, Smith devoted much of his time to the writing of articles and historical books, including his memoirs. He was notable in many circles, held important positions in several states, and touched many aspects of American life. He was an active participant in politics, the military, academia, filibustering, business, and industry.

This biography, the first book-length work on Smith places him as a leading participant during those tumultuous times of the nineteenth century. Smith's multifaceted life, replete with successes and failures, serves as an example of one man's roles, illuminated against the backdrop of our most controversial historical period.

≈

Gustavus Woodson Smith, the son of Byrd and Sarah Hatcher Woodson Smith,[1] could proudly trace his genealogy through many generations to England from which his ancestors had emigrated to North America. On his maternal side, Gustavus was a descendant of John Woodson of Devonshire, England who came to America with his wife Sarah in 1619 aboard the ship "George".[2] In April of that year, the thirty-three year old Woodson and his wife disembarked at the Jamestown settlement in the Virginia Colony. The Woodsons were men of outstanding reputations, many of whom had achieved impressive records in the legal, military, and medical professions. The traditions of high attainment and distinction continued with John Woodson. The Virginia Company sent Woodson to Jamestown because of his proficiency as a surgeon. Woodson's primary responsibility was to the British soldiers who were there to provide protection to the colonists from Indian attacks.[3] There in the wilderness, the surgeon tended the sick of whom there were many, and mourned the passing of those who were quietly lifted from his care by the hands of death.

In addition to the harsh conditions of the wilderness, the colonists were also fearful of being attacked by neighboring Indians, who deeply resented the intrusion of white men into their territory. On April 14, 1644, the Indians under the leadership of Chief Opechankano, assayed a surprise and deadly attack upon Jamestown. Before they were repulsed, more than 300 of the settlers had been killed. Among the dead was John Woodson, the progenitor of the name in America, who was killed in sight of his home while returning from visiting the sick. What happened to Sarah after the death of her husband in the April massacre is unknown.[4]

On the paternal side, Gustavus W. Smith also could trace his lineage to Europe. His grandfather John Smith, who was of English ancestry, was born in Halifax County, Virginia, in June 1764. In 1785 at the age of twenty-one, he married a local girl named Mary Byrd. After their marriage, the Smiths crossed the Appalachian mountains when it was still Indian country and settled in Scott County in what was later the state of Kentucky.[5] The Smiths raised a log cabin in Georgetown, the county seat of Scott, and settled down to a life of farming and the rearing of a family that soon included several children. Mary died in April 1794, leaving behind her husband of less than ten years and five young children. Shortly after the death of Mary, John visited Botetourt County, Virginia, and returned to Georgetown with his new bride, Anna. For reasons unknown, John moved the family to Arkansas in 1808. His son Byrd, who was eighteen at the time refused to relocate with the family because of his dislike for his stepmother. Smith's grandfather died at Little Rock in 1821 at the age of fifty-seven.

Gustavus' father, Byrd Smith, was born in Georgetown, Kentucky, in May 1790. Byrd who was the third oldest child, witnessed the death of his mother for whom he was named when he was but four years old. Following his undistinguished tour of duty in the War of 1812, he returned to Georgetown to pursue his trade as a tanner, which he continued for many years. Though the tannery was his main trade, he was also a farmer. In June 1818, Byrd visited Cumberland, Virginia, and brought back his bride, Sarah Hatcher Woodson. Byrd Smith had some education and was active in the political life of Georgetown.[6] He was a product of the frontier; rough in manners, calculating in thought, and reserved in demeanor. He cherished individualism and honesty. His wife Sarah was a Woodson and she extolled the virtues that had been a trademark of the Woodson family for many generations. She was frugal, industrious, intelligent, and conscientious. The Woodson women were gracious, God-fearing, and unbending in their fidelity.[7]

Byrd and Sarah adjusted to life on the frontier. Georgetown, when first settled in 1775, was called McClelland's Station, but was renamed in 1790 by the Virginia legislature to honor the nation's first president.[8] Originally, Scott was a part of Woodward County, but it became a separate jurisdiction in 1792, the same year that Kentucky entered the Union as the fifteenth state. Located in the famous Blue Grass Region of Kentucky near Elkhorn Stream,[9] Georgetown was situated twelve miles north of Lexington, seventeen miles east of Frankfort, and sixty-six miles south of Cincinnati.[10] In spite of its proximity to Lexington and Frankfort, Georgetown flourished as a manufacturing center of light industries such as flour, whiskey, and guns. Georgetownians were proud that the first bourbon whiskey made in Kentucky was distilled there in 1789. Georgetown also had the distinction of being home to the first paper mill built in the state. Because of the abundance of game and the excellent soil, this country was known as the "Eden of the Red Man".[11] The victory at Fallen Timbers in 1794 ended any threat from Indians north of the Ohio River.

Gustavus W. Smith was born in Georgetown on January 1, 1822. He was reared in a family whose puritanical virtues of hard-work, thrift, and morality were the guiding forces. His parents were ardent supporters of the Baptist church that was organized in Georgetown in 1811. There was nothing outstanding about Smith's boyhood. He did most of the things that boys of Georgetown did in those days such as farm work, fishing, and hunting. Smith received his early education from the local schools of Scott County.[12] Prior to the act of the Kentucky legislature in 1821, little attention was paid to the school houses.[13] This act not only provided for the amelioration of the physical condition of the schools, but sought an improvement in the curriculum as well. Latin, Greek, and science became standard courses in the curriculum of some of the schools. A solid academic background would help those seeking admission to the United States Military Academy. As Smith approached the end of his school years the possibility of attending the Academy seemed more realistic.

When President Thomas Jefferson signed a bill in March 1802, West Point as a national institution became a reality. The fundamental purpose of the Academy was to transform civilians into soldiers. The creation of the Military Academy represented Jefferson's idea of American democracy in which deserving young men of the masses could be trained free of charge in exchange for a tour of duty in the regular army.[14] West Point during the antebellum years was a small and intimate Academy where cadets from across the United States matriculated on equal terms irrespective of social or economic differences. Because of the many reform measures initiated by Superintendent Sylvanus Thayer, he was commonly referred to as the father of the Military Academy.[15] He expanded the curriculum placing greater emphasis on science, mathematics, and engineering. It was under Thayer's leadership that West Point earned its reputation for producing first-rate engineers. Thayer's penchant for order and discipline left a lasting impression on the military college. Perhaps his most outstanding reform was the introduction of the order of merit ranking of the Academy.[16]

The schools of Scott County had prepared Smith as well as could be expected for a West Point career. Those Virginians who had helped to settle Scott were of the better class of citizens. Since schools were established in parts of Virginia, it was not surprising that they would take the lead in fostering education in Kentucky.[17] By attending secondary school, Smith had fulfilled an important prerequisite in his quest for a place at the Academy. The advantages of receiving a West Point education were many. To gain admission to the military college was difficult because of the limited number of vacancies available there each year. West Point also had an outstanding reputation as an institution of high academic quality. Furthermore, to serve the nation in the army was a prestigious profession. In terms of academic programs, it was comparable with other colleges and universities in the United States at that time. West Point was in fact the first engineering school in the nation. The Academy's greatest strength was its engineering curriculum and for its time, no better general engineering training was available in the nation. A degree from the Military Academy also would guarantee a lucrative salary upon graduation.[18] The fact that Gustavus' father had fought in the War of 1812 to help the United States maintain its independence from Great Britain was not lost on the young Smith. Smith's strict upbringing had suited him well for the regimented life that a military career demanded. He easily met the basic qualifications that required a candidate to be between the ages of sixteen and twenty-one. A candidate could not be afflicted with any disease or infirmity that would render him unfit for military service. The successful cadet had to be at least five feet in height and of good moral character. Candidates were required to demonstrate the ability to read, write, and perform basic mathematical functions accurately.[19]

Smith was elated when he received the political support of Richard

M. Johnson, Vice President to Martin Van Buren. Johnson was born in Louisville but relocated with his family to Bryant's Station near Lexington at a young age. He was known as a champion of education. While serving in the House of Representatives, Johnson introduced resolutions aimed at the establishment of military academies throughout the country. He was a founder and trustee of George Washington University.[20] The Democratic Vice President nominated Smith for an academy appointment on January 31, 1838. In his letter to War Secretary Joel A. Poinsett, Johnson wrote, "I give you the name of Gustavus Woodson Smith to fill the vacancy ... in my old congressional district."[21] It was the responsibility of the War Secretary to make selections to fill the several vacancies each year at the Academy. As prescribed by law, the nominee had to proffer a letter of acceptance or refusal to the War Secretary. Smith in his letter of April 12, 1838, stated, "I accept my conditional appointment as a cadet and I hope that in six months I shall prove myself worthy of a commission in the service of the United States."[22] In the spring of the year, Smith received instructions to report to summer camp. After several days' journey, he arrived at the Academy on the Hudson River and was assigned quarters. With pride and confidence, Smith entered West Point in June 1838 at the age of sixteen. Upon the completion of a series of physical and mental examinations, the appointees became full-fledged cadets. During the summer encampment, there was no academic instruction. With reveille at 5:30 a.m., the cadets were kept busy throughout the day with instruction in drilling, riding, fencing, and infantry tactics. Their introduction to military life also included instruction in arms, standing guard, and academy regulations. The cadets were prohibited from using alcohol, tobacco, or visiting taverns. Card-playing, fighting, and the wearing of mustaches were also forbidden. Obviously, life at the Military Academy was governed by the strict enforcement of regulations. One such stipulation was the required attendance of cadets at chapel services on Sundays. Although attending church was mandatory, there was no evidence that Smith was a religious enthusiast.

Life for the aspiring soldiers was not easy at the Academy. Their physical and mental endurance was tested daily under the watchful eyes of their instructors. The small classes allowed the cadets to receive personal attention and supervision. The transition from civilian to military life was difficult as evidenced by the frequency with which demerits were issued. Regimentation commenced as soon as the cadets arrived at the West Point campus. Their first order of business was to confirm their identity at the adjutant's office, and then deposit their money with the treasurer. Next, the cadet or plebe reported to the quartermaster to obtain furniture and other supplies for his room. Overcrowding, poor ventilation, and unregulated temperature made the barracks uncomfortable. The cadets could escape from the rigors of the Academy by swimming in the Hudson River, hiking through the nearby hills, or engaging in sports. The only holidays of the academic year were Christmas and New Year's Day. Students who were fortunate enough to live near the Academy could go home during the holidays. However, most cadets lived too far away to take advantage of this luxury.[23] Smith eagerly awaited the beginning of his academic studies at West Point. In appearance, Smith was impressive in his gray uniform. Tall and muscularly built, his physical strength had been developed through hard work, a characteristic not unfamiliar to one of frontier heritage. His broad shoulders were suggestive of strength and stamina.

As Smith entered the Academy, the graduating class of 1838 saw the departure of cadets William J. Hardee, Irvin McDowell, and Pierre G. T. Beauregard, all of whom were to distinguish themselves during the Civil War. Smith's enrollment at West Point came at a critical time. The Academy had just survived an attempt by Congress to close it down.[24] Critics of the military training institution pointed to the resignations of some of the men during the 1830s as evidence of disloyalty. Congress responded by passing a law in July of 1838, which stipulated that the cadet had to serve four years in the military upon graduation.[25] Among others who matriculated with Smith in the class of 1842 were James Longstreet, William S. Rosecrans, Mansfield Lovell, Alexander P. Stewart, John Pope, Abner Doubleday, Earl Van Dorn, Lafayette McLaws, Robert M. Anderson, and Daniel Harvey Hill. These young cadets were destined to make names for themselves during the Civil War.[26] A total of 112 were admitted to West Point in June 1838, but the demanding work that lay ahead caused many of them to leave. Smith, however, adjusted easily to cadet life and made several friends at the Academy. From the beginning, Smith enthusiastically embraced his studies at West Point. He distinguished himself as a serious and hard-working cadet, judiciously budgeting his time to allow adequate concentration on his courses. He settled down to an array of subjects such as mathematics, French, tactics, natural philosophy, and artillery. Smith knew that failure to perform would result in a recommendation from the Academic Board for dismissal. The Board was vitally important to the academic bureaucracy of West Point. Comprised of faculty members, it established curriculum guidelines, evaluated the cadets, and gave the Superintendent advice on academic matters. The results of the general examination of cadets in June 1839 revealed that after his first year, Smith ranked sixth with his strongest subject being mathematics. Smith had also accumulated sixty demerits during his first year.[27] These demerits resulted from minor transgressions, not serious infractions. However, shortly after Smith's arrival at the Academy, he along with cadets Napoleon Buford, John Newton, and Theodore S. Laidley, were arrested for going to Meads Landing without authorization.[28] They received extra guard duty as punishment for their offense.

At the end of his second year, the official report of his conduct and standing at the Academy ranked Smith third in mathematics, twelfth in French, and thirty-seventh in drawing, a subject he was unable to grasp with skill.[29] Smith ranked sixth and twelfth in 1840 and 1841, respectively. The conduct roll indicated that in general, Smith was well-behaved and usually stayed clear of trouble. On several occasions during his stay at West Point, he was recognized as a distinguished cadet for correct deportment. While in his third year, however, Smith was sentenced to extra guard duty for disrespectful conduct to one of his instructors.[30] As graduation approached, it was obvious that Smith would rank in the upper echelon of his class. The Corps of Engineers was particularly attractive to superior graduating cadets who had the choice of selecting their branch of service.

The merit roll in June 1842, one month prior to graduation disclosed the final standing of Smith's class. Although there was no commencement convocation, July 1, 1842, was a happy day for the fifty-six men who graduated. The only official acknowledgments that the cadets had finished their course of study were a congratulatory sermon in honor of the cadets and publication of an order terminating them from further duty at the Academy. The inaugural commencement was held in 1853. From this time forward, commencement was celebrated yearly with speeches, music, and the presentation of diplomas.[31] Handsomely dressed in their uniforms, the class of 1842 would earn the reputation as one of the most distinguished classes in the history of the United States Military Academy. In fact, fourteen graduates of that class would eventually reach the rank of general.[32] Rosecrans graduated fifth, Smith eighth, Lovell ninth, Van Dorn fifty-second, and Longstreet fifty-fourth.[33] The top graduate was cadet Henry L. Eustis of Massachusetts who would in 1849 chair the first engineering department of Harvard University.[34]

The standard of study and discipline at West Point had further sharpened Smith's leadership abilities and character. Smith's years there had not only developed his intellectual capacity but his body as well. The body had been trained to endure the physical demands of service and the mind to think logically and analytically. His talents for both military and civil pursuits became apparent at West Point. Officers graduating from the Military Academy were fully capable of superintending the construction of fortifications for the defense of the nation's maritime frontier. They also had the capacity to extend beyond military pursuits and embrace the construction of public buildings, railroads, canals, and bridges as civil engineers.[35] Those cadets graduating at the top of their class were recommended for promotion into the much coveted United States Army Corps of Engineers with the charge of fortifying rivers and harbors. Those of lower rank were relegated to serve in the infantry, artillery, or cavalry with duties at various army stations throughout the country.[36] Smith's fine academic record secured him a place in the elite corps of engineers after West Point. When he received his commission as Lieutenant in July 1842, his ambition had turned into achievement. Smith would now become a soldier in active service for the United States. The young engineer officer treasured his West Point experience and looked forward to the new challenges that lay ahead.

Smith's first duty was in the port town of New London located in the southeastern section of Connecticut. At the time of his appointment, the sectional discord between the North and South manifested itself almost exclusively around the issue of slavery. Smith, while on furlough in 1840 told his family in no uncertain terms that the two sections would clash over the issue of slavery within twenty years. He reached this conclusion based on his observation of the North's opposition to the peculiar institution and the South's strong attachment to it. Smith's prediction would become a painful reality in less than twenty-one years and he would find himself as a major participant in the Civil War.[37] Abolitionism had reached full stride, and the public was made aware of the evil nature of chattel slavery. By the early 1840s the Industrial Revolution was changing the Northern way of life. New towns were springing up around factories and the developing transportation system of roads, canals, and railroads was connecting rural America with larger cities. The United States was rapidly becoming an industrialized nation. During the mid-1840s with the expansionist James K. Polk in the White House, the United States initiated an aggressive campaign of annexation based on the ideology of Manifest Destiny. This doctrine was the belief that America was "divinely" inspired to expand its boundaries from coast to coast, not for selfish motives but as an altruistic attempt to spread American culture, traditions, and institutions.

Situated on the Thames River which was a tributary of Long Island Sound, New London was forty-two miles southeast of Hartford and fifty-three miles east of New Haven. Beautiful homes and elegant buildings were scattered throughout the town. New London's life blood was its harbor which facilitated the development of a maritime economy. The town was defended by two forts, Trumbull and Griswold. Fort Griswold was located on the east side of the Thames in the village of Groton.[38] Smith served as the assistant engineer in the construction of Fort Trumbull from 1842-44. The twenty-year old Smith could now put into practice what he had learned at the Academy. Fort Trumbull was situated on a strip of land extending into the Thames River that flowed through the center of town. During the Revolutionary War, Fort Trumbull defended the port of entry at New London. At that time it was the only fortification in the state of Connecticut. Because of many years of neglect, the old revolutionary fortress was in desperate need of repair. It was demolished about 1840 and rebuilt from the ground up under the supervision of Captain George W. Cullum of the United States engineers. This massive fort, completed in 1849, was the pride of New London.[39]

Soon after arriving at New London, Smith met Lucretia Bassett, the woman who was to become his wife. She was the daughter of sea captain Abner Bassett, who had relocated to New London from Savannah in the early 1830s. Smith and Lucretia were married in

October 1844.[40] Smith's work at New London came to an end with a vacancy on the West Point faculty. Colonel Joseph G. Totten, chief engineer of the United States, appointed Smith an assistant professor of engineering at the college beginning in the fall of 1844. To teach at the Military Academy was a prestigious assignment. In addition to intellectual ability the West Point faculty were expected to be loyal, enthusiastic, and resourceful.

# Notes

1. Jon L. Wakelyn, *Biographical Dictionary of the Confederacy* (Westport and London: Greenwood Press, 1977) 299.

2. Henry Morton Woodson, *Historical Genealogy of the Woodsons and Their Connections* (Columbia: E. W. Stephens Publishing Co., 1915) 11.

3. Ibid., 21.

4. Ibid., 22.

5. *Encylopaedia of Contemporary Biography of New York*, 11 vols. (New York: Atlantic Publishing and Engraving Co., 1882), vol. 2, p. 58.

6. *Twenty-Eighth Annual Reunion of the Association of the United States Military Academy at West Point, New York* (Saginaw: Seeman and Peters, Printers and Binders, 1897) 13.

7. Woodson, *Historical Genealogy*, 16.

8. David C. Roller and Robert W. Twyman, eds., *The Encylopedia of Southern History* (Baton Rouge: Louisiana State University Press, 1979) 518.

9. William Henry Perrin, ed., *History of Bourbon, Scott, Harrison, and Nicholas Counties of Kentucky* (Chicago: O. L. Baskin and Company, Historical Publishers, 1882) 180.

10. B. O. Gaines, *The B. O. Gaines History of Scott County*, 2 vols. (Georgetown: Frye Printing Co., 1957) 1:234. Nearly all the records of Scott County were destroyed by fire when the Court House burned in 1837 and again in 1876.

11. Ibid., 76.

12. *The National Cyclopaedia of American Biography*, 63 vols. (New York: James T. White and Company, 1944) 7:515.

13. Gaines, *The B. O. Gaines History*, 1:130-131.

14. James L. Morrison, Jr., *The Best School in the World: West Point, the Pre-Civil War Years, 1833-1866* (Kent: Kent State University Press, 1986) 2.

15. *New York Times*, February 22, 1860. Thayer served as Superintendent of West Point for sixteen years from 1817-1833.

16. Morrison, *The Best School in the World*, 23-24.

17. Perrin, *History*, 160.

18. Sidney Forman, *West Point: A History of the United States Military Academy* (New York: Columbia University Press, 1950) 85.

19. RG94: Qualifications for Admission to the United States Military Academy. Letters Received. Records of the Adjutant General's Office, National Archives, Washington.

20. Allen Jones and Dumas Malone, *Dictionary of American Biography* (New York: Charles Scribner's Sons, 1933) 10:114-16.

21. RG688: Richard M. Johnson to Joel A. Poinsett, January 31, 1838. United States Military Academy Cadet Application Papers, 1805-1866, National Archives, Washington.

22. Ibid., Gustavus to Poinsett, April 12, 1838. United States Military Academy Cadet Application Papers, 1805-1866, National Archives, Washington. Because of the limited number of vacancies designated to Kentucky in 1838, only 13, Gustavus was actually appointed as an at-large cadet.

23. Morrison, *The Best School in the World*, 64-77.

24. Robert G. Hartje, *Van Dorn: The Life and Times of a Confederate General* (Nashville: Vanderbilt University Press, 1967) 9.

25. Forman, *West Point*, 66.

26. William A. Courtenay, "The Coast Defense of South Carolina, 1861-5: The Battle of Honey Hill," *Southern Historical Society Papers* 26 (January-December 1898): 79.

27. Merit Roll of the Cadets of the United States Military Academy Showing the Results of the General Examination, June 1839, National Archives, Washington.

28. Records of the Office of the Adjutant General: Monthly Consolidation of the Weekly Class Report Including the Conduct Roll of the Cadets of the United States Military Academy for September 1838, National Archives, Washington.

29. Merit Roll of the Results of the United States Military Academy Showing the Results of the General Examination, June 1840, National Archives, Washington.

30. Records of the Office of the Adjutant General: United States Military Academy Weekly Class Reports, January 1835 December 1841, National Archives, Washington.

31. Morrison, *The Best School in the World*, 110, 122.

32. Hartje, *Van Dorn*, 15.

33. Merit Roll of the Cadets of the United States Military Academy Showing the Results of the General Examinations, June 1842, National Archives, Washington.

34. Forman, *West Point*, 89.

35. Ibid., 75.

36. Ellsworth Eliot, Jr., *West Point in the Confederacy* (New York: G. A. Baker and Co., Inc., 1941) 22.

37. *Twenty-Eighth Annual Reunion*, 13.

38. John W. Barber, *Connecticut Historical Collections* (New Haven: Durrie, Peck, and Barber, 1836) 272-273.

39. Frances M. Caulkins, *History of New London, Connecticut* (New London: Published by the Author, 1852) 652-653.

40. Wakelyn, *Biographical Dictionary of the Confederacy*, 299.

# CHAPTER TWO

# At War in a Foreign Country

The 1840s, a decade of American expansionism saw Texas come into the Union as the twenty-eighth state. Washington promptly dismissed the warnings coming out of Mexico City that the annexation of Texas would produce war. The Mexican government had never recognized the independence of Texas. With the annexation complete, the United States then had the obligation of protecting this large state against foreign attacks. Prior to the start of the Mexican War, the United States had enjoyed more than thirty years of continual peace.

The start of the war between the United States and Mexico found Smith at West Point. As Smith stood at the threshold of engineering prominence, the years of study at the Military Academy and his work at New London had broadened his knowledge and sharpened his skills. Smith was ready to accept the challenge that history was about to force upon him as the curtain lifted on the stage of the Mexican War. This conflict would provide the young engineer officer with an opportunity to practice his chosen profession and thereby attract the attention of his army's chief.

Before the outbreak of hostilities, Colonel Totten had tried on several occasions to persuade Congress to pass legislation to authorize the enlistment of a company of engineer soldiers. Totten of Connecticut, who graduated from West Point in 1805, had achieved fame as an engineer officer in the War of 1812. Totten's promotion to the rank of Colonel and his appointment as chief engineer of the United States Army occurred in December 1838. When General Winfield Scott began his invasion of Mexico, he took Totten with him as a member of his inner circle.[1]

Totten finally succeeded in winning the establishment of a new unit of engineers. Congress had sent Captain Alexander J. Swift, an 1830 graduate of West Point, to the school at Metz in France for additional engineer training. Following the completion of his study at the French school, Swift returned to the Military Academy where Totten had won an opportunity to put his training to use. On May 15, less than a week after the start of the Mexican War, Congress passed an act that authorized the formation of a company of engineer soldiers.[2] Undoubtedly, the conflict with Mexico had convinced the lawmakers of the importance of forming such a company.

The act called for the enlistment of one hundred men into an engineer company as part of the regular army. Captain Swift assumed command of the company. On August 11, Colonel Totten relieved Smith from his professorship at West Point and assigned him to the company of engineer soldiers as the second ranking officer.[3] Smith instructed the company as an infantry command, for which duty his teaching experience would doubtless be helpful. While at the Military Academy, George B. McClellan appreciated the personal interest Smith had taken in him and gladly accepted invitations to visit Smith at his home. McClellan remembered Smith as the "kindest friend" he had at "the Point."[4] Upon the recommendation of Smith, Totten designated McClellan as the third officer in command of the engineer company. Smith, who had taught McClellan during his last year at West Point, had knowledge of the officer's character, aptitude, and skills at soldiering. McClellan, who had recently graduated second in his class was excited about his appointment because it would provide him with an opportunity to achieve fame on the battlefield. A cordial and cooperative spirit existed among the leadership of the new company. Smith rhapsodized, "no three officers of a company of soldiers ever worked together with less friction … there was [sic] no jars—no doubts or cross purposes—and no conflict of opinion or of action."[5] A Negro named Songo accompanied Smith and McClellan to Mexico to assist them in the capacity of a servant.

In September 1846, Company A of the Corps of Engineers, sailed from the Military Academy for Brazos Santiago, near the mouth of the Rio Grande. Strong winds and filthy water made camp life there miserable. McClellan called Brazos Santiago "the worst port on the Texas coast."[6] President James K. Polk had deployed American soldiers into Texas to protect its boundary in the fall of 1845 under the command of Zachary B. Taylor. An important aspect of Taylor's leadership was that he afforded his subordinates opportunities for distinction during the Mexican War. In return, his soldiers catapulted him into national fame, and this was good enough to earn him a tenure in the White House as the twelfth president of the United States.[7]

Volunteers who had returned to the United States from the Rio Grande later gave vivid descriptions of the conditions there. According to a volunteer of the Third Regiment of Ohio, lizards and frogs covered the turbid Rio Grande River. In describing one of the more loathsome aspects of military life, the soldier wrote, "when you break a biscuit, you can see it move if the critters are not dead from eating the bad flour."[8] Camp life was filled with long days and dreary nights. The impatient soldiers toiled in the heat and drilled amidst snakes. The morning sun was a welcome relief from the discomfort of sleeping on wet blankets. The harsh conditions of camp prepared the soldiers for the ordeals of the long and bitter campaign that lay ahead.[9]

From West Point, families watched in agony as their loved ones departed for Mexico. Illness, which was common among the troops, had reduced the engineer company to about seventy-five men. McClellan voiced the sentiments of many engineer soldiers when he said, "if the Lord and Santa Anna will only condescend to give us a chance to fight—I'll be the most confoundly mistaken if we don't thrash them some."[10] Both officers and men realized that promotions came slowly during peace time. They saw in the Mexican War a chance for rapid advancement and opportunities to enhance their reputations and military careers. The engineers were motivated by a desire to practice their profession in the heat of battle. The true value of their training would be determined on the battlefield.[11] The conflict with Mexico was the first major military test for the graduates of West Point.

The engineer company arrived at the town of Camargo in early November 1846, via the Rio Grande. The disgraceful behavior of the volunteer troops there was a topic of discussion among the soldiers of Company A. George Gordon Meade noted that "they are always drunk, and are in a measure irresponsible for their conduct. They rob and steal the cattle and corn of the poor farmers ...."[12] Both officers and enlisted men complained about the monotony of camp life brought on by long periods of inactivity. While at Camargo, Smith kept his troops busy practicing drills. Meanwhile, large quantities of supplies arrived in preparation for the march to the interior, and General Taylor reorganized his army into two divisions. The first division was commanded by General David E. Twiggs and the second by General William J. Worth. From Camargo, the engineer company marched to Matamoros, reaching that place in December. The engineer company suffered heavily from diseases. And when the army marched out of Matamoros, several men of Company A including Captain Swift were left there to recover.

Before the army left Matamoros for Victoria and Tampico, Smith discovered that the cook of the company was disobedient and clumsy. Smith marched the impudent recruit into the dense forest a few hundred yards from camp and informed him that he had brought him into the chaparral for the purpose of making the cook obey him. Smith then proceeded to give him a compelling lecture telling the young man, "we were in the enemy's country in time of war; all of our lives were in peril, and that persistent disobedience on the part of any officer or soldier to the legal authority of those over him was punishable with death."[13] After a few hours of strenuous drilling, the cook agreed to obey his superiors.

Except for the cook, Smith had not experienced any difficulty with his men. His demand for excellence had brought the engineer company to a high standard of drill and discipline as an infantry company. Smith thought of himself as a tough disciplinarian. Smith, however, appeared to have been a poor judge of stamina, as he frequently pushed his men to the edge of their physical endurance. Fatigue was a common complaint of the troops under his command. Smith's work with the engineer company endeared him to his superiors. Both Colonel Totten and General Scott praised the engineer soldiers as the best company in the United States Army.

The preeminent American commander during the Mexican War was General Scott of Virginia. His first test as a soldier came in the War of 1812 from which he emerged with an exalted reputation. Though not as popular as Taylor, Scott was superior to him in terms of organization, strategy, and tactics. Standing over six feet tall and always in full uniform, his appearance was one of dignity and strength. Eager for combat, Scott taught his men that an American soldier should never entertain the thought of retreat or defeat.[14] Among the qualities that made up Scott's greatness was the recognition of his shortcomings and weaknesses. Foremost among his deficiencies was the lack of formal military training. However, Scott surrounded himsef with West Point graduates who provided him with the technical knowledge and specialized skills he did not possess.[15] Among those skills admired by Scott was engineering, therefore, Smith would have the opportunity to impress the general.

Because of Swift's illness, General Taylor ordered Smith to repair the road from Matamoros to Victoria. When Company A departed from Matamoros on December 21, 1846, it had been reduced to two officers and forty-five men.[16] The volunteers worked under the supervision of the engineer troops also known as the "pick and shovel brigade." The duties of an engineer officer were at times both tedious and dangerous. The road between the two towns required an enormous amount of work to make it passable for artillery and transport wagons. Smith never complained about the difficulty associated with the repairing and building of roads "in the enemy's country." On the way to Victoria, the Americans were faced with the crossing of a river more than a hundred yards wide, and with banks more than a hundred feet high. After a survey of the river, Smith decided that drag-ropes would be the most efficient method to use to make it possible for the wagons to ford the stream. This method was the most practical because it required less time and fewer men to construct than an ordinary bridge. Smith secured a work force of several hundred men and explained to them the nature of the work to be done. The working party responded expeditiously and in a few hours wagons were crossing the river.[17]

With the engineer company leading the way, the American forces under General Taylor entered Victoria in January 1847. On January 12, Taylor relieved the engineer company from duty under General Robert Patterson and ordered it to report to General Twiggs. At Victoria, Taylor received word from Scott announcing his intention to lead the army into Mexico City. General Scott requested Taylor to release the greater part of his army to him. General Taylor, with chagrin parted with his courageous troops, many of whom had shared with him the thrill of victory in several battles. Taylor thus stripped of his men, was ordered by Scott to defend the line at Monterey. It would be Scott who would operate on the Mexican coast and therefore, attack Vera Cruz.[18]

Smith constructed bridges and repaired roads as the army departed from Victoria for Tampico on January 13. It was not uncommon to find the men working from dawn to dusk. In less than two weeks the soldiers had marched more than a hundred miles, arriving at Tampico on January 23. From Matamoros to Tampico via Victoria, the troops had traveled more than 300 miles in a little more than six weeks. In spite of the hard labor, the soldiers had acquired valuable experience in practical engineering during the many miles of road building.[19] Tampico was a delightful place with all the luxuries and comforts of a modern town: good markets, fine cafes, excellent shops, and beautiful rivers.[20] The cultural life of the town was elevated with the arrival of a theatrical group brought from Monterey by the United States troops. As on previous occasions the soldiers had worked up a great deal of excitement in anticipation of a fight there. Their elation changed to disappointment with the news that Tampico had capitulated to the Navy several weeks earlier. Scott arrived at Tampico on February 19, 1847. The Mexican troops had marched to the interior where they would make a stand against the quick advancing American troops. After about a month's delay at Tampico, Scott's army reembarked and set sail for the port city of Vera Cruz on the Gulf of Mexico about 200 miles away. Except for a token force, Vera Cruz had been evacuated by orders of Santa Anna.

The engineer company sailed for Vera Cruz by the way of Lobos Island and Anton Lizardo. The sappers and miners learned upon their arrival at Anton Lizardo that their Captain had arrived there from Matamoros, and was recuperating aboard a vessel in the harbor. Immediately upon learning that Swift was ashore, Smith reported to him and the feeble Captain resumed command of the company. The soldiers languished at Anton Lizardo for a few days before Scott ordered them to make preparations for a movement against Vera Cruz. On March 9, 1847, the army sailed for the Island of Sacrificios, located three miles south of Vera Cruz.[21]

En route to Sacrificios, McClellan informed Smith that Captain Swift intended to lead the engineers ashore once they reached their destination. The physical condition of Swift had worsened since his departure from Matamoros to the point that he could not walk without assistance. Upon reaching the Island, Smith took McClellan's advice and visited the convalescent Swift to make a request that he not lead the engineer company ashore. This was a delicate situation for Smith. For him to advise Swift not to go ashore with Company A was in effect asking him to relinquish command to Smith in the most important operation of the Mexican War up to that time. Smith showed both compassion and tact in handling this matter. After listening patiently to Smith, Swift replied, "My mind is made up, I will lead the company in this; and would do so even if I knew that the bare attempt would certainly cost me my life."[22] Upon reaching the shore, Swift showed a remarkable increase of vitality and, as promised, directed the engineer soldiers to their proper place in the line of investment. Swift's resurgence of strength, however, was only temporary and within a few hours he had collapsed beneath the Mexican sun. He never regained his health and died at New Orleans in April 1847.[23] With the death of Captain Swift, command of the engineer company devolved upon Smith.

General Scott's landing of 12,000 troops at Vera Cruz was a remarkable military operation. Not a single soldier was lost, and every detail was carried out in a skilled manner. As the troops approached the shore, loud shouts of joy reverberated from nearby trees. The disembarkation was one of enthusiasm and wild excitement resembling that of an afternoon picnic. Anxious men waving the United States flag leaped into the water before they reached the shore; each soldier coveted the distinction of being the first to plant the American flag on that shore of Mexico.[24] On March 10, the day after the initial landing, Scott moved his forces ashore and began to invest the city.

Paramount to the successful investment of Vera Cruz was the work of the engineer company. Smith was in charge of constructing the works there. Chief among his duties were reconnoitering expeditions to locate suitable sites for artillery. For the engineer troops, the three-week siege provided them with an excellent opportunity to put their academic and professional training to work. To better his position, General Patterson ordered Smith to build a road through the thick forest to Milibran, an old monastery. Within a few hours of this request, Patterson was moving up the newly opened road to the Milibran ruins. To expedite the surrender of the besieged city, Colonel Totten ordered Smith to locate and shut off the aqueduct that carried water to the city.[25] General Scott acknowledged the work of his troops during the first days after the siege. He wrote, "In extending the line of investment around the city the troops, for three days have performed the heaviest labors in getting over the hills and cutting through the intervening forests."[26]

Three days after the landing, Smith and McClellan reconnoitered to within a few hundred yards of the old walled city. When they returned to camp to inform Totten of their expedition, he replied that Smith and McClellan had provided him with more valuable information than any of the other officers.[27] On March 15, Colonel Totten ordered Smith to reconnoiter the enemy's works to find a location in which to erect gun batteries. With the assistance of Pierre G. T. Beauregard, the construction of the works began under enemy fire. Of the five batteries that ultimately reduced the city, Smith and Beauregard had selected the position of three.[28]

The greatest discomfort for the Americans at Vera Cruz came from the fleas of which Dabney H. Maury gave a lurid description. He noted that the Vera Cruz fleas stood ready to swarm all over the troops by the hundreds in search of a change of diet. The engineer officers Smith and McClellan came up with an ingenious method of escaping from the parasitic insects. They greased themselves with salt pork and slept in canvas bags. Smith and McClellan were safe, but those soldiers who did not take such precautions were left to the mercy of the fleas.[29]

✧

On March 29, the Mexican General Jose Juan De Landero surrendered Vera Cruz to Commanding General Scott. Later that evening, Scott informed Secretary of War William L. Marcy that the flag of the United States floated victoriously over Vera Cruz and the castle of San Juan. Though Smith had rendered valuable service to the army during the siege, the engineer company did not take part in the official ceremonies marking the surrender. Totten lauded Smith and the other officers of the engineer company for their heroism during the siege. In his official report of the operations against Vera Cruz, he stated that the engineer officers provided meritorious service during the attack against the heavily fortified city. Totten also noted that had the engineers not been so few in numbers, the capitulation of Vera Cruz would have been accelerated.[30]

After the surrender of Vera Cruz the engineer company disassembled the batteries and magazines. In early April, Scott issued orders for the army to begin its march to the interior that would lead to Mexico City. The engineer company arrived at Plan Del Rio, a short distance from Cerro Gordo on April 17. Upon Smith's arrival at camp,

Robert E. Lee instructed him to construct a battery that night on a previously selected hill. Smith secured a large working party, and, despite their exhaustion and the difficulty of the ground, the battery was erected.

Cerro Gordo was on an immense hill where the road from Vera Cruz to Mexico City passed through the mountains. This well-fortified hamlet was fifteen miles east of Jalapa situated between perpendicular hills where Santa Anna had intended to defeat the American army.[31] The possibility of death was the one aspect of war that Smith and the other soldiers feared the most. And corpses served as a constant reminder that perishing in battle was a reality of combat. Smith remembered the encounter he had with a Mexican corpse at Cerro Gordo. He wrote:

I started to join the company and became sound asleep whilst walking down the hill. Stumbling into a quarry hole, I found myself sprawling on a dead Mexican soldier—his glazed eyes wide open, within a few inches of mine. For a moment I felt that horror of a corpse which many persons have, at times experienced. The probability that in a short time after daylight—in storming the position of the enemy—I might be as dead as the man upon whom I was laying, [sic] forced itself upon me.[32]

Once at Cerro Gordo, Smith was attached to General Persifer Smith's brigade commanded by Colonel William S. Harney. Scott had decided to attack Santa Anna at Cerro Gordo on April 18, 1847. Like Lee and McClellan, Smith made several reconnaissances of the enemy's works there. Smith informed Harney that their defensive line was not heavily fortified.

Smith led the advance guard of the brigade when Colonel Harney ordered the attack. A fierce fight occurred on a hill in front of the American battery. After a short struggle, the Mexican soldiers retreated in disorder and confusion. The American soldiers had gained control of the key point of the hill, and there they planted the nation's flag. Smith displayed courage in victory and compassion for the defeated Mexicans. He provided a Mexican officer with a comfortable place to lie and a blanket. Smith then went in search of a physician for him and the other wounded prisoners.[33] The battle of Cerro Gordo was the first major engagement for Scott's army since leaving Vera Cruz. The engineers were as comfortable with muskets as they were with picks and shovels; the facility with which they handled weapons at Cerro Gordo made their officers proud.[34]

It was obvious that Scott had a high opinion of the engineers in general and of the twenty-five-year old Smith in particular. In his report following the triumph at Cerro Gordo, he wrote, "Lieutenant G. W. Smith led the engineer company as part of the storming force; and is noticed with distinction."[35] General Twiggs also spoke favorably of Smith's courage at Cerro Gordo. He reported that while leading the engineer company in its assault of the main enemy work, Smith "killed two men with his own hand."[36] Colonel Harney, who commanded Smith at the battle noted that "Lieutenant G. W. Smith, of the engineers, with his company rendered very efficient service in his own department, as well as in the storming of the fort."[37]

From Jalapa, Scott's army marched to Puebla; the second largest city in Mexico. The army reached this city of about 80,000 on May 15, 1847. On August 7, General Twigg's division with Smith and his engineer company at its head left Puebla. This march was the genesis of the movement of the United States Army into the valley of Mexico. General Scott's army halted at Ayolta, until the engineer company reconnoitered the most feasible path for the continuation of the march. Following Smith's reconnaissance, General Worth instructed him to make the road passable to the interior. After a few hours of work, Smith and his men had improved the condition of the road to the point that artillery and wagons could traverse it.

The army continued to advance reaching the town of San Augustine on August 19. Once there, Smith received orders from Scott's headquarters instructing him to report to Lee. Lee directed Smith to secure the necessary tools from the engineer train and make the road from San Augustine to Contreras practicable for artillery.[38] The village of San Augustine was about twelve miles south of Mexico City. Midway between San Augustine and the capital stood the entrenchments on the heights of Contreras. This fortified camp was situated on the side of a mountain and protected with both heavy guns and a garrison of 7,000 troops under General Gabriel Valencia. These were the best soldiers in the Mexican army. They were supported by Santa Anna with an additional 12,000 men.

After reaching San Augustine, Scott instructed his engineers to survey the works in the vicinity of Contreras in preparation for an assault on that citadel on August 20. Smith had ventured several hundred yards down the road in the direction of the fort when he heard shots coming from the Mexicans. General Twiggs responded to the report of musket fire by ordering the regiment of rifles to march forward. Twiggs also enjoined the Third Infantry to proceed to the front to provide support and reinforcement to this regiment. The engineer company occupied the position to the left of the Third Infantry. Upon learning from John G. Foster that the American troops would soon attack, Smith requested permission from Lee to allow the engineer company to fight with General Smith's brigade.

Once Smith had attached himself to General Persifer Smith's brigade, he surveyed the Contreras village to ascertain whether Colonel Bennet Riley's brigade was near the front. Following this inspection, Smith reported that Riley had advanced very close to the Mexican battery. Later into the night of August 19, General Smith informed the leader of the engineer company that battery of the enemy would be stormed early the next morning. At 3:00 a.m. on August 20, the soldiers commenced their movement through nearly impenetrable forests and underbrush in the direction of Fort Contreras. By daybreak, they had secured positions in the front and flanks of the enemy's main works. Smith's company and the rifle regiment occupied a position in the line on the left of Colonel Riley's brigade. With the completion of this disposition, Smith suddenly found himself at the head of one of the columns of attack.[39] Methodically, the American forces stormed the Mexican stronghold. The assault by the invading army was so effective that the actual battle lasted less than twenty minutes.[40]

The confused and dispirited Mexicans retreated to the capital city. Competent leadership combined with the heroic service of the enlisted men to give the American army a victory at the battle of Contreras. In his official report of the battle, Gustavus W. Smith wrote, "my men acted with great gallantry; their promptness in obeying every order and the effect with which they used their muskets, entitle them to all the highest praise."[41] With the defeat of the enemy at Contreras, the road to Churubusco, less than six miles from the Mexican capital, was opened. This formidable position was garrisoned by the very best officers and soldiers in General Santa Anna's army.

From his headquarters at Coyohacan, about one mile from Churubusco, General Scott ordered Twiggs' division to lead the advance on that village. Early in the afternoon of August 20, 1847, General Twiggs ordered the engineer company to survey the works of the enemy surrounding Churubusco. Despite a tremendous volley, Smith and Foster ascertained the strategic location of the enemy's artillery. This exploration revealed that nothing heavier than a six-pounder had been discharged by the Mexicans. With this information, Smith sent Foster to General Twiggs to tell him that he believed the entire force under Twigg's command should be employed to turn the enemy's left.[42] The strong position of the Mexicans at Churubusco made the battle a fierce one. Writing some years after the war, Ulysses S. Grant recalled the Churubusco fight as the "severest battle fought in the valley of Mexico."[43] In spite of the victory, Smith's one major criticism of the battle was that it was fought haphazardly with insufficient time to reconnoiter the enemy's works.

In his report, General Smith noted that Smith and McClellan distinguished themselves during the engagements on August 19 and 20. He stated that "nothing seemed too bold to be undertaken ... and their services as engineers were as valuable as those rendered in battle at the head of their gallant men."[44] Smith was especially pleased that none of the engineers of Company A were wounded or killed in the action at Churubusco. It was obvious that he was maturing as an officer, and the welfare of his men were of utmost importance. He recognized that his success as a military officer depended on the quality of work produced by his men. They served him well; and in return he recorded for posterity their exploits and achievements in his official reports.

With the defeat of the enemy at Molino Del Rey on September 8, another vestige of Mexican resistance had been eliminated. General Scott now focused his attention on the castle of Chapultepec, a well-fortified citadel located on a hill a short distance from Mexico City. Three days after the Molino victory, Smith received instructions to detail several men to provide assistance to the engineer officers who were in charge of superintending the construction of batteries. Once completed, these batteries would be used to reduce the fort of Chapultepec. Smith was charged with supervising the construction of Battery No. I, which would essay an attack on the castle from the south. Battery No. II was constructed by McClellan. Construction on the batteries commenced early in the morning of September 12, and was completed quickly.[45] When the bombardment occurred the next day, Chapultepec capitulated to the ensuing assault.

After the fall of Chapultepec, the only resistance standing between the American army and the Halls of Montezuma were strong breastworks at the gates of the city. Scott's forces continued their advance to the Mexican capital by marching down the San Cosme road. Upon reaching General Worth on the outskirts of the city, he informed Smith that Isaac I. Stevens had been wounded while surveying the enemy's defenses near the front. The wound to Stevens made Smith the Senior Engineer with Worth's division.[46] Worth immediately instructed him to examine the enemy's defensive line, and to make a recommendation to him as to the most practical method of storming the fortified gates. Following Smith's scouting, he advised Worth that infantry alone was sufficient to capture the gates. Satisfied with what he had heard, Worth ordered Smith to execute the plan.

Before dark on the evening of September 13, 1847, the stubborn Mexicans were routed from the San Cosme Garitas. General Worth's division effected a lodgement at the gates after a bitter fight with the enemy there. The road into Mexico City now lay open before the victorious Americans. However, the Mexicans were not yet ready to surrender their capital city. In the meantime, Worth learned that a large convent a few hundred yards in front was occupied. Worth ordered a brigade forward to take up position near the well-fortified church. Smith directed the brigade against the convent.

As night fell over the capital city like an enormous curtain, it was symbolic of the fading Mexican resistance. Smith, disappointed with Worth's decision to halt the army for the night, asked him for permission to continue the advance. Smith was confident that he could reach the National Palace before daybreak with a force of about 500. Worth, unimpressed with Smith's argument, denied his request because his troops were exhausted. Worth also instructed him and McClellan to remain at his tent until he gave orders for them to resume their operations at the front. Shortly after midnight on September 14, General Worth received a Mexican delegation that tendered the surrender of the city and informed him that General Santa Anna had evacuated the capital. Because Worth doubted the authenticity of the commission, he ordered Smith to press forward and to conduct a survey of the city to confirm that it was vacated. Smith also searched all the large buildings leading to the capital city to make certain that Mexican troops did not occupy any of them. Following Smith's examination, he communicated to Worth that all the buildings were abandoned and that the enemy had indeed withdrawn from the city.[47]

When the United States flag was unfolded over the National Palace on the morning of September 14, it signaled that the occupation was complete. With the exception of sporadic outbursts in the capital, the Mexicans had given up the contest as hopeless. The war was virtually over. With the end of the fighting, the officers submitted their official reports to the War Department. General Scott noted that Smith and several other engineers "won the admiration of all about them."[48] While in Mexico City, Smith joined the Aztec Club as a charter member in 1847.[49] This organization served as a forum to promote social interaction among officers of the army of which John A. Quitman was its president.[50]

Smith and his comrades had learned a great deal about military life and had been baptized under fire during the American invasion of Mexico. One year to the month after departing from the West Point post, the engineer company found itself as part of the victorious army then occupying Mexico City. They had left the Military Academy as inexperienced troops. By the time they descended upon the enemy's capital, they had become seasoned soldiers and the veterans of several important battles. Smith was impressed with the work of his company during the war; particularly in view of the paucity of troops under his charge. Upon reaching Mexico City in September 1847, the engineer company had been reduced to less than forty men. Smith was disappointed that only a few engineers had been added to Company A since its departure from West Point in 1846. During the year that Smith commanded the company, he advocated for more companies of engineer soldiers in the army. He suggested that if additional companies were not forthcoming, plans should be made to bring the engineer company up to its authorized maximum strength of one hundred.

In February 1848, Smith requested that Colonel Totten relieve him from duty as commander of the only engineer company in the army. Perhaps the lack of a positive response to his suggestion was a factor in his decision to relinquish command of his company. Smith was a realist who understood that because of his low rank, his recommendation was not likely to find a receptive ear in Washington. However, Smith left the door open when he offered himself as commander of a future engineer battalion. Smith indicated that he would gladly serve in this capacity based upon the stipulation that he be made major, by brevet.

On May 22, 1848, Lee ordered Smith to go to Vera Cruz to procure all the property of Company A and prepare it for shipment to West Point.[51] Before the engineer company left Mexico City in May, Smith handed over command of the company to McClellan. The new commander marched with his company to Vera Cruz to begin the long journey home.[52] From there, the American army returned by steamers to the United States. It was a joyous occasion when the engineer company arrived at West Point in June. Smith departed from the Mexican coast a few days after McClellan and did not reach the Military Academy until early July. Once there, he applied for a six-month leave of absence. At the end of his leave, Smith was officially relieved from duty with Company A. Before leaving, Smith accepted the invitation of Colonel Totten to recruit young men for the company to replace those who had been discharged. When Smith fulfilled this obligation, his tour of duty with the first engineer company came to an unceremonious end.

The American soldiers faced many trials of war including death, sickness, disease, lack of supplies, and an unfriendly climate. Despite these hardships, Scott's army had achieved a magnificent triumph. The land acquired from Mexico, however, would later prove to be the focal point of a national controversy regarding slavery in the territories. Credit for this victory must be given to the officers who planned the strategy and tactics and to the soldiers who carried them out with near perfection.[53] Looking through the telescope of retrospect, General Scott articulated one of the reasons for his success against the Mexicans. He stated:

I give it as my fixed opinion that but for our graduated cadets the war between the United States and Mexico might, and probably would, have lasted some four or five years, with, in its first half, more defeats than victories falling to our share; whereas in less than two campaigns we conquered a great country and a peace without the loss of a single battle or skirmish.[54]

The leaders of the army found West Point graduates not only essential for technical and organizational assistance, but they also provided "knowledge, skill, and sometimes resolution."[55] Secretary Marcy also acknowledged the value of the West Pointers. Writing in December 1848, he stated that "the graduates of the institution contributed in an eminent degree to our unexampled career of success."[56] Their success proved that the United States Military Academy was an institution worthy of the government's investment.

The engineers formed what could be called an unofficial General Staff at a time when the army did not have one in the modern sense.[57] From a military perspective, the engineer company formed but a small part of Scott's army. However, it executed the perilous work assigned to it with aplomb. This involved work not only of an engineering nature, but as fighting soldiers as well. Because of Smith's courageous leadership, he was honored twice with the brevet rank. He was made Brevet First Lieutenant for his meritorious conduct at the battle of Cerro Gordo and Brevet Captain for his gallant services at the battle of Contreras.[58] Undoubtedly, Smith made a lasting impression on General Scott. In 1854, Scott wrote to the War Department to request the brevet rank of major for him. Scott stated that he had "never known a young officer so frequently and so highly distinguished as Captain G. W. Smith in the campaign of Mexico."[59] Scott's request, however, went unfulfilled.

Obviously, this recognition brought to Smith the distinction most cherished by a soldier. After all, it was on the battlefield where a soldier can test himself and gain valuable experience. An unknown or obscure soldier also can win the admiration and respect of his commanding officers. Another important aspect of the Mexican War for Smith was that it provided him with an opportunity to learn about those men who would be both his allies and enemies in the Civil War. The Mexican campaign served as a training ground for American soldiers who would fight each other in opposing armies in less than fifteen years. The Mexican War gave Smith a chance to improve his engineering skills and to develop his leadership qualities. He emerged from this conflict at the age of twenty-six with an established reputation as an engineer soldier of exceptional talents. The physically fit Smith was blessed with remarkably good health during the Mexican campaign. The energetic and intrepid Kentuckian enthusiastically led his troops into battle. Smith would long remember the contributions he made to the United States Army while at war in a foreign country.

# Notes

1. Charles J. Peterson, *The Military Heroes of the United States: With Narratives of the War of Independence, the War of 1812, and the War With Mexico*, 2 vols. (Philadelphia: William A. Leary, 1848) 2:237-238. See also Allen Jones and Dumas Malone, *Dictionary of American Biography*, vol. 18 (New York: Charles Scribner's Sons, 1931-1932) 598-599.

2. Gustavus Woodson Smith, *Company "A" Corps of Engineers, U.S.A. 1846-1848 in the Mexican War* (New York: The Batallion Press, 1896) 7.

3. *Records of the Adjutant General*, Roll #398 the National Archives; Washington, D.C.

4. Stephen W. Sears, *George B. McClellan: Young Napoleon* (New York: Ticknor & Fields, 1988) 10.

5. Smith, *Company "A" Corps of Engineers*, 8.

6. Sears, *George B. McClellan*, 14.

7. Peterson, *The Military Heroes of the United States*, 2:160. See also Ulysses S. Grant, *Personal Memoirs of U.S. Grant*, 2 Vols. (New York: Charles L. Webster and Company, 1885) 1:138-39.

8. *New York Tribune*, September 8, 1846.

9. Robert G. Hartje, *Van Dorn: The Life and Times of a Confederate General* (Nashville: Vanderbilt University Press, 1967) 21.

10. William Starr Myers, ed., *The Mexican War Diary of George B. McClellan* (Princeton: Princeton University Press, 1917) 7. Antonio Lopez de Santa Anna, who assumed the presidency of Mexico on three separate occasions, ruled with dictatorial powers. He was toppled each time. He defeated the Texans at the Alamo in 1836.

11. T. Harry Williams, ed., *With Beauregard in Mexico: The Mexican War Reminiscences of P.G.T. Beauregard* (Baton Rouge: Louisiana State University Press, 1956) 7.

12. George Meade, *The Life and Letters of General George Gordon Meade*, 2 vols. (New York: Charles Scribner's Sons, 1913) 1:41.

13. Smith, *Company "A" Corps of Engineers*, 11.

14. Peter, *The Military Heroes of the United States*, 2:212, 222. See also Grant, *Personal Memoirs*, 1:138-139.

15. Williams, *With Beauregard in Mexico*, 8-9.

16. Smith, *Company "A" Corps of Engineers*, 13. The engineer company was attached to General Robert Patterson's command at Matamoros.

17. Ibid.

18. Meade, *The Life and Letters of General Meade*, 1:175. Vera Cruz was the most important seaport in Mexico. This heavily fortified city was surrounded with hills of thick forest. It was guarded by the massive fortress of San Juan d'Ulua.

19. Smith, *Company "A" Corps of Engineers*, 14.

20. Meade, *The Life and Letters of General Meade*, 1:175-77.

21. Myers, *The Mexican War Diary of McClellan*, 53. See also George A. McCall, *Letters From the Frontiers* (Philadelphia; J. B. Lippincott and Co., 1868; Knoxville: University of Tennessee Microfilms, Reel, # 339) 476.

22. Smith, *Company "A" Corps of Engineers*, 18.

23. Myers, *The Mexican War Diary of McClellan*, 55.

24. Edward D. Mansfield, *Life and Services of General Winfield Scott* (New Haven: H. Mansfield, 1852) 369. See also D. H. Strother, *Illustrated Life of General Winfield Scott Commander-In-Chief of the Army in Mexico* (New York: A. S. Barnes and Company, 1848) 136.

25. Smith, *Company "A" Corps of Engineers*, 21.

26. U.S. Congress, Senate, Report of General Scott, March 1847, Executive Doc. No. 1, 30th Congress, 1st session, 1847, 216. See also Cadmus M. Wilcox, *History of the Mexican War* (Washington, D.C.: The Church News Publishing Company, 1892) 246.

27. Myers, *The Mexican War Diary of McClellan*, 56-57.

28. Williams, *With Beauregard in Mexico*, 30.

29. Dabney Herndon Maury, *Recollections of a Virginian in the Mexican, Indian and Civil Wars* (New York: Charles Scribner's Sons, 1895) 34.

30. Report of Colonel Totten, Executive Doc. No. 1, 30th Congress, 1st session, 1847, p. 245.

31. Strother, *Illustrated Life of General Scott*, 156.

32. Smith, *Company "A" Corps of Engineers*, 30-31.

33. Sidney Forman, *West Point: A History of The USMA* (New York: Columbia University Press, 1950) 72.

34. Peter S. Michie, *General McClellan* (New York: D. Appleton and Company, 1901) 21.

35. Report of General Scott, April 1847, Executive Doc., No. 1, 30th Congress, 1st session, 263.

36. Ibid., Report of General Twiggs, 278.

37. Ibid., Report of Colonel Harney, 281.

38. Report of Gustavus W. Smith, Appendix, August 1847, Executive Doc., No. 1, 30th Congress, 1st session, p. 68. The struggle which took place at Contreras was also known as the battle of Padierna.

39. Report of Gustavus W. Smith, Appendix, August 1847, Executive Doc., No. 1, 30th Congress, 1st session, p. 68.

40. Mansfield, *Life and Services of General Scott*, 420. See also Horatio O. Ladd, *History of the War with Mexico* (New York: Dodd, Mead and Company, 1883) 235.

41. Report of Gustavus W. Smith, Appendix, August 1847, Executive Doc., No. 1, 30th Congress, 1st sesssion, p. 69.

42. RG 94: Report of Gustavus Woodson Smith's Company of Engineers in the action at Churubusco in the afternoon of August 2, 1847: Letters received by the Adjutant General's office 1822-1860. Roll #359. National Archives:

Washington, D. C.

43. Grant, *Personal Memoirs*, 1:145.

44. Report of General Persifer F. Smith, August 1847, Executive Doc., No. 1, 30th Congress, 1st session, 332.

45. Wilcox, *History of the Mexican War*, 452-453.

46. Smith, *Company "A" Corps of Engineers*, 48-49.

47. Wilcox, *History of the Mexican War*, 478-82.

48. Report of General Scott, September 1847, Executive Doc. No. 1, 30th Congress, 1st session p. 385.

49. "Smith's Membership Application," *Aztec Club Papers*, United States Army Military History Institute, Carlisle Barracks, Pennsylvania.

50. Robert E. May, *John A. Quitman: Old South Crusader* (Baton Rouge: Louisiana State University Press, 1985) 197-198.

51. Lee to Smith, May 22, 1848, *Robert E. Lee Letter Book*, Virginia Historical Society, Richmond.

52. Myers, *The Mexican War Diary of McClellan*, 93. See also Michie, *General McClellan*, 23. See Smith, *Company "A" Corps of Engineers*, 62-63. Smith believed that because of his low rank, he was detrimental to the company. He felt that an officer with a higher rank was needed to command the company in order to give it the prestige it deserved.

53. Grant, *Personal Memoirs*, 1:167.

54. William A. Shunk, "The Services of Graduates in the Mexican War," *The Centennial of the United States Military Academy at West Point New York 1802-1902*, 2 vols. (Washington: Government Printing Office, 1904) 1:602.

55. Justin H. Smith, *The War with Mexico*, 2 vols. (New York: The MacMillan Company, 1919) 1:320.

56. Shunk "The Services of the Graduates in the Mexican War," 627.

57. Williams, *With Beauregard in Mexico*, 9.

58. *Twenty-Eighth Annual Reunion of the Association of Graduates of the United States Military Academy at West Point, New York* (Saginaw: Seeman and Peters, Printers and Binders, 1897) 16.

59. Ibid.

# CHAPTER THREE

# Resignation and Relocation

The long and bitter campaign with Mexico had convinced Smith of the need to seek a respite from the drudgery of military life. He was officially relieved from duty with the engineer company at the end of his six-month furlough. Smith accepted Totten's offer to return to the West Point faculty in 1849. He commenced his second tenure as principal assistant professor of science of war and military and civil engineering in the fall of that year. Totten was impressed with Smith's work as an engineer officer and his ability to grasp complex situations. With the Mexican War behind him, Smith had the advantage of bringing to the classroom the experience of the battlefield and could then combine practical knowledge with theoretical concepts.

Of all the courses taught by Smith, civil engineering was his least favorite. This was somewhat of a paradox, especially since he had acquired valuable experience as an engineer after leaving West Point in 1842. Writing to his friend Barton S. Alexander in April 1853, Smith admitted that his knowledge of civil engineering did not go beyond the course taught at West Point. This admission of a weakness was uncharacteristic of Smith. In that same correspondence, Smith also expressed a sardonic view of the cadets at the military institution. With a bit of cynicism, he said, "what little I know [it is] a d----d sight more than these grey coated chaps manage to learn."[1] Smith was displeased by the attitude of some of the cadets toward their academic work.

In 1851, Smith competed with several other engineers for a position on the Virginia Military Institute faculty as a professor of natural sciences and artillery tactics. Others recommended by the

West Point faculty were George B. McClellan and John G. Foster. Despite the support of the faculty, these men were passed over in favor of Thomas J. Jackson.[2]

In March 1853, Smith was promoted to the grade of First Lieutenant of the corps of engineers. This was Smith's first military advancement since he was commissioned a Second Lieutenant at the time of his graduation. Promotions were cherished events in the military career of a soldier, particularly in peace time. Smith, however, accepted his new rank with tepid enthusiasm because of the long wait between promotions. He was disappointed that after many years of military service he had not yet made captain. In a letter to Alexander at the time of his promotion Smith said, "so we are 1st Lts. Well better late than never. One more turn of the wheel the thing will be worth talking about."[3]

By 1853, Smith had grown tired of the quiet life at West Point; therefore, it was not surprising when he left the army the next year. Smith's official resignation on December 18, 1854, marked the end of his affiliation with the United States Army. Smith had matured both as an engineer and professor during the twelve years of his military career. He also had worked on several engineering projects and had emerged from the Mexican War with an impressive record.

Several factors contributed to Smith's decision to resign his commission. He had grown dissatisfied with the lack of enthusiasm for military life by some of the cadets. In his 1853 letter to Alexander, he said of them, "Cadets, ignorant, ill-natured — resenting as affront not to be submitted to any attempt to teach them."[4] Doubtless, Smith had become disillusioned with teaching which he described as "excruciatingly boring and frustrating."[5] Smith also had a desire to return to private life to work as a civil engineer. Moreover, the slow rate of promotions angered him. In fact, Lee contacted Totten after the Mexican War to find out why Smith had not been promoted.[6] Lee's inquiry, however, did not produce any results on Smith's behalf. Low pay combined with the slow rate of promotions caused many officers to leave the military during the postwar years. In 1856, Beauregard contemplated resigning his commission to join forces with the filibuster William Walker in Nicaragua.[7] On the occasion of Smith's resignation, Totten reflected upon the military career of one of his favorite engineers. Writing to Smith on December 26, 1854, he said: "I am parting in the present case, with an officer whose services in the field have, by their marked gallantry and high professional character, added to the reputation of the corps and the army. These considerations strengthen my regret at the loss we are now sustaining."[8]

Another contributing factor to Smith's resignation, and perhaps the most important one, was his desire to join the filibustering movement. After Smith's departure from the army, he selected New Orleans, the fifth largest city in the nation as his new home. Once in the Crescent City, he renewed his acquaintance with General John A. Quitman, with whom he had served in the Mexican War. Both Smith and Quitman were active filibusters during the decade of the fifties. It should be noted that Smith's association with Quitman at this time was important because it marked the beginning of his involvement with Southern nationalism and the development of an orientation that would cause him to join the secessionists a few years later.

The decade preceding the Civil War was both an exciting and turbulent period in nineteenth-century America. Of the many events and activities that made it memorable, filibustering must rate near the top. The filibusters were "self-appointed agents of Manifest Destiny" whose adventurism and elaborate schemes were often motivated by vanity. Imagination, however, did not tell the whole story behind these grandiose expeditions. The filibustering movement was deeply rooted in sectionalism and slavery, two issues which were dividing the nation at that time.[9] One of the more colorful personalities of the filibustering phenomenon was the quixotic John A. Quitman.

Quitman, who was born in New York, moved to Mississippi in 1827 and established his residence at Natchez where he quickly became a leading planter and slaveholder. He immediately submerged himself in the politics of his adopted state and became prominent in the Democratic party. In the 1830s, he sided with South Carolina during the Nullification controversy. He believed that the federal government was determined to maintain control over the states with the sword and bayonet.[10] The ambitious Quitman moved up the political ladder with amazing ease and was elected Governor of Mississippi in 1851.[11] An ardent Southern nationalist, and a leading proponent of secession, Quitman campaigned diligently to maintain and spread the institution of slavery. He possessed a forceful personality and craved to always impress those with whom he was intimate.[12] Quitman, a man of intrigue, was the acknowledged leader of one of the largest planned filibuster expeditions in the 1850s.

As early as 1852, Quitman had begun to lay the ground work for his expedition to Cuba. His main objective was to topple Spanish hegemony on the island and convert Cuba into a slave state. However, other factors such as "unhappy family lives, broken romances, debts, and troubles with the law were as likely to make a filibuster as was proslavery fanaticism."[13] Crucial to Quitman's success was the selection of men who shared his beliefs and possessed military experience. Therefore, he depended heavily on veterans of the Mexican War to staff his expeditionary force. In addition to veterans, Quitman's army consisted of adventure seekers, unemployed workers, and men in search of land. One of the more critical periods during the preparation of the expedition was between November 1854 and February 1855. During those decisive four months, General Quitman made appointments within his command structure. Though specific "ranks and assignments" remain nebulous, important positions were assigned to Mansfield Lovell and Smith.[14] Writing to the influential Southerner Charles A. L. Lamar in Savannah, Smith indicated that "in the absence of Gen. Quitman," he had "authority to act in all matters referring to Cuban Affairs."[15] Lovell, a Washington, DC native and West Point graduate served as aide-de-camp to General Quitman in the Mexican War. During the time he served on Quitman's staff, a close relationship developed between the two men. He would be appointed a major general in the Confederate army in October 1861.[16]

Both Smith and Lovell, obsessively committed to the invasion of Cuba, were men with proven skills and abilities. Smith's engineering experience would have been a valuable asset to any invading army; therefore, Quitman was happy to have him join his force. Lovell's resignation from the army became effective the same day as did Smith's. Undoubtedly, Smith and his close friend were in communication and had decided to resign their commissions simultaneously once the expedition had the possibility of success. By December 1854, Smith and Lovell were convinced the plans had progressed to that point. It did not take much perception for the Commandant of the Military Academy, William H. T. Walker to conclude that the resignations of Smith and Lovell had some connection to General Quitman's expedition against Cuba.[17] The *Richmond Examiner* later stated as a "noteworthy fact" that both Smith and Lovell had resigned their commissions for the purpose of assuming leadership positions in the Cuban enterprise.[18] The filibusters waited anxiously for the signal from General Quitman for the vessels to set sail from New Orleans for the invasion of Cuba, but it never came. Circumstances had changed since 1852; and the success that Quitman had hoped for faded with the passage of time. Quitman was frequently under attack by federal authorities because of his blatant defiance of the neutrality laws that prohibited American citizens from engaging in private military ventures against foreign nations.[19] To save the administration the embarrassment of appearing to be a tool of the slave power, Franklin Pierce had issued a presidential proclamation in May 1854 stipulating that persons implicated in the designs against Cuba would be prosecuted.[20] Furthermore, President Pierce summoned Quitman to the White House for a private meeting during which time he appealed to him to call off the expedition. When Pierce showed Quitman information on the strong Cuban fortifications, the filibuster leader understood that an invasion would have been futile. The expedition disbanded in April 1855, when Quitman resigned from the Junta.[21] Smith's dream of adventure collapsed with the downfall of Quitman. For Smith and the other recruits, the much anticipated filibustering expedition against Cuba was an empty dream filled with more rhetoric than reality.

Throughout the filibustering movement, Smith held firmly to the code of confidentiality. In a note sent to George W. Cullum some years after the planned expedition, Smith did not divulge his activities during the period of December 1854 through June 1855. Smith informed Cullum that he was "accounted for" during those months and suggested to Cullum that he fill in the gap as he pleased.[22] Smith, with all of his drive and imagination, was undoubtedly disappointed that the expedition faltered. Perhaps it was a blessing in disguise that it was a failure in the United States because it probably prevented an even greater catastrophe from occurring in Cuba.

George B. McClellan, another West Point graduate and Mexican War veteran, gave serious consideration to joining one of the filibustering movements of the 1850s. He corresponded frequently with Smith, Lovell, and Beauregard concerning filibustering expeditions. He intimated to them that he would have gladly accepted a high position in a filibustering army if the opportunity presented itself. Whereas Smith and Lovell were motivated by a desire to spread slavery, McClellan was driven by the nationalistic doctrine of Manifest Destiny.[23] Like his friends, McClellan's vanity exceeded his sense of pragmatism, and his ambition remained unfulfilled.

Having been out of service for a few years, the lure of the military proved too great for Smith. He informed Robert E. Lee that he had submitted through Totten an application for the position of field officer in any new regiments that Congress might create. To aid Smith's return to active duty, Lee wrote to Totten in February 1856. Lee's letter was full of praise for the Kentuckian. He reminded Totten that he was Smith's immediate commander during a portion of the march from Vera Cruz to Mexico City in which Smith displayed gallant conduct in several battles. Lee said that Smith had "exhibited on all occasions Military Conduct with professional skill; was ready with his command for every duty; eager in its discharge [and] prompt in its execution ... the Official reports, prove him to be an active [and] efficient commander [and] a good soldier."[24] Lee's intervention was to no avail. Smith would remain inactive until the fall of 1861 when he would join the Confederate army.

A few months after the abortive Cuban expedition, Smith found himself on the move again. Smith, at the request of Treasury Secretary James B. Guthrie, relocated to the nation's capital. Guthrie, who had gained prominence in the Democratic party, was a man of sound judgment, honesty, and integrity. When Smith arrived in

Washington after a long trip from New Orleans in the summer of 1855, he immediately reported to the Treasury Department. The Treasury Building, the first executive building to be erected in the nation's capital, had an interesting history of its own. This thirty-room structure was completed in 1800 at a cost of about $40,000. The original edifice was torched by British soldiers in August 1814. A second building was erected, and in 1833 it too was destroyed by fire. In July 1855, Guthrie appointed Smith as superintendent of constructing the extension to the United States Treasury Building. Guthrie understood the success of a construction project depended on the competency of the person in charge; therefore, it was necessary to select a superintendent who was industrious, honest, and possessed technical training. Guthrie was certain that Smith would show the same enthusiasm for civil work that had characterized his military career.

Foremost among Smith's duties was the negotiating of contracts for the purpose of obtaining the required building supplies. After the procurement of materials, it was then necessary for the superintendent to employ the most efficient labor to carry out the work. In addition to supervising workers, the superintendent also had to maintain accurate records of expenditures. Upon the completion of a construction project, the superintendent had to present it to the engineer in charge of the Treasury Department for final inspection.[25]

Smith began his work under the supervision of Alexander H. Bowman, the engineer in charge of the Treasury Department. The decade of the fifties saw a proliferation of the construction of government buildings such as marine hospitals, branch mints, custom-houses, and post-offices. With an eye toward efficient management in his department, Guthrie recognized the need for a trained engineer to oversee the construction of such works. He had appointed Bowman to head the newly-created department for the construction of government buildings.[26]

Smith's training and experience had prepared him well. His special aptitude for engineering and the eagerness with which he always threw himself into anything in the line of his duty made him an excellent choice for the superintendency of the extension work on the Treasury Building. The third building was constructed in 1836. The extension was necessary because the existing building was insufficient to accommodate all of the offices and workers. The lack of space had forced the Department to rent nearby buildings at exorbitant prices.[27] One of the major decisions concerning the extension project had to do with the type of material to be used in its construction. After several days of debate between Guthrie and Bowman, the Treasury Secretary accepted the recommendation of the latter to use granite instead of marble. The determining factor in this decision was that granite was durable, beautiful, and less expensive.[28] The blueprint for the extension called for each floor of the Treasury Building to have 54,000 square feet of space when completed.[29]

Smith's first order of business was the procurement of the necessary supplies. Once a substantial amount of construction material had been purchased, Smith could then engage his labor force. Many of the skills that Smith had acquired during his military career were applicable to civilian life. He was particularly adept at organizing men for their most effective use. Under Smith's supervision, the excavation work for the cellar was completed and the laying of stone for the basement had begun. Smith's propensity for construction engineering was evident by the amount of work completed in a short time. Following a personal inspection of the construction site, Bowman reported to Guthrie that the work was progressing satisfactorily.[30]

In July 1855, Bowman informed Guthrie that he had inspected all of the proposed sites for the new marine hospital at New Orleans. Bowman recommended the square at the corner of Common and Broad Streets because of its proximity to a city reservoir and a cost of only $12,000.[31] Following the selection of the site and a construction company, the next order of business was the appointment of a superintendent to oversee the work. Guthrie did not have to look very far, and once again called upon Smith to assist him. In December 1855, Guthrie relieved Smith of his duties at the Treasury Building and sent him to New Orleans where he assumed the superintendency of the repairs of the Branch Mint, and of the construction of the new marine hospital there. The purpose for the construction of the hospital was to accommodate the sick and disabled sailors at the port of New Orleans. The repairs to the New Orleans Branch Mint included replacing some walls and making the depository both burglar and fire proof, of which iron beams were used for the latter.[32]

During the 1850s, wrought-iron replaced cast-iron in the construction of government buildings. One of the major suppliers of wrought-iron to the federal government was the Cooper and Hewitt Company of Trenton, New Jersey. The major irritant to Smith was the interruption of work due to delays in receiving wrought-iron beams from the North that were transported to the Crescent City in slow-moving steamers. Despite the occasional delay, both Bowman and Smith were pleased with the rate of progress.

Because of Smith's work on various government projects, his aptitude for construction engineering had become well known; not only in political circles but in the business community as well. Smith did not enjoy the satisfaction of seeing a construction project to its completion in either Washington or New Orleans. This, however, did not lessen his sense of achievement. Smith's work with the federal government had provided him with an opportunity to acquire valuable administrative experience. This experience would serve him well in his later careers. Construction work required extensive travel. The constant traveling precluded Smith from enjoying the luxuries and comforts of a permanent home. Perhaps his decision to travel was made easier since his eleven-year marriage to Lucretia had produced no offspring.

Smith had worked in New Orleans for less than a year when he relocated again. He resigned his superintendency there in the fall of 1856 to accept the position of chief engineer with the Cooper and Hewitt Company.[33] By accepting the position in the capital of New Jersey, Smith was moving into a city known for its production of iron and steel. Between 1840 and 1860, the population of Trenton increased from a little over 4,000 to well over 17,000.[34] The ambitious Smith was not one to pass up an opportunity for advancement; particularly in the vicinity of New York City where the possibility existed for even greater opportunities.

Smith embarked upon his new challenge with the same fervor

and determination that had brought him so much success in the past. He was qualified for his new occupation. He had gained a wealth of experience in both private and public engineering undertakings. No doubt Smith's transition from government work to the business sector was easier because of his close association with Lovell. He had preceded Smith by one year in employment at the Cooper and Hewitt industrial plant. The chief engineer of an industrial complex was expected to have practical skills acquired through specialized and technical training. In Europe, it was common for factories to have first-rate engineering departments with scientifically trained workers who were involved with the actual operation of the plants. When America placed university educated engineers in its mills, the nation was following a trend that had been well-established abroad.[35]

Smith embarked upon his career in the iron industry when the nation was enjoying phenomenal economic growth brought on in part by the production of iron and steel. Iron foundries were the foundation pillars upon which the industrial base of the nation rested. One of the largest iron works in the country was the Cooper and Hewitt Company which employed almost 800 workers in 1860.[36]

The Trenton Iron Works was founded by the inventor, manufacturer, and philanthropist, Peter Cooper in 1845.[37] He was ably assisted in the operation of the Company by his son-in-law Abram S. Hewitt and his son, Edward Cooper. Abram and Edward were classmates at Columbia College, from which Hewitt graduated in 1842. He represented the United States at the Paris Exposition in 1867 and was elected mayor of New York in 1886. Hewitt's resourcefulness and incisive mind made him a valuable partner in the operation. Hewitt, the more meticulous of the threesome, was in charge of the business affairs of the iron company.[38] The mechanical and technical operations of the Company were entrusted to the superintendence of Cooper. He invented the regenerative hot blast stove for blast furnaces that improved and lessened the cost of iron production. He became one of the nation's foremost experts in the field of metallurgical engineering. Cooper was elected mayor of New York City in 1879 and worked enthusiastically for municipal reforms.[39]

Impressed with the work of Hewitt and Cooper, and the success of the Company, Peter Cooper decided to set up a more permanent organizational structure. In 1847, the elder Cooper permitted the two young men to form a partnership under the firm name of Cooper and Hewitt. Satisfied with this arrangement, the two lieutenants began to manufacture iron under the new name of Cooper and Hewitt Iron Works. This Company assured its place in the annals of industrial history in 1854 with the successful manufacturing of wrought-iron beams and girders that were used primarily to fire-proof buildings. This was the Company's greatest contribution to the iron industry in the United States.[40] Cooper and Hewitt's production of wrought-iron, could not have come at a more opportune moment. They were the principal suppliers of beams and girders used in the construction of many government buildings during the decade preceding the Civil War.

The manufacturing of iron and steel were not the only preoccupations of Edward Cooper and Abram Hewitt. Their interests included politics as well. And both industrialists became prominent in the Democratic party of New York City. In addition to wealth, the two business magnates had name recognition as well. When Smith was accepted in the house of Cooper and Hewitt, this was an important step in the nurturing process of a political career. In time, Smith would embrace politics as naturally as did his employers. Smith arrived in New York City in October 1856, and then proceeded to Trenton to assume his position as chief engineer at the Cooper and Hewitt Company.

Shortly thereafter, the paths of Smith and McClellan crossed again. Like many other soldiers of his generation, McClellan also had resigned his military commission during the fifties. The limited opportunities the army offered and low pay were the reasons for his departure. Before submitting his official letter of resignation in November 1856, McClellan discussed employment possibilities with his closest friends; one of whom was Smith. Smith introduced the Philadelphia native to Hewitt. Among many of Hewitt's activities was an interest in railroad expansion in the middle west, and, in 1852, the Cooper and Hewitt Company began selling rails to the Illinois Central Railroad Company. Two years later, Hewitt was elected to the Illinois Central board of directors.

Based on a recommendation from Hewitt, the thirty-year old McClellan was made vice-president of the Illinois Central. In recommending McClellan, Hewitt said, "He is a gentleman of lengthened education, and for mental and physical endurance has no rival in the army. He is ... in my judgement the best man to be secured in the country."[41] McClellan commenced his new vocation in January 1857. The main line of the Illinois Central measured 700 miles and opened the center of the state to farmers and settlers. This vital railroad line fostered internal improvements in the West and made Illinois an important part of the United States' economic system. The Illinois Central was under the dynamic and energetic leadership of its president William H. Osborn who was unquestionably the dominant figure in the history of the Company.[42] At an early age, Osborn had developed a special aptitude for business and administration.

Not long after McClellan's appointment with the Illinois Central, Smith was named to its board of directors. The permanent meeting place of the board was New York City. Doubtless, Smith's association with Hewitt and McClellan were instrumental in his being elected a director of the Company. After less than a year on the job, McClellan contemplated resigning because of boredom and several contentious encounters with Osborn. Smith reminded McClellan of his three-year commitment and warned him that the board would not accept his resignation.[43] McClellan, who valued Smith's opinions, remained with the Illinois Central until the start of the Civil War.

Smith found the nation's largest metropolis steeped in political corruption. City officials violated laws with such impunity that it became difficult to distinguish between those whose responsibility it was to uphold the law and those who abused it. Corruption had become so widespread in the police department that the state legislature was forced to intervene and take over the police in 1857. However, Fernando Wood, the Democratic mayor of New York City, was not about to relinquish control of the police department to the State without a fight. For a short time two police forces existed in New York City, the one created by the Republican-controlled State legislature and the old municipal force.[44]

Wood was one of the more interesting mayors ever to occupy City Hall. Born in Philadelphia in 1812, he relocated to New York City with his family at a young age. His mayoralties, to say the least, were stormy.[45] The ambitious Wood was elected to the House of Representatives on the Tammany Hall ticket in 1840 at the age of twenty-eight. Mayor Wood was a sagacious politician, whose soft-spokeness concealed the enormous power he wielded in the city. Wood was as intelligent as he was corrupt.[46]

The Street Commissioner directed the activities of the Street Department, one of the more important branches of the city government. The commissioner was responsible for making appointments, supervising workers, and advertising for contracts. He negotiated all contracts in his department and made payment for work upon the authorization of the Common Council. The Street Commissioner also served as a surveyor of the city. The Street Department consisted of several bureaus that functioned as the administrative arm of the department.[47] Assisting the Street Commissioner was a deputy who assumed control of the department in his absence.

The Street Department was as corrupt as it was expansive and many of the city's most notorious scandals had originated there. It had a long history of political contractors who lined their pockets with fraudulent funds secured from the city treasury through the office of the Street Commissioner. With the death of Street Commissioner Joseph R. Taylor in June 1857, Mayor Wood, prompted by a substantial bribe, appointed Charles Devlin to the position.[48] Devlin was one of the more dishonest Street Commissioners of New York City during the nineteenth century. An editorial of the *New York Times* remembered Devlin as "the most unscrupulous plunderer of the treasury that New York has ever seen."[49]

As the mayoral election of 1857 approached, the political opponents of Wood nominated Daniel F. Tiemann as the Tammany Hall candidate. The Democrat was a formidable campaigner, who had made a great deal of money as a paint manufacturer.[50] Tiemann campaigned on a platform to reform the municipal government. In return for his promise to restore decency to the city and to sweep away the last vestiges of the Wood regime, Tiemann was elected mayor in December 1857. A leading newspaper of the city recalled the election of Tiemann as a blessing in which "the city escaped from the mischief of having a bold, unscrupulous politician entrusted for two years longer ... who appointed notorious swindlers to lucrative public offices."[51] In truth, Tiemann was politically inept, but as virtuous and honest as Wood was larcenous.

When Tiemann occupied the mayoral seat of New York on January 1, 1858, the major problem facing him was how to curb the rampant corruption that had permeated the various departments of the city. Of particular concern to him was cleaning up the corruption in the Street Department. According to Tiemann, the best way of restoring respectability to this branch of government was the removal of Devlin. With the support of the Board of Aldermen, Tiemann terminated Devlin on April 12, 1858. In announcing the departure of Devlin and his underlings, Tiemann said, "They are most unscrupulous knaves, and if they ever get their deserts they will do the State some service at Sing Sing."[52]

To fill the vacancy created by Devlin's termination, Mayor Tiemann recommended the iron-maker Edward Cooper to the office of Street Commissioner. Cooper agreed to take the position with the stipulation that he would retire once order had been restored and the department reorganized. The *New York Times* called the appointment of Cooper, "one of the most substantial of the many benefits conferred upon our City by the active honesty of Mayor Tiemann."[53] Cooper named Smith to serve as his deputy. Smith possessed the formal training in engineering that Cooper lacked. By selecting Smith, Cooper had opened the door of politics for him. Cooper also appointed Lovell to serve as superintendent of the bureau of street improvements. These officials occupied their municipal seats on April 20, 1858. This date marked the end of Smith's affiliation with the Cooper and Hewitt Company and the beginning of his political career. Smith's principal tutor in the political arena was Edward Cooper, a man of honesty and compassion.

Against seemingly insuperable obstacles, both Cooper and Smith enthusiastically accepted the challenge of extricating the troubled Street Department from its chaotic condition. Cooper uncovered several speculative schemes that had originated in Devlin's administration. Smith acceded to the top position at the Street Department when Cooper resigned after six months on the job. Based on the recommendations of Cooper and Hewitt, Mayor Tiemann nominated Smith to the Board of Aldermen for confirmation as Street Commissioner of New York City. He was unanimously confirmed to fill the vacancy created by Cooper's departure. The *New York Tribune* acknowledged that Smith's education and experience qualified him for the municipal post. The editorial concluded that Tiemann had "selected about the most competent officer he could find for the place."[54] On November 12, 1858, Smith took his seat as Street Commissioner of the nation's largest city. The new commissioner named his friend and colleague Lovell to serve as his deputy. Within a few years after Smith's resignation from the army, he had catapulted himself from a construction engineer to the Street Commissionership of New York City.

# Notes

1. Gustavus W. Smith to Barton S. Alexander, April 22, 1853. Smith Collection, United States Military Academy, West Point, New York.
2. Hunter McGuire, "General Thomas J. Jackson," *Southern Historical Society Papers* 19 (January 1891): 315-16. Following Thomas "Stonewall" Jackson's graduation from West Point in 1846, he was ordered to Mexico where he was twice brevetted for meritorious service. When the Civil War started, he offered his services to the Confederate States and was commissioned a major-general in August 1861.
3. Smith to Alexander, April 23, 1853. Smith Collection, USMA.
4. Ibid.
5. Robert E. May, "Young American Males and Filibustering in the Age of Manifest Destiny: The United States Army as a Cultural Mirror," *The Journal of America History* 78 (December 1991): 882.
6. See Lee to Totten, May 21, 1848, *Robert E. Lee Letter Book*, Virginia Historical Society, Richmond.
7. T. Harry Williams, ed., *With Beauregard in Mexico: The Mexican War Reminiscences of P.G.T. Beauregard* (Baton Rouge: Louisiana State University Press, 1956) 106.
8. *Encyclopedia of Contemporary Biography of New York*, 11 vols. (New York: Atlantic Publishing and Engraving Co., 1882) 2:59.
9. Charles H. Brown, *Agents of Manifest Destiny: The Lives and Times of Filibusters* (Chapel Hill: University of North Carolina Press, 1980) 108.
10. See the Address to the People of Mississippi by the Committee appointed by the States's Rights Convention, May 21, 1834, *Hunter Family Papers*, Virginia Historical Society, Richmond.
11. James T. McIntosh, ed. *The Papers of Jefferson Davis* 5 vols. (Baton Rouge: Louisiana State University Press, 1974) 106-08.
12. Charles J. Peterson, *The Military Heroes of the United States: With Narratives of the War of Independence, the War of 1812, and the War With Mexico*, 2 vols. (Philadelphia: William A. Leary, 1848) 2:262.
13. May, "Young American Males," 864.
14. May, *John A. Quitman*, 290.
15. Smith to Lamar, February 21, 1855, Box 4, Folder 12, *John A. Quitman Papers*, Mississippi Department of Archives and History, Jackson.
16. *New York Times*, June 2, 1884. See also Ezra J. Warner, *Generals in Gray, Lives of the Confederate Commanders* (Baton Rouge: Louisiana State University Press, 1959) 194-95.

17. May, *John A. Quitman*, 293.

18. *Richmond Examiner*, October 14, 1861.

19. William Barney, *The Road to Secession: A New Perspective on the Old South*, with a Foreword by James P. Shenton (New York. Praeger Publishers, 1972) 17-18.

20. Chester Stanley Urban, "The Abortive Quitman Filibustering Expedition 1853-1855," *Journal of Mississippi History* 18 (1956): 183.

21. John F. Claiborne, *Life and Correspondence of John A. Quitman*, 2 vols. (New York: Harper and Brothers Publishers, 1860) 2:392. The Junta which was headquartered in New York City consisted of Cuban exiles who were determined to drive the Spanish from the island.

22. Smith to George W. Cullum, n.d. Smith Collection, USMA. During the post Civil War years, Cullum compiled a compendium of graduates of the USMA which included terse biographical sketches.

23. Stephen W. Sears, *George B. McClellan: The Young Napoleon* (New York: Ticknor & Fields, 1988) 52.

24. Lee to Totten, February 15, 1856, *Robert E. Lee Letter Book*, Virginia Historical Society, Richmond.

25. U.S. Congress, Senate, Report of the Secretary of the Treasury, December 1853, Executive Doc. No. 2, 33rd Congress, 1st session, 10: 279-85.

26. Report of the Secretary of the Treasury, December 1853, Executive Doc. No. 2, 33rd Congress, 1st session, Vol. 10, pp. 17-19.

27. Report of the Secretary of the Treasury, December 1853, Executive Doc. No. 2, 33rd Congress, 1st session, Vol. 10, p. 22.

28. RG:121: Office of Construction, Treasury Department, (Roll #2) National Archives: Washington. Bowman to Guthrie, October 5, 1855, p. 230.

29. Proofs of Office Letters: Office of Construction, Treasury Department, January 3, 1855–November 15, 1856. National Archives: Washington.

30. Report of Alexander H. Bowman, November 1855, Executive Doc. No. 2, 34th Congress, 1st session, 1856, Vol. 12, pp. 32, 218-19.

31. Proofs of Letters: Office of Construction, Treasury Department, National Archives: Washington, Bowman to Guthrie, July 21, 1855, p. 162.

32. Report of Alexander H. Bowman, Executive Doc. No. 2, 34th Congress, 1st Session, 1855, 12: 234-36.

33. *Twenty Eighth Annual Reunion of the Association of the Graduates of the United States Military Academy at West Point*, New York (Saginaw: Seeman and Peters, Printers and Binders, 1897) 17.

34. Harold F. Wilson, *Outline History of New Jersey* (New Brunswick: Rutgers University Press, 1950) 85.

35. Duncan Burn, *The Economic History of Steelmaking, 1867-1939: A Study in Competition* (Cambridge: The University Press, 1940; reprinted 1961) 215-226.

36. Peter Temin, *Iron and Steel in Nineteenth-Century America: An*

*Economic Inquiry* (Cambridge: The Massachusetts Institute of Technology Press, 1964) 109. The Trenton Iron Company was the fourth largest iron works in the country in 1860. The top three were: The Montour Iron Works, Wood Morrell and Co., and the Phoenix Iron Company.

37. *Encyclopaedia of Contemporary Biography of New York*, 2:25-26. See also Howard Carroll, *Twelve Americans: Their Lives and Times* (New York: Harper and Brothers, 1883) 77-116.

38. Allen Jones and Dumas Malone, *Dictionary of American Biography*, (New York: Charles Scribner's Sons, 1932) 2:396. See also the *New York Times*, February 26, 1905.

39. Allen Nevins, *Abram S. Hewitt: With Some Account of Peter Cooper* (New York: Octagon Books, Inc., 1935; reprinted ed. 1967) 83. See also *The New York Times*, January 19, 1903.

40. Peter Mack, *Peter Cooper: Citizen of New York* (New York: Duell, Sloan and Pearce, 1949) 205-06, 210-11. See also William T. Hogan, *Economic History of the Iron and Steel Industry in the United States*, 5 vols. (Lexington, Toronto, and London: D.C. Heath and Company, 1971) 1:95-96.

41. Nevins, *Abram S. Hewitt*, 158.

42. Osborn of Massachusetts was made president of the Illinois Central Railroad in 1855 while the line was still incomplete and on the verge of financial ruin. He rescued the line from its chaotic condition and earned the reputation as a man of indomitable will and integrity. After almost thirty years of service to the Company, he retired in 1882. Osborn died in 1894 in New York City. See Jones and Malone, *Dictionary of American Biography*, 14:72-73; *New York Tribune*, March 4, 1894. See also Paul W. Gates, *The Illinois Central Railroad and Its Colonization Work* (Cambridge: Harvard University Press, 1934) 77-78.

43. Sears, *George B. McClellan*, 56.

44. Edward Robb Ellis, *The Epic of New York City* (New York: Coward-McCann, Inc., 1966) 277.

45. Note appended to letter of Fernando Wood to Henry Alexander Wise, April 11, 1859. Misc. Mss. Wood, F. The New York Historical Society, New York.

46. Jerry Patterson, *The City of New York: A History* (New York: Harry N. Abrams, Publisher, 1978) 34-35. Ellis, *The Epic of New York City*, 277; *The New York Times*, February 14, 1881.

47. The Street Department consisted of the following bureaus: Street Improvements, Wharves, Roads, Lands and Places, Lamps and Gas, and Collection of Assessments. For a description of the duties of each bureau see *The New York Times*, December 30, 1858.

48. Samuel Augustus Pleasants, *Fernando Wood of New York* (New York: Columbia University Press, 1948) 78. Ellis, *The Epic of New City*, 278. See also Jerome Mushkat, *Fernando Wood: A Political Biography* (Kent: The Kent

State University Press, 1990) 73-74.

49. *New York Times*, November 24, 1859.

50. Mushkat, *Fernando Wood*, 79.

51. *New York Times*, November 24, 1859.

52. *New York Tribune*, April 25, 1858.

53. *New York Times*, October 25, 1860.

54. *New York Tribune*, November 12, 1858.

# CHAPTER FOUR

# From Triumph to Treason

The thirty-six-year old Smith understood that the responsibility of directing the business of the Street Department would not be easy; but like a true soldier he was ready to accept the challenge. The Street Department was an amorphous operation that touched virtually every interest of New York's largest city. This included several bureaus and an annual appropriation of $3,000,000. The engineering and administrative skills that Smith had acquired over the years would serve him well as commissioner. A noticeable aspect of Smith's life was that he had developed a habit of careful attention to technical details.

Smith inherited an office with a long history of fraudulent activity. He was careful not to breach the trust of New Yorkers for personal gain. Ambition, not avarice, was the guiding principle of his administration. Smith's honesty and integrity were a sharp departure from that of several of his predecessors; many of whom had occupied the office of Street Commissioner with the intent of lining their pockets at the public's expense.

A few days after Smith took the oath of office, an editorial in The New York Times called his attention to the condition of the city streets. A survey of the city revealed that many of them were unpaved, uncleaned, and unfinished. And of particular concern was the pathetic condition of side streets. The editor reminded the new commissioner that the taxpayers would not tolerate poorly maintained streets. The editorial concluded by appealing to Smith to give his "prompt and efficient attention" to this problem.[1] Smith understood the power of both the press and that of public opinion and made the improvement of city streets a priority of his administration.

Though street improvement was important to Smith, it was not his most urgent concern. The major problem confronting him was the lack of fiscal management. Smith's mathematical background and training as head of the engineering department at the Cooper and Hewitt plant had prepared him well for the supervision of financial matters. One of the more enduring contributions made by Smith was the introduction of a new system of financial record keeping. The system called for vouchers to be prepared in triplicate with a copy in the office of Street Commissioner, the comptroller, and the bureau where the contract originated. This was essentially the same record keeping system used at the Treasury Department by Secretary Guthrie. The success of the triplicate voucher system at the Treasury Department's bureau of Construction where Smith had worked a few years earlier had convinced him of its merit. Furthermore, Smith's familiarity with the system made its implementation a routine procedure. The triplicate voucher system called for three separate offices to maintain original documentation relating to each business transaction. Smith was aware that each office would have to participate if fraud were to occur.[2] The chance for fraudulent payments to contractors, whether accidental or intentional, was effectively curtailed.

Commissioner Smith had learned through the uncovering of profligate schemes of previous administrations that the alteration of price figures on contracts was a common method of fraud. To remedy this problem, Smith required his superintendents to write out in full the negotiated price on such documents. He also mandated that each contract contain comprehensive descriptions and specifications as to the nature of the work to be done. With the successful implementation of these reform measures, Smith had taken a monumental step toward the elimination of corruption at the Street Department. But more importantly, he had inaugurated an efficient fiscal management policy.

Smith was satisfied with the manner in which the record keeping system was carried out under his governance. He had succeeded in bringing order to what was once a confusing and chaotic situation. In doing so, Smith had affirmed what many had already known; that he was a man of superb administrative talents. Commenting on the nature of voucher payments under his supervision, Smith said, "the system itself is correct and well adapted to the varied and important business of this department but it has been carried out in most cases by the officers under me with zeal and industry."[3] To insure accountability among his superintendents, Smith required that they transmit monthly reports to him detailing the business transactions of their bureaus. The superintendents' reports were to contain the amount and kind of work completed, the cost of materials and supplies, and a statement about the budget.

The year 1859 opened with Mayor Daniel F. Tiemann delivering his Annual Message on January 3 to the Common Council. The mayor painted a rosy picture of the city by assuring New Yorkers that his administration had made significant strides toward the elimination of political corruption.[4] Mayor Tiemann announced to the Council that when he began his term as mayor in January 1858, the Street Department was steeped in corruption and disorder. Speaking of Smith, Tiemann said his training as an engineer and his high moral character qualified him to direct the activities of the Street Department.

In January 1859, Edward Ewen, superintendent of street improvements, sent a letter to the Street Department and the Common Council to solicit Smith's support for the completion of the Battery Enlargement in the city. The slow rate of progress on the Battery and the lack of attention given to it by Smith angered Ewen. In the same letter Ewen offered the following resolution for the consideration of the Common Council. It read in part, "that the Street Commissioner is hereby authorized and directed to advertise for proposals and enter into a contract for the completion of the Battery."[5] Undoubtedly, Superintendent Ewen believed that by writing directly to Smith and invoking the name of the Common Council he could gain the Street Commissioner's support for his pet project. Ewen's resolution did not receive the slightest attention from Smith or the Common Council. Obviously, the improvement to the Battery was not high on the Street Commissioner's priority list, and the mere writing of a letter did not cause Smith to change his mind. Also, a recommendation emanating from the Street Department without the endorsement of its chief was not likely to be received by the Common Council.

Smith adjusted comfortably into the social and political circles of New York City. As Street Commissioner, Smith was gaining valuable knowledge in the school of Democratic party politics. With the passage of time, he was gaining more notice as an influential political figure in the Tammany Hall wing of the Democratic party. Tammany Hall was a powerful nineteenth century political phenomenon that gained its strength through exploitation. The burgeoning city bureaucracy was controlled by strong men. As the city expanded so did the influence of the Tammanyites. This organization maintained its power for many years through a system of patronage. Although openly dishonest and corrupt, Tammany Hall was an institution to be reckoned with in politics.

Smith clearly understood that he had secured his position as the result of a political appointment. And to ignore the wishes of his party was tantamount to political suicide. The outside influence of Tammany Hall proved to be powerful, and Smith responded by removing two clerks from the Street Commissioner's office, effective February 1, 1859. The Republican *New York Tribune* stated as a well-known fact that the "urgent demands for Democrats to take their places" had caused the positions of William V. Leggett and Joseph B. Pollock to be sacrificed.[6] The little opposition in the Street Department that had been tolerated was gradually being weeded out. The termination of these clerks was indicative of the political reality of the time. It also underscored that partisan politics was a constant companion in the Street Department. Mayor Tiemann had called for the heads of departments to take a non-partisan approach to the staffing of their respective departments, but adherence to this request was disregarded with impunity. Though he valued fairness, Smith was unable to escape the tentacles of partisan politics. But to give the impression that Smith was motivated more by politics than by competence would be inaccurate. He expected quality work from his large staff. Smith retained William Allen as his assistant from the previous administration because he was too valuable to discharge.[7] Though politics might have been the overriding factor in the dismissal of the Street Department clerks, perhaps a lack of competence also played a role in their departure. After all, Allen was a Republican.

Hard work and stress eventually took their toll on Smith. The preparation of bids, contracts, reports, and staff supervision consumed his time. Smith was absent from the Street Department for several weeks during the spring of 1859 because of a serious throat disease. On the advice of his physician, Smith went South for the benefit of his health. During his absence, the duties of the office devolved to Mansfield Lovell.

Smith resumed his duties in May 1859. Smith noted that he was "perfectly satisfied" with Lovell's work during his convalescence. Upon returning, Smith found the accounts of the bureau of collection and assessments in total disarray, and he appointed William Kelly to head the troubled office. Kelly accepted the appointment with the stipulation that he would leave after completing his work. Smith instructed him to conduct a review of the affairs of that bureau. Kelly's laborious investigation revealed that inadequate record keeping was the source of the problem. Smith directed him to implement the necessary corrective procedures to bring the record keeping of that bureau in line with the other departments. Believing his work was done, Kelly left his post on December 31. On the occasion of Kelly's departure, Smith reflected on the municipal career of one of his more capable superintendents. "He discharged the duties of his office to my entire satisfaction," Smith said, "and the city by his resignation loses the services of a thoroughly competent and efficient officer."[8]

Because of the complex nature of the Street Department it was impossible for Smith to supervise every aspect of its operation. He was quick to acknowledge that irregularities and abuses occurred in the various branches under his administration. Smith insisted that every transaction be accompanied with documentation so thoroughly written as to require no explanation. He also issued a directive to his subordinates requiring them to make the official records of their departments available for public inspection. Smith told his staff that all papers pertaining to the activities of the Street Department were public property belonging to the office, and not the officer. Smith's penchant for documentation forced his workers to be accountable not only to him, but to the public as well.

Smith constantly searched for ways to improve the operations of the Street Department. A particularly disturbing problem was the lack of a permanent corps of qualified Inspectors to supervise the contractual work of the various branches of his department. He realized that work was not always done in accordance with the specifications of the contracts. To insure that contractual obligations were met, Smith recommended to the Board of Aldermen the appointment of several Inspectors to his department. His formal request called for eight Inspectors to be attached to the bureau of street improvements; four to the bureau of wharves; and two to the bureau of roads, for a total of fourteen. Smith suggested an annual salary of $900 for each Inspector.

Smith's recommendation was a dramatic departure from the existing system that called for Inspectors to be appointed to supervise each contract at a rate of $2 a day regardless of the length or importance of the work. According to Smith, this arrangement was unacceptable. Smith argued that the appointment of a sufficient number of competent Inspectors would eliminate this problem and greatly improve the affairs of the Street Department. The Board of Aldermen's Committee on Ordinances recommended that the amendment for appointing the Inspectors be adopted. After a discussion of some length, the Board president Thomas McSpedon called for a vote, and the measure passed.[9]

The Street Commissioner, however, had his share of controversy as well. Smith and Henry H. Howard, chief engineer of the Fire Department, found themselves locked in a sharp debate over appropriations for the Fire Department. In September 1859, Smith informed the Common Council that the funds for the Fire Department were nearly exhausted with four months remaining in the fiscal year. The balance was encumbered as a result of vouchers drawn against the account by Howard. Smith told the Council that the City Charter prohibited any department head from incurring an expense when there was no appropriation to cover it. Smith recommended that the Common Council appropriate a little more than $11,000 to cover the expenses for the remainder of the year.

On September 17, Howard responded to the letter Smith had written to the Common Council. In his correspondence to the Street Commissioner, Howard stated that "every article of the Fire apparatus is in perfect working condition," and "no fresh amount of appropriation will be needed for this Bureau."[10] Smith said that he could not understand this assertion when requisitions amounting to several thousand dollars were still awaiting his approval. The quarrel between the two men was rapidly degenerating into anger. Smith sent a vitriolic note to Howard demanding that he not incur any further expense in his department until the Common Council had made the necessary appropriation. The controversy ended when the Common Council approved Smith's recommended appropriation.

Among Smith's accomplishments in New York was the repair and construction of public buildings. One of the city's outstanding structures was City Hall. In August 1858, a wave of excitement engulfed the city and indeed the nation with word of the successful laying of the Atlantic telegraph cable under the direction of the New York merchant, Cyrus W. Field. This technological achievement revolutionized the commercial and communication relationship between the Old World and the New. The city celebrated the event amidst the pageantry of parades, banquets, and fireworks.[11] The brilliant display of fireworks resulted in the burning of City Hall on September 1. The occasion was thus rendered ironically memorable by the devastation of the roof, the cupola, and the statue of justice.

Almost a year after the fire, the Common Council passed a resolution authorizing Smith to prepare specifications and advertise for proposals to have the City Hall repaired.[13] Smith secured the services of an architect and by the end of July 1859 the blueprint was ready for Council approval. The Council appropriated $50,000 for this work. Smith was well-suited to supervise the repair work at City Hall because of his prior experience as a construction engineer. By the end of the year, Smith was ready to present the repaired City Hall to City Inspector Charles Delavan for his approval.

The repair work to City Hall was not the only construction project under the supervision of the Street Department. Smith was also in charge of completing the construction of the three- story building at Tompkins Square. The Square was named in honor of Daniel D. Tompkins, Governor of New York during the War of 1812 and vice president under James Monroe.[14] Construction for the market at Tompkins Square began in August 1857. Until that time, the Square was no more than an open field showing all the signs of neglect. The construction at Tompkins was among the more notable improvements taking place in the eastern section of New York in 1857. Upon completion, the building would house offices and stores and would serve as the headquarters for the Seventh Regiment of the New York State Militia.

As the Tompkins Square market neared completion, Smith's combativeness propelled him into a controversy with Comptroller Robert T. Haws, who was elected to that position in 1858. The *Tribune* stated that Haws owed his election "to a spirit of political revolution on the one hand and to the independent action of upright citizens on the other, rather than to the machine of party organization."[15] During the campaign, Smith had given not only his moral but financial[16] support as well to Haws' opponent, James Purser of Tammany Hall. Haws' mercantile and business experience would serve him well in his new position as head of the city's finance department. He had been a prominent Whig and, after that party's demise, placed his allegiance with the Republican party.[17]

The awarding of the contract for the construction of the roof on the building at Tompkins Square embroiled Haws and Smith in a memorable controversy. In the spring of 1859, Smith accepted bids for the roof work. Much to Smith's disappointment, he received only two estimates, one for $14,500 and another for $10,500. In June, Smith forwarded the highest bid to Haws for approval of payment. Due to a technicality, Smith concluded that the lowest bid was unacceptable and refused to submit it. Therefore, he believed it was his duty to award the contract to the highest bidder. Subsequently, Haws declined to approve payment. He also noted that the difference between the two bids was so great that the action by Smith was not justified. By denying the sureties, Haws claimed to have saved the treasury $4,000 on the roof contract.

Smith appealed Haws' decision to the Board of Aldermen. While awaiting the decision of the Board, Smith without explanation readvertised for the roof job. During the second round of bidding, the Street Department received an estimate of $10,000 from the contractor, Theodore Hunt. This estimate being lower than the lowest bid of a few weeks earlier, Smith gave the job to him. When Smith contacted Hunt to confirm acceptance, Hunt informed the commissioner of a serious omission from the original bid. Hunt had failed to include the estimate for the iron that amounted to $3,500 and because of this error wished to have his bid voided. Smith informed him that he did not have the authority to disallow the bid. At its meeting on September 13, 1859, the Board of Aldermen granted Hunt his wish and relieved him from his pending contractual obligation. The controversy finally ended when the Aldermen directed Smith to award the roof contract to Gillespie and Maitlang, who were among the two original bidders for the Tompkins project. The adoption of Alderman John H. Brady's resolution required Haws to approve the sureties for Gillespie and Maitlang for $14,500 for the construction of the roof at Tompkins Market.[18] Once the roof contract controversy was settled, it was only a matter of months before the work on Tompkins Square was completed.

The year 1859 closed with the mayoral election in December. This election was important because of its implications for the national conventions of the coming year. The prestige of victory in this contest would greatly increase the importance of the state of New York in the nomination of candidates for the major political parties in 1860. Because of the number of candidates, opposition was divided which made the election of Fernando Wood possible.[19] Tiemann's last official act as mayor was the swearing in of Wood and Bronson C. Greene as Corporation Counsel on December 28. The situation in the Empire City at the beginning of Wood's third term was contentious for the incoming mayor. His success depended on the support of the heads of departments, many of whom were Tiemann's appointees. In most cases they had a year left in office. Mayor Wood was powerless to remove them without the approval of the Board of Aldermen.[20] Mayor Wood delivered his Annual Message to the Common Council on January 2, 1860. He opened his address with the lament that the municipal government of New York appeared "to have become the more demoralized and feeble" as the metropolis itself had grown to become one of the great and powerful cities of the Western World.[21] The excessive cold of early January was symbolic of the ubiquitous dark shadows of political strife that hovered about the nation at that time.

In early 1860, the nation commenced readying itself for the political conventions that were to draft platforms and nominate candidates for the upcoming presidential election.[22] The election of 1860, to say the least, was an unforgettable one and the most important ever held in terms of its results. More than in any other election of the nineteenth century, the issue of slavery dominated the campaign. In great halls of the North, orators argued the merits and constitutionality of extending or restricting the institution of slavery. The tremendous excitement generated by the campaign swept through the nation as though it were a tidal wave. Most of the excitement centered on the Midwesterner Abraham Lincoln. On the occasion of his first visit to New York City, Lincoln made his famous Cooper Institute Address on February 27, 1860.[23] There he stood in the Great Hall, face to face with about 1,500 eastern urbanites and the New York press. Though a bit nervous, Lincoln delivered a powerful speech that helped to prepare the way for his nomination as the Republican presidential candidate.[24]

In almost ritualistic fashion night after night, thousands of New Yorkers listened to the rhetoric on either side of the slavery question. The inflammatory oratory of the campaign did not cool off as summer slowly gave way to autumn. The fiery speeches served as a warning of an impending crisis. New York was home to many Southerners who had migrated there in earlier years in search of economic prosperity. Also, a strong economic bond tied New York to the states below the Potomac that helped to produce a strong pro-Southern sentiment in the city.[25]

As the campaign unfolded it became clear that of the two major political parties of New York the Republicans enjoyed far greater unity than their rivals. There were three competing forces vying for hegemony of the Democratic party of New York. The first was the Albany Regency, the regular state organization. Its strength lay almost exclusively in the up-state districts of the state. The second rival faction was Tammany Hall, the local Democratic organization in New York City. Though not as powerful or influential as it once was or was to become, Tammany remained a force to be reckoned with. The final Democratic faction was Mozart Hall, the creation of Fernando Wood. Mozart Hall also controlled New York City Hall in 1860 and the political patronage that went with it. It also had the support of a major newspaper in the city, the *New York Herald*.[26] Wood had been a member of Tammany, but unable to dominate it, he withdrew and established the rival Mozart Hall of which he was the leader.

After the nominating conventions were over, supporters of the candidates began to campaign in earnest for the White House. New York was important to them because of its thirty-five electoral votes. Among the prominent New Yorkers caught up in the excitement of the historical campaign was Smith.[27] Smith, a cautious and perceptive politician, followed the campaign very carefully before deciding who to support. After listening to the harangue of several politicians and presidential candidates, Smith decided to endorse the ticket of John C. Breckinridge of Kentucky and Senator Joseph Lane of Oregon. That Smith would support the Southern wing of the Democratic party was not surprising. After all, he was a Southerner by birth and his affection was with that region of the country.

The New York City delegates to the Breckinridge-Lane State Convention met at the Irving Building on Broadway on August 1, 1860. Smith chaired the meeting that was called to organize for the state convention that was scheduled for Syracuse a week later. Smith told the gathering that New York City representation to the Breckinridge Convention at Syracuse on August 7, would include one delegate and one alternate from each Assembly District. Smith and George Baldwin were the delegate and alternate respectively from the fourteenth district.[28] Smith appointed a committee to draft a resolution on the idea of fusion. The committee reported to the Irving group that the city delegates to the Syracuse convention would not accept any form of fusion with Stephen A. Douglas. The resolution was unanimously adopted. Before adjourning, Smith announced that state officers for the Breckinridge ticket would be nominated at the Syracuse convention.

The Breckinridge-Lane State Convention convened at Syracuse in the Corinthian Hall on the morning of August 7. More than 300 enthusiastic supporters had gathered there to nominate state and electoral tickets. Many influential Democrats were in attendance including Richard Lathers and Smith of the New York delegation of Tammany Hall. The harmonious proceedings of the convention were not only important for the smooth transaction of business, but also for a show of unity and strength as well. The Breckinridge Convention adopted, as was expected, a proslavery platform calling for the protection of slavery in the territories. The delegates also adopted a resolution criticizing Abraham Lincoln for his uncompromising stand against the spread of slavery into the new territories. Before the Convention adjourned, presidential electors pledged to Breckinridge and a state ticket led by the prominent attorney James T. Brady for Governor had been nominated. Brady possessed one of the best legal minds in the state.[29] Nonetheless, Lincoln and the Republicans carried both New York and the national majority. No doubt the factionalism in the Democratic party contributed to the Republican triumph. The Democratic party of New York also had its share of discord. The turbulent decade of the 1850s witnessed bitter factional fights within Tammany Hall over the slavery issue. Tammany had always been vocal in its opposition to the abolition of slavery and in its excoriation of abolitionists.[30] With Lincoln's victory, South Carolina prepared to leave the Union.

A few days after the November 6 election, the Breckinridge-Lane General Committee held a meeting at Thorp's Hotel in New York City to draft an address to the country on the secession threat. Smith called the near capacity crowd to order and announced that it was a special meeting for a special purpose. Because of the meeting's importance to the nation, Smith invited the New York press. The climax of the meeting was the reading of the memorial by Phillip W. Engs of the Executive Committee entitled "An Address to the Nation." The Address was as much an attack on Lincoln as it was a defense of the social and political institutions of the South. The Executive Committee wrote that the clouds of apprehension that engulfed the nation were the result of Lincoln's election. And that the gathering storm on the horizon was directly attributable to his hostility toward the expansion of slavery. When Engs stated that the Republicans would "attempt to reverse the order of nature and elevate the negro to an equality with the white," the crowd erupted into a thunderous applause. The Address concluded by predicting a bleak outlook for the nation with the inauguration of Lincoln in March 1861.[31] The Address was unanimously adopted by the meeting. In a letter to Joseph Lane on November 15 (signed by Smith and three other members of the Breckinridge-Lane Committee), the signatories asked him to give his opinions in regard to the threat of secession. Lane's reply echoed the same theme as did the "Address to the Nation." He defended the right of slave masters to carry their property into the territories. Lane concluded his letter with a warning that the Union was not formed by force and that force should not be used to maintain it.

After the presidential election, the talk of secession coming from the Southern states became more ominous. Less than two months after Lincoln's victory, the secessionists proceeded confidently, perhaps even arrogantly to make good on their pre-election threat of disunion.[32] When South Carolina called for a convention to draft its Ordinance of Secession, the *New York Journal of Commerce* urged that State to exercise patience and not to precipitate a civil war. The editorial also counseled South Carolina that it was possible for it to maintain dignity and honor while preserving peace and order.[33] By then, however, the secession movement had progressed to the point of no return and the Palmetto State was in no mood to exercise restraint. South Carolina threw down the gauntlet on December 20, 1860. The reality of secession occurred on that day when South Carolina "the proudest and most aristocratic of all Southern States" declared its independence from the Union.[34] The culmination of secessionism was the formation of the Confederate States of America at Montgomery in early 1861.

By the time of Lincoln's inauguration, seven states had left the Union. Perhaps no other border state of the Confederate South was watched with more interest during the secession controversy than Smith's native state of Kentucky. Not only was Kentucky the birthplace of Presidents Abraham Lincoln and Jefferson Davis, but also a state with strong attachments in both sections of the country. The separation of the union and the advent of civil war caused Kentucky to adopt a unique policy in response to these unprecedented events. By May 20, the Kentucky legislature had declared a "position of strict neutrality" for its state.[35] This policy of neutrality placed Smith in a precarious position. Kentucky's neutrality, however, was ephemeral. On September 11, 1861, the Kentucky legislature ordered the Confederates to leave the state. This settled the issue, Kentucky had decided to place its allegiance unequivocally with the United States.[36]

Despite the insurmountable odds of holding the nation together, a conservative wing of the Democratic party still hoped for reconciliation. One of the last attempts to bring about a peaceful solution to the crisis was the efforts of a group of conservative Democrats. These men voiced their hope in a forum that came to be known as the Pine Street meeting. A circular announcing the meeting was mailed on December 10, 1860, to nearly 200 of the most prominent and influential citizens of New York.[37] The by-invitation-only meeting convened on December 15 in the offices of Richard Lathers on Pine Street, the heart of the city's commercial district. According to the invitation, the purpose of the meeting was to devise and adopt measures which could heal the nation and restore the country to "peaceful and harmonious relations." Smith was one of the seventeen prominent conservatives who had signed the invitation calling for the meeting on Pine Street.[38] The most influential person behind this peace movement was the statesman, Richard Lathers. He was born in Ireland and brought to South Carolina before he was one year old. He remained in the Palmetto State until he relocated to New York City in 1848 at the age of twenty-seven. Two years later, he founded the Great Western Insurance Company. Lathers, who died in 1903 at the age of eighty-two, was a Tammany Democrat.[39]

The prominent New York attorney Charles O'Conor was selected as chairman of the meeting. He then appointed a committee of twenty-four, one of whom was Smith. O'Conor gave them instructions to prepare resolutions and to draft an address to be delivered to Southern leaders. Before the close of the Pine Street meeting, the Committee through its chairman, John A. Dix, presented a lengthy essay known as the "Address and Resolution," which after considerable debate was adopted by the Pine Street meeting. The enthusiastic acceptance of the

Address as a peace panacea by the press and leading citizens of New York was satisfying to the committee that had labored so diligently to produce it.[40] It should be noted that the Pine Street meeting was a pro-slavery and anti-Republican gathering.

The document stated that the rights of the South should not be usurped by the federal government and the people of the territories alone should decide whether a state should be admitted into the Union free or slave. The memorial articulated not only the principle of peaceable secession but also an appeal for time to solve the difficulties that existed between the two sections.[41] Before the meeting adjourned, a delegation consisting of Millard Fillmore, Bronson C. Greene, and Richard Lathers was appointed to proceed to the South with the Address. Both the ex-President and Greene had to withdraw; therefore, Lathers was left alone to undertake the delicate mission. In spite of the overwhelming odds against halting secession and the impending war, the efforts of the Pine Street meeting were not abandoned.[42] Lathers departed from New York for the South in February 1861, with the Address in hand. Although he visited several cities and presented the celebrated document to many Southern leaders, in the end the effort to hold the nation together was hopeless.[43] Though nothing came of the Pine Street effort to avert disunion, Smith could find satisfaction in knowing that he had played a role in trying to save the nation from the madness of war.

Years after the war, Lathers recalled the memorable occasions in which high ranking officers of both the Union and Confederate armies gathered at his home in Charleston to reminisce about their days on the battlefield. Among those who engaged in the friendly exchange in South Carolina were George B. McClellan, Irvin McDowell, John A. Dix, Gustavus W. Smith, Mansfield Lovell, and Joseph E. Johnston. Though Lathers had been unable to prevent the war, he found comfort in knowing that in a small way he had helped to bring the two sections of the country back together, even if it were underneath a tree in his yard.[44]

There were many in New York City who sympathized with the South during the secession controversy. Once disunion had become a reality they moved away from a posture of compromise to one of advocating nonintervention in the South on the part of the federal government. This position found expression in the form of a large anticoercion meeting held at Brooks Hall on January 15, 1861. The meeting was called by pro-Southern men to voice their opposition to the use of force by the federal government in preventing a state from leaving the Union or forcing a state to return to it. Among the leaders of the Brooks Hall meeting were its chairman P. W. Groot, Smith, and his deputy, Mansfield Lovell, both of whom were appointed vice-presidents of the meeting. The Brooks Hall meeting passed a resolution warning the federal government that any attempt to coerce the South to submit to the will of the North would be opposed by all legitimate means. It also declared that the United States was a white man's government and that slaves should be freely spread over the entire nation.[45]

The bold act of secession by South Carolina was the pretext Mayor Wood needed to deliver one of the more extraordinary messages ever received by the Common Council. On January 7, 1861, he suggested that New York become an independent city should war occur between the North and the South. He called for the establishment of a free Manhattan Island, "peaceably, if possible, forcibly, if necessary." The mayor's proposition was not a popular one. It represented a long-standing feud between Wood and upstate New York over control of the city. Wood used the opportunity to denounce bitterly the state legislature for interference in the corporate life of the municipality.[46] Wood's audacious memorandum was less of a serious proposal than an attempt to please his pro-compromise business supporters of the South. Wood believed that the dissolution of the federal government was inevitable and that the city should not jeopardize its profitable trade with the Southern states. The ties between Wood and New York businessmen made it easy for advocates of the South including Smith to continue to operate amidst his most avid supporters.

Mayor Wood, the quintessential politician, miscalculated the secession crisis and the war itself. He believed that when the unavoidable military conflict was over, the country would be permanently divided as a result of a Southern victory. During the whole secession movement, Wood's sympathies were with the Southern states.[47] In keeping with his pro-Southern ideology, Wood denounced the Negro population as inferior and declared that "the profits, luxuries, the necessities—nay even the physical existence depended upon labor and the prosperity of the slave master."[48] In the Proclamation, Wood issued to New York in January 1861, he stated that the special rights and demands of the South were misunderstood. In an effort to avert the calamity of civil war, Wood dispatched a commission to the South with instructions to preserve the peace and to secure the rights of the Southern people.[49] It would appear that Wood devoted more of his time to national issues than to governing the city.

Smith, however, never neglected his duties during the political controversy. On November 12, 1860, Smith wrote to the Common Council informing them that his official term of two years had expired the day before. It then became the duty of the mayor to nominate a candidate to the Board of Aldermen for confirmation as commissioner. As Smith's expiration date approached, City Hall officials and Street Department workers anxiously awaited the announcement from the mayor as to who would be the next chief of the department. As expected, there was a tremendous amount of gossip and speculation in political circles about Smith's successor. But as November slowly gave way to December, the city was still awaiting the formal announcement of Smith's replacement. As required by law, the present commissioner was to remain in office until the appointment of his successor.

It was well-known that the mayor was campaigning tirelessly to have his brother Henry Wood replace Smith. Fernando Wood expended a good deal of time and energy canvassing the members of the Board to determine whether he had enough votes to win the seat for his brother before officially submitting his name for confirmation. A few days before Smith's term expired, Mayor Wood invited to his office for a private meeting those members of the Board whom he deemed approachable to the idea of his brother's becoming commissioner. He intimated to them that nine aldermen had agreed to Smith's replacement; the requisite number for confirmation. However, a comparison of notes produced laughter when it was revealed that only Aldermen Nicholas Seagrist and Gilbert M. Platt supported Mayor Wood's plan.[50] When Wood returned to New York City in late December after celebrating his third marriage, he was disappointed to learn that the chance of Henry becoming commissioner was exceedingly slim. In warning the Board not to accept the mayor's brother a leading newspaper of New York lamented, "the threat of Henry Wood's nomination" portended ill for the public treasury of the city.[51]

Because of inimical feelings toward Mayor Wood, the Board of Aldermen was not ready to support his effort to aid his brother.

However, bitterness and a preponderance of Democrats on the Board did not fully explain their rejection of Wood's proposal. To begin with, the city had not forgotten the mayor's chicanery in securing the office of Street Commissioner in 1857 for the corrupt Charles Devlin. But paramount to the defeat of Wood's scheme was the fact that Smith was a competent commissioner whose reputation had not been tarnished by corruption. The Board regarded Smith as a capable and judicious official and could not see any advantage to be gained by his removal. A few weeks before Smith's term had officially expired, the *Times* praised him for his efficiency and honesty at the Street Department. The newspaper characterized Smith as an "officer against whose official purity not even slander has dared to wag a tongue."[52] The endorsement of Smith by the Board combined with the support of the major newspapers convinced Wood that his effort to secure the municipal office for his brother was hopeless. And he refrained from submitting the name of Henry Wood to the Board. Smith never involved himself in the squabble between the Board and Mayor Wood concerning his replacement. A cordial and professional relationship existed between Smith and Wood. Nonetheless, Smith was willing to wage political war against the attempt to remove him.

Despite the attempt by Mayor Wood to remove Smith, the new year found him firmly entrenched as Street Commissioner of New York City. In early January 1861, Smith terminated John H. Chambers from the office of deputy collector of assessments. Chambers was a casualty because of his sympathy with Wood during the recent attempt to oust Smith. His replacement was the Democrat, John Y. Savage, who competently carried out the duties of his office. Smith devoted his attention and time almost exclusively to the business of his department during the winter of 1860 while patiently awaiting the appointment of any replacement.

Though Smith continued to carry out the duties entrusted to his office, he was not oblivious to the political situation around him. As Smith looked into the distance, he could clearly see the gathering clouds of war on the horizon. Smith still had hoped even during these tumultuous days that war could be averted. But the pragmatic Smith was faced with the somber reflection that time could not be made to stand still and that patriotism alone could not impart the common sense men seem to lose during a war. The highest statesmanship was needed to deal with the awful difficulties before the country. But such leadership was conspicuously absent in both the North and the South. The firing on Fort Sumter by the Confederates on April 12, 1861, began a new chapter in the saga between the sections. The day after the capitulation of the Fort, Lovell wrote to McClellan to inform him that he and Smith would never acquiesce to "throat-cutting" abolitionists, who wanted to give American Negroes "political [and] civil equality with the white man." They were convinced that the South would vigorously oppose a doctrine of racial equality. Lovell concluded, "I trust that mature reflection and close investigation of the whole subject will result in your siding with us." Although unofficial, Lovell's invitation was as close as McClellan came to being offered an opportunity to join the Southern cause.[53] Obviously, Smith and Lovell shared the racial ideology of Negro inferiority that was prevalent among the planter aristocracy.

Both Smith and Lovell still hoped that reason would prevail, thereby preventing the nation from becoming involved in the conflict. They were quick to learn, however, that the war would not be restricted to South Carolina or the South. When it became clear that the war would be of longer duration and that the federal government was determined to preserve the Union with the bayonet, Mansfield Lovell began the necessary preparations to relocate his family to the South. He had made up his mind to give his support to the Confederacy in the fearful struggle that was underway. Before leaving New York, Mayor Wood called upon Lovell to lead the Mozart Regiment into battle. In making the offer Wood said, "you would confer on its members and myself, the greatest obligation by affording them an early opportunity to show their zeal in defence [sic] of their country if placed under your command."[54] Flattering though it was, Lovell rejected the offer and resigned as Deputy Commissioner in September 1861.

General Joseph E. Johnston made an appeal to Davis on August 19, 1861, for commissions for Smith and Lovell. He recommended them "as two of the best officers whose services" the Confederate army could obtain. Johnston stated that they were as fit to command divisions as any officer then in the Confederate army. Johnston called Smith, "a man of high ability." Johnston said that both Smith and Lovell had "always wanted" to join the Confederate effort.[55]

When Lovell's resignation was announced, it was circulated in the

New York press that he had pledged not to leave the city during the war. The *Tribune* stated as a fact that "Lovell was among the first who was suspected in New York, and it was only by giving his parole of honor that he escaped arrest months ago."[56] Writing many years after the war, Smith sought to defend his friend and set the record straight on this matter. Smith emphatically argued that Lovell had never given his parole or promise to the superintendent of police or anyone else that he would not leave the city to avoid arrest and imprisonment.[57] Lovell proceeded to Richmond and offered his services to the Confederate States of America. On October 7, 1861, Davis appointed him to the rank of major general and placed him in command of the Department of Louisiana with headquarters in New Orleans.

Meanwhile Lovell's former superior was preparing to join him. Approximately two weeks before the Confederate attack on Fort Sumter, Smith was suddenly struck down by a stroke of paralysis reportedly brought on by overwork in his department. During Smith's protracted illness, he was confined to his room and with the exception of medical personnel and his wife, no other guests were permitted to visit him. When Smith had sufficiently regained his strength, his physician advised him to travel to Hot Springs, Arkansas for the benefit of his health. Smith took his doctor's advice and near the end of July 1861, departed from New York for Hot Springs.[58] While at Lexington, Smith detailed his illness to General Beauregard. He reported:

On the 29th of March to my utter surprise and horror, I had an attack of paralysis-one half of my face became rigid as marble. It extended to my arm and hand. But by prompt and energetic treatment the disease was checked and in two weeks I could wink my eyes very slightly-this was the first indication that the disease was checked and that I had begun to recover. I am well aware of the fact that my disease is of a fearful character. I have been five weeks at Pharne Springs, New York for the benefit of hot·sulphuric baths and my health is greatly improved.[59]

Shortly after the outbreak of the war, the federal government exerted a new power for the protection of public safety. Arrest orders were arbitrarily issued for persons in the North whom the government deemed disloyal and dangerous. This also included persons who sympathized with the Confederate cause or engaged in a secessionist talk. It was the responsibility of the Secretary of State to determine who would be arrested and placed in confinement. The government had decided that it would not tolerate open opposition or the utterance of treasonable sentiments.[60]

Soon after Smith's arrival in Kentucky, he learned that the authorities in Washington intended to arrest and imprison him because of his known pro-Southern views. The government had misconstrued his motives and ordered his arrest as a disloyalist.[61] It was commonly known that Smith, as a states' rights advocate, was opposed to the election of Abraham Lincoln. He believed the Republicans were antislavery men who were determined to effect a strong centralized government at Washington with the support of the United States Military.[62] Also disturbing to Smith was the belief that the Republican party intended to emancipate the slaves and maintain its domination over the South through force. From Smith's vantage point of having lived on both sides of the Mason-Dixon, he fully understood the temper of the people both North and South. He was aware of the deep resentment of Southerners to what they called Northern aggression.[63] Smith also knew that the North enjoyed a tremendous advantage over the South in terms of population, supplies, materials, and resources.

During Smith's absence from New York, there was considerable speculation at City Hall and the Street Department concerning his whereabouts. One rumor had placed Smith in Missouri. Another rumor had circulated about town to the effect that he had gone to St. Mary's, Canada, where he left his wife, Lucretia. The word from City Hall, however, was that if he did not immediately report to his office he would be superseded by the deputy Street Commissioner.[64]

On September 8, 1861, Smith ended the mystery concerning his location. In a letter to Henry W. Genet, president of the Board of Aldermen, Smith announced his resignation as Street Commissioner of New York:

> I have determined not to return to the City of New York to reside at the expiration of the period during which my physician directed me to travel for the benefit of my health. I tender to you, and through you to the Board of Aldermen, my sincere thanks for the kind and courteous treatment uniformly

extended to me by the Board over which you preside during our official intercourse.[65]

Less than two weeks after resigning because of previous ill health, Smith went to Richmond and offered his services to the Confederacy. Smith's sickness should have cast doubt on his capacity for the rigors of field command. But Davis accepted Smith's self-appraisal of his health. Writing to the Confederate President from Nashville on September 3, Smith said, "I am glad to be able to say that I have entirely and perfectly recovered from my recent illness, at one time it was feared that perfect recovery would not take place for a year, if ever."[66] On September 19, Davis conferred the rank of major general upon him.

Davis, himself a graduate of the Military Academy and a veteran of the Mexican War, valued such experience in his appointees. As Secretary of War in the Pierce administration, he had ample opportunity to become aware of Smith's reputation won in these arenas. Moreover, he had selected as the Confederacy's Adjutant General Samuel Cooper whose principal qualification was his administrative experience that gave him thorough knowledge of officers' reputations in the prewar Army. Smith went South with a great reputation and was appointed commander of the Second Corps of the Army of the Potomac. With the addition of Smith and Lovell to the Confederate army, the *New York Herald* editorialized them as ranking "among the ablest officers in the country ... that both Beauregard and Johnston have been thrown into the shade by their superior reputation."[67] A Richmond newspaper stated that Generals Joseph E. Johnston, Pierre G. T. Beauregard, and Smith presented "an array of talent and skill not be equaled on the continent."[68] At the age of thirty-nine, the soldierly looking Smith was in the prime of his life. Possessing extraordinary mental strength, his conduct and character were impeccable. His civil and military training and Mexican War experience were exemplary.

Because of Smith's defection to the South, the United States considered him a traitor. As a major general in the Confedrate army, he had taken an important role in assisting the Confederacy in its attempt to overthrow the federal government. Smith had achieved distinction under the American flag; now he was committed to using his talents to topple the same. On the theory of whether or not Smith would have become a traitor had his arrest not been imminent, one can only speculate. However, the evidence strongly suggests that in all likelihood he would have cast his lot with the Confederacy.

To begin with, Smith was in frequent communication with Southern leaders during the secession crisis and after the creation of the Confederate government.[69] In January 1861, while en route to assume the superintendency of the United States Military Academy, Beauregard visited with Smith in New York City for a few days. No doubt the topic of discussion was what their course of action would be if the nation plunged into an internal war. Beauregard made no secret as to where he would place his loyalty if civil war came. He had informed General Joseph G. Totten, chief engineer, of his intention of going with his home state of Louisiana if it seceded from the Union.[70]

Writing to Smith in New York from Montgomery in February 1861, Beauregard requested his services in obtaining ten first-class Drummond lights to be used at New Orleans and Charleston. Beauregard told Smith that this transaction was to be executed in total secrecy. He concluded by asking Smith, "When shall we have the benefit of your services and those of Lovell?"[71] In early March, Smith assured Beauregard that his request had been carried out. Since Smith could not attend to this matter without attracting attention, he called on his friend Harmon Livingston to facilitate the purchase. Thus Smith had assisted in procuring equipment to be used to defend Confederate harbors against the United States. In response to Beauregard's question, Smith intimated to him that he and Lovell would favorably consider joining the Confederacy if asked by Davis or his Secretary of War, Leroy P. Walker.[72] While the Confederate government was still in its infant stages, its president had already expressed to Captain Raphael Semmes his desire to have Smith join the Confederate army. Writing to Semmes on February 21, Davis said, "Capt. G. W. Smith and Capt. Lovell, late of the U.S. Army and now of New York City ... please say to them that we would be happy to have their services in our army."[73] By August, Smith had reached a definitive decision as to the side he would take in the hostilities between the North and the South. In a letter to Beauregard, Smith wrote, "I would serve with satisfaction and pride under such men as yourself."[74] An important fact that should not be overlooked was that Smith had traveled to Richmond and was appointed to high command a week after Kentucky had ended its neutrality.

The three years that Smith served as Street Commissioner of New York City were filled with both excitement and controversy. He received the commendation of the press and the public for the efficient manner with which he performed his duties. Smith's combination of honesty and hard work were the main ingredients that he used to weed out corruption at the Street Department. It should be noted that corruption was not endemic to the Democratic party. Since the Democrats held power for longer periods of time, they had greater opportunities to foster corruption.

Smith continued in office for almost a year longer after his official expiration date while awaiting the appointment of his successor. On September 20, 1861, the Board of Aldermen confirmed Shepherd F. Knapp as Street Commissioner of New York. He was a conscientious man with superb executive ability who had made a name for himself in the business world. Knapp was known around New York for his devotion to horse-racing and cock-fighting.

Smith served New York to the satisfaction of both Tiemann and Wood. Of course, he did not operate in a vacuum. With few exceptions, he was ably supported by competent officers whom he rewarded with both praise and promotion. However, he never hesitated to punish those who were found guilty of misconduct. Smith was an educated engineer who made a difference as head of the Street Department. Smith's illustrious and triumphant career in New York was marred by his decision to become a traitor to the United States. Once he had defected to the South, only time would tell whether he would duplicate the success of his early military life as a General in the Confederate army.

# Notes

1. *New York Times*, November 17, 1858.
2. *New York Tribune*, December 30, 1858; *New York Times*, February 8, 1859.
3. *New York Times*, January 2, 1860.
4. James Grant Wilson, *The Memorial History of the City of New York: From Its First Settlement to the Year 1892*, 3 vols. (New York: New York History Company, 1893) 3: 453.
5. *New York Times*, January 16, 1859. The first contract issued for work to be done on the Battery Enlargement was in 1852. It was not completed until after Smith left office in 1861.
6. *New York Tribune*, January 12, 1859.
7. Attorney William Allen resigned that position to become Deputy Comptroller to Robert Haws in 1859.
8. *New York Times*, January 2, 1860.
9. *New York Tribune*, October 28, 1859; *New York Times*, June 15, 1859.
10. *New York Tribune*, September 20, 1859.
11. Mary L. Booth, *History of the City of New York: From Its Earliest Settlement to the Present Time* (New York: W.R.C. Clark and Meeker, 1867) 767. See also Wilson, *The Memorial History*, 3:465-466.
12. Maxwell F. Marcuse, *This was New York: A Nostalgic Picture of Gotham in Gaslight Era* (New York: LIM Press, 1965; reprint ed., 1969) 248-251.
13. *New York Tribune*, June 28, 1859.
14. Edward Robb Ellis, *The Epic of New York City* (New York: Coward-McCann, Inc., 1966) 212-213. See also the *New York Tribune*, October 21, 1859.
15. *New York Tribune*, December 10, 1858.
16. There is no indication of how much money Smith donated to the Purser campaign. Smith's salary in 1861 was $5,378.
17. *New York Tribune*, March 23, 1863; *New York Times*, January 3, 1859. See also Jerome Mushkat, *Fernando Wood: A Political Biography* (Kent: The Kent State University Press, 1990) 104.
18. *New York Times*, November 4, 1859; *New York Tribune*, September 13, 1859.
19. The four candidates in the mayoral election of 1859 were: George Opdyke, Republican, he would be elected mayor in 1861; William F. Havemeyer, Tammany Hall, Fernando Wood, Mozart Hall, and DePeyster Ogden, American Party.
20. Samuel Augustus Pleasants, *Fernando Wood of New York* (New York: Columbia University Press, 1948) 103.
21. *New York Times*, January 3, 1860.
22. Daniel Wait Howe, *Political History of Secession: To the Beginning of the American Civil War* (New York: The Knickerbocker Press, 1914) 410.
23. Cooper Institute was originally known as the Cooper Union for the Advancement of Science and Art. It was presented to the city in 1859 by the

philanthropist Peter Cooper. Cooper Union was an institution of higher learning where race, religion, or nationality were not factors in admission.

24. Marcuse, *This Was New York*, 109. See also Ellis, *The Epic of New York City*, 289-91.

25. Leonard, *History of the City of New York*, 367.

26. Sidney D. Brummer, *Political History of New York State During the Period of the Civil War* (New York: Longmans, Green and Company, 1911) 24-36.

27. In May 1860, Smith took time out of his busy schedule to participate in the wedding of his friend and comrade, George B. McClellan. McClellan selected his West Point friends including Smith, Cadmus Wilcox, Henry Clitz, and Seth Williams to serve as his groomsmen. See Stephen W. Sears, *George B. McClellan; The Young Napoleon* (New York: Ticknor and Fields, 1988) 63.

28. *New York Tribune*, August 2, 1860. See also William C. Wright, *The Secession Movement in the Middle Atlantic States* (Rutherford, Madison, and Teaneck: Fairleigh Dickinson University Press, 1973) 167-69.

29. Brummer, *Political History*, 76-77. *New York Herald*, August 8, 1860; *New York Tribune*, August 8, 1860; *New York Times*, November 30, 1859.

30. Morris R. Werner, *Tammany Hall* (New York: Doubleday, Doran and Company, Inc., 1928) 89.

31. For a complete text of the Address, see the *New York Tribune*, November 15, 1860.

32. Philip S. Foner, *Business and Slavery: The New York Merchants and the Irrepressible Conflict* (Chapel Hill: The University of North Carolina Press, 1941; reprinted, New York: Russell and Russell, 1968) 239-40.

33. *New York Journal of Commerce*, December 21, 1860.

34. Ellis, *The Epic of New York City*, 290-91. *New York Tribune*, December 21, 1860. For an excellent account of South Carolina's move toward secession see, Walter Brian Cisco, *States Rights Gist: A South Carolina General of the Civil War* (Shippensburg: White Mane Publishing Company, 1991).

35. Lowell H. Harrison, *The Civil War in Kentucky* (Lexington: University of Kentucky Press, 1975) ix, 8, 9, 14.

36. James G. Randall and David Donald, *The Civil War and Reconstruction*, 2nd ed., (Lexington: D.C. Heath and Company, 1969) 229-31.

37. For a complete roster of those persons who were invited to attend the Pine Street meeting, see the *New York Tribune*, December 17, 1860.

38. The most complete newspaper account of the Pine Street meeting is to be found in the *New York Journal of Commerce*, December 17, 1860. *New York Times*, December 17, 1860; See also Kenneth M. Stampp, *And the War Came: The North and the Secession Crisis 1860-1861* (Baton Rouge: Louisiana State University Press, 1950) 127. Alvan F. Sanborn, ed., *Reminiscences of Richard Lathers* (New York: Grafton Press, 1907) 91-92.

39. *New York Times*, September 18, 1903. See Wright, *The Secession Movement*, 194-95.

40. Sanborn, *Reminiscences of Richard Lathers*, 91-92.

41. *New York Journal of Commerce*, December 17, 1860. Also Wright, *The*

*Secession Movement,* 196-97.

42. Sanborn, *Reminiscences of Richard Lathers,* 112, 121.

43. Brummer, *Political History,* 102.

44. Sanborn, *Reminiscences of Richard Lathers,* 406. Also the *New York Times,* September 18, 1903.

45. Wright, *The Secession Movement,* 201-203. Also *New York Tribune,* January 16, 1861.

46. Werner, *Tammany Hall,* 92-94.

47. Jerry Patterson, *The City of New York: A History* (New York: Harry N. Abrams, Publisher, 1978) 34-35.

48. Ellis, *The Epic of New York City,* 285.

49. "Appointment & Certification of New York City's Commissioners to the South," Misc. Mss. Wood, F. The New-York Historical Society, New York.

50. *New York Tribune,* November 6, 1860.

51. *New York Times,* November 30, 1860.

52. Ibid, October 25, 1860.

53. Sears, *George B. McClellan,* 66. At any rate, Smith and Lovell did not join the Confederate army until the war had been in progress for five months.

54. Wood to Maj. Gen'l Mansfield, 2nd July, 1861. Misc. Mss. Wood, F. The New-York Historical Society.

55. U.S. War Department, *The War of the Rebellion: A Compilation of the Official Records of the Union and Confederate Armies,* 128 volumes and Index (Washington: Government Printing Office, 1880-1901) Series 1, 5:797-98. Johnston stated that the reason why Smith and Lovell had not come forward was because they were not from a seceded state (New York); therefore, they did not know how they would be received as officers in the Southern army.

56. *New York Tribune,* September 21, 1861.

57. *Fifteenth Annual Reunion of the Association of the Graduates of the United States Military Academy at West Point, New York* (Saiginaw: Carrier Printing Co, 1884) 116-17.

58. *Twenty-Eighth Annual Reunion of the Association of the United States Military Academy at West Point, New York* (Saiginaw: Seeman and Peters, Printers and Binders, 1897) 17.

59. Smith to Beauregard, August 12, 1861, Gustavus Woodson Smith Collection, William R. Perkins Library, Duke University, Durham.

60. Wilson, *The Memorial History,* 3:497-98. Also *New York Tribune,* May 17, 1861.

61. Mark Mayo Boatner, *The Civil War Dictionary* (New York: David McKay Company, Inc., 1959) 771-72.

62. *Twenty-Eighth Annual Reunion of the Association,* 19.

63. Encyclopedia of Contemporary Biography of New York, 11 vols. (New York: Atlantic Publishing and Engraving Co., 1882) 2:60.

64. *New York Tribune,* September 20, 1861.

65. Ibid., September 21, 1861.

66. Smith to Davis, September 3, 1861, Jefferson Davis Papers, William L.

Clements Library, University of Michigan, Ann Arbor.

67. *New York Herald*, October 11, 1861.

68. *Richmond Dispatch*, September 20, 1861.

69. Douglas Southall Freeman, *Lee's Lieutenants: A Study in Command*, 3 vols. (New York: Charles Scribner's Sons, 1944) 1:162.

70. T. Harry Williams, *P.G.T. Beauregard: Napoleon in Gray* (Baton Rouge: Louisiana State University Press, 1955) 45.

71. *Official Records*, Series 1, 53:126-27.

72. Ibid., 129-30.

73. Davis to R. Semmes, February 21, 1861, Jefferson Davis Papers, Louisiana Historical Association Collection, Manuscripts Department, Tulane University Library, New Orleans.

74. Smith to Beauregard, August 12, 1861, Smith Collection, Duke University.

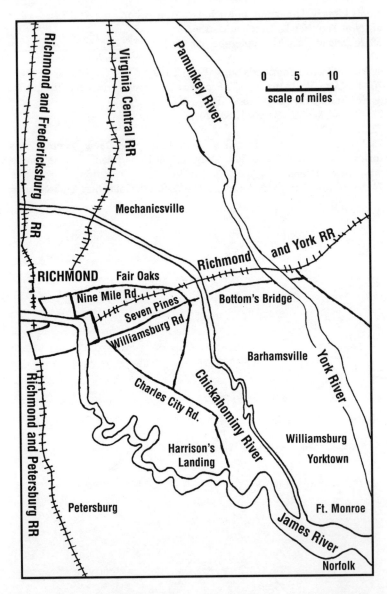

Map 2. Positions between Norfolk and Richmond including the location of Seven Pines.

# CHAPTER FIVE

# Tried in the Test of Battle

Generals Joseph E. Johnston and Pierre G. T. Beauregard emerged as two of the most influential and respected military leaders during the early months of the Confederacy. In the beginning, they commanded independent armies; each reporting to and receiving instructions from the War Department. It was after the Confederate victory at the battle of Bull Run in July 1861 that the War Office reorganized the forces then stationed in the Northern Virginia area. Beauregard's Confederate Army of the Potomac formed the First Corps and Johnston's Army of the Shenandoah was designated the Second Corps in what came to be known as the Confederate Army of the Potomac.

Johnston and Beauregard urged President Jefferson Davis to appoint Gustavus Woodson Smith to a high rank. Beauregard of Louisiana was a West Point graduate and a veteran of the Mexican War. He joined the Confederate army in February 1861 and was commissioned a brigadier general. A man of quiet confidence and cordial manner, he was in command at Fort Sumter and had served under Johnston at the first battle of Manassas.[1] As the war progressed, Beauregard found himself numbered among the anti-Davis general officers who quarreled incessantly with their chief. The Confederate administration's war policy left the Louisianian wishing only to be allowed to fight battles as he pleased without interference from Davis.[2]

Davis commissioned Smith a major general in the Confederate army on September 19, 1861, and he was confirmed by the Confederate Senate a few weeks later.[3] This appointment marked the beginning of a new chapter in the life of the old soldier. His first order from the War Office was to proceed to Manassas, Virginia. Once there, he reported to Johnston, the Commanding General of the army who on September 25 assigned Smith to the command of the Second Corps. Having relinquished his corps command, Johnston could now devote his full attention to the general operations of the army.

With the addition of Smith, both civil and military leaders in Richmond sparkled with high hopes for the Southern army. There was an abundance of praise in the Confederate capital for the newly minted major general. President Davis had a high opinion of him and looked forward to the Confederacy benefiting from Smith's wisdom and administrative experience. Johnston noted that his new subordinate was a man of exceptional ability, and one of the most promising officers that the Southern government could commission at that time. To Smith, Johnston was "Joe" and their relations were both intimate and cordial.[4] The confederate army was now entrusted to the military wisdom and leadership of Johnston, Beauregard, and Smith.

By then, President Abraham Lincoln had conferred the rank of major general upon George B. McClellan and had assigned him to the superior command on the Federal side. One of the many ironies of the Civil War was that those who were friends during peace time often found themselves opposing each other on the battlefield. This was more than evident in the case of Smith and McClellan. The close friendship that developed while they were at West Point continued during their service together in the Mexican War. McClellan of Philadelphia was welcomed to the Union army with open arms. He had graduated second of fifty-nine from West Point in 1846 in a class which sent twenty general officers to the United States and Confederate armies. His admirable service during the Mexican conflict brought him commendation from his superiors. In November of 1861, he replaced the aging hero of Mexican War fame, Winfield Scott, as the General-in-Chief of the Federal army.[5] With this young and scholarly officer the United States had placed its hope for victory.

Among Confederates, General Smith's reputation had also preceded him to the battlefield. He was highly regarded by the authorities at Richmond as a fine administrator, an excellent engineer, and an officer of more than adequate leadership ability. The Kentuckian was determined to impress his superiors and subordinates alike with his comprehension of military knowledge, not only at the conference table, but in camp as well. Only a few other Confederate soldiers had been the recipient of so high a first appointment as Smith's. When Smith received this important commission, he was four months short of his fortieth birthday. In appearance, Smith was bulky with a sense of strength, power, and pride emanating from his broad shoulders and full chest. He was a man of more than average height, with deep and penetrating eyes and hair that had begun to recede.

In actuality, Smith's appointment and confirmation as a major general was perplexing. The Confederate administration allowed itself to accept Smith's self-evaluation, an assessment confirmed by his superiors. His qualifications were "more imagined than real and … in his bluff and self-confident manner he looked the part" of a general.[6] Smith's career was void of any evidence of greatness on the battlefield as a commander. The Mexican War had provided his only military experience in combat. However, that conflict had failed to present him with an opportunity to formulate strategy or to command a large body of troops. Furthermore, there was no comparison between Mexico in 1846 and the United States fifteen years later. General Smith enjoyed the benefit and prestige of a high rank though he had only limited experience with soldiers. Both governments appointed to high rank soldiers with only limited military experience resulting in blunders made as these generals received on the job training. Smith had established a creditable reputation as an engineer and administrator, but was untried as a military leader.

When Smith arrived at Richmond, he was elated to learn that his friend Mansfield Lovell was already there. Smith wasted no time in recommending the appointment of Lovell to a high command. In his letter of September 26, 1861, he urged the President to confer upon Lovell an appointment equal in rank to Smith's own and suggested that he be assigned duty with the Confederate army.[7] Smith's endorsement of Lovell undoubtedly impressed Davis. On October 7, he commissioned Lovell a major general and assigned him to command at New Orleans, replacing General David Twiggs. The evacuation of the Crescent City in the spring of 1862 destroyed Lovell's reputation and caused the Confederate administration to lose confidence in him.

Jefferson Davis of Mississippi, like many others of his generation, had served in the Mexican War. Davis' political career included two terms as senator from his home state and as Secretary of War in the Franklin Pierce administration. He was a Southern nationalist who extolled the virtues of his region and defended its way of life. Slave labor worked the fields of his plantation. Among his shortcomings were a lack of humor, a contentious personality, and delicate health. It came as a surprise to Davis when he received word of his election to the Confederate presidency. He believed that there were others eminently more qualified and better suited for the President's mansion than he was. Accordingly, Davis believed that his strength was as a military rather than as a civil leader. It was no secret that he had hoped to be the supreme commander of the Confederate armies. Referring to his election, Davis remarked, "I thought myself better adopted to command in the field."[8] But as president, he was the commander-in-chief of the military. In that capacity, he was responsible for the overall planning of strategy. With the exception of Robert E. Lee, Davis believed himself to be the equal of any of his commanders as a strategist. Davis' presidency was a stormy one in part because his relationship with many of his field commanders was characterized by confrontation and dissension.

One of Davis' more controversial subordinates was the enigmatic Joseph E. Johnston of Virginia, who had graduated from West Point in 1829, the same year as Lee. His distinguished service during the Mexican War earned him several brevets. A few days after the capitulation of Fort Sumter, Johnston volunteered for service in the Confederate army. His magnetic personality won him many friends, many of whom remained loyal to him for life. Though small of stature, Johnston was confident, stubborn, and an outstanding strategist.[9] He was as proud and fiesty as a gamecock. The military and ideological differences between Johnston and Davis degenerated into a feud which hampered the war effort of the South.

The origin of the animosity between Davis and Johnston was the confirmation of rank by the Confederate Congress of several generals in August 1861. According to Confederate law, the rank of the officers of each grade was to correspond with their former commissions in the United States Army. Therefore, of the five generals confirmed, Johnston should have ranked first instead of fourth. The President was determined to advance the career of his longtime friend Albert Sidney Johnston, and in the process he slighted the Virginia native. It was obvious, though, that Davis was calculating in his actions. He had waited until the arrival of Albert Johnston to the Confederacy before submitting the nominations of the generals for confirmation. On September 12, 1861, Joseph Johnston wrote a long letter to the Confederate President in which he articulated his displeasure at being insulted. In reference to his relative position of fourth, he said, "It seeks to tarnish my fair fame as a soldier and as a man, earned by more than thirty years of laborious and perilous service."[10] The Virginia general believed that the treatment he received from the Richmond authorities was due to the President's dislike for him.

During the latter part of September 1861, General Joseph E. Johnston wrote to the Secretary of War, Judah P. Benjamin, to invite either him or Davis to visit the army which was headquartered at the Fairfax County Court House for a conference on military strategy.[11] Davis accepted the invitation and proceeded there via train. Following a review of the Army, Davis convened a council of war on the evening of October 1 at Beauregard's headquarters where they were joined by Johnston and Smith. This was the first of several important meetings that General Smith would be invited to attend. Smith found himself in conference with the President, though he had been in service for less than a month.

The topic of discussion at the Fairfax conference was whether the Army of the Potomac could be sufficiently reinforced to undertake an offensive across the Potomac River before winter set in. A pensive Smith sat silently during much of the meeting. When he had joined the Army, he was convinced that the leaders in Richmond were floundering and had not developed a comprehensive war policy. This was not accurate. Davis had adopted a defensive strategy for the war because of limited men and resources in the Southern states. Nonetheless, with lightning suddenness, Smith interrupted the conversation with a question directed to Davis. "Mr. President," he said, "is it not possible to increase the effective strength of this army, and put us in condition to cross the Potomac and carry the war into the enemy's country."[12] It appeared that Smith was speaking for Beauregard who had already been attacked by Davis. Therefore, the Louisianian believed that his plan would have a better a chance of being accepted by the Confederate leader if presented by Smith. Beauregard, however, was unaware that Davis when secretary of war had "begrudged" Smith his resignation in 1854.[13] All the discussants agreed that the military strength of the Southern army was at its best since the creation of the Confederacy. It was also the unanimous opinion of the council that the Confederate States of America Army of the Potomac alone was incapable of launching an offensive movement against the Northern capital.

During the debate, Davis turned to General Smith and asked him how many troops would be needed. Smith calmly answered 50,000 "seasoned soldiers" and suggested that the additional troops be withdrawn from other places including Yorktown and Pensacola. Both Johnston and Beauregard gave an estimate of 60,000 as the total number of effectives necessary to assay an assault beyond the Potomac.[14] At the time of the October conference, Johnston's army numbered 40,000 men. The two-hour meeting ended with Davis rejecting the idea of invading the North. The fundamental reason for Davis' decision not to reinforce the Army was the inability of the Confederate government to provide its soldiers with an adequate supply of weapons and ammunition. He confided to a friend that the men offered themselves for war faster than arms could be procured.[15] Another of Davis' concerns was that a troop withdrawal would leave other positions in the Confederacy vulnerable to capture by the Union army. The triumvirate of generals were disappointed with Davis' decision not to reinforce the Army for an immediate campaign of invasion.

The Confederate President, however, was keenly aware that no Southern general had yet emerged who gave much indication of being capable of conducting a successful offensive operation. Therefore, Davis was reluctant to authorize such a monumental campaign without an aggressive and able field commander. General Smith thus far had shown potential of being loquacious, and not much else. Although none of his generals had demonstrated great promise, perhaps it would have been prudent for Davis to have authorized the invasion. In the fall of 1861, the generalship of the North was no better than that of the South. The Confederacy lost a brilliant opportunity to achieve victory. Seldom in the long and bitter Civil War would the South have such an opportunity to emerge victorious.[16] Although Smith's suggestion was not accepted at the meeting, he welcomed the opportunity to provide input to the Confederate army at the highest level. Writing several years after the war, Smith acknowledged the lasting impression the council of war had made on him. It was Smith's first chance to impress Davis as well as the beginning of a rift between the two that would last for many years. The feud between Davis and Smith during the war was carried over to the postbellum period in the form of literary battles. On October 19, the Confederate Army of the Potomac moved from its Fairfax location to the village of Centreville, a distance of less than ten miles. Johnston was totally devoted to Smith and insisted that he remain with him at all times, to the extent that Smith occupied a room adjacent to Johnston's on the second floor of an old building there.[17]

A few days after the Fairfax conference, Smith counseled the President about the negative effects of repressing the enthusiasm of the volunteers for an advance against their adversary. As Commander-in-Chief, Davis was also concerned about the morale of his troops and, on October 10, addressed a letter to Smith in which he suggested that small expeditions be carried out against detachments of the enemy as a means of keeping up the spirit of the soldiers. Furthermore, Davis insisted that immediate gratification could be gained by destroying the enemy's line of communication.[18]

Shortly after the Fairfax conference, Smith asked the President to appoint Horace Randal as Inspector General of the Second Corps. Randal, who was appointed to West Point from Texas, graduated in 1854. He enjoyed a fine reputation as a cavalryman and had fought Indians on the frontier before the outbreak of the Civil War. When Texas seceded, he resigned his commission in the United States Army and joined the Confederacy at the rank of Lieutenant.[19] While stationed in Pensacola in the late summer of 1861, he resigned his commission and went to Richmond, arriving there shortly after Smith had assumed command of the Second Corps. From there he proceeded to Smith's headquarters where he served Smith in the capacity of a volunteer assistant without benefit of rank or compensation.

President Davis was slow to respond to Smith's recommendation of Randal. Writing to the Confederate President on October 14, Smith urged him to appoint his nominee without delay, giving him rank corresponding to the duties of Inspector General.[20] A few days later, Secretary Benjamin informed Smith that because of Randal's previous resignation from the Confederate army without explanation, the request could not be approved. After a careful review of the Randal case, Davis concluded that no such office was provided for under the law of organization.[21]

Writing to General Beauregard during the Randal controversy, Smith confided to him that he was happy to have the services of the courageous Texan, "I wish we had a dozen such men in this army."[22] Though Smith had failed in his attempt to secure the position of Inspector General for Randal, he did not believe the action taken by the

Secretary and the President would preclude Randal from serving as his aide-de-camp. Davis was both surprised and incensed when he learned that Smith had permitted Randal to affiliate with his Army in that capacity. Even more irritating to Davis was Smith's announcement to his troops of his nominating Randal to serve as the senior aide-de-camp. Near the end of October, Davis communicated to Smith that the appointment of an aide from civil life could only be conferred at the discretion of the President. He went on to lecture General Smith that had Randal rescinded his resignation and returned to General Braxton Bragg at Pensacola, his nomination in all likelihood would have been approved.[23] A very angry Smith recorded his displeasure with Davis' decision not to appoint Randal in a memorandum. He wrote, "My requests and recommendations in regard to this and pretty much all other matters ... seem to be entirely ignored; if not systematically opposed."[24]

In the meantime, Davis did an about face and moved from a position of confrontation to one of accommodation. The two-month battle that had produced a voluminous amount of correspondence between Smith and the authorities in Richmond was coming to an end. On November 22, the President informed Smith of the possibility of appointing Randal as his senior aide noting that "Neither the circumstances nor the state of my feelings incline me to alienation from anyone who confronts our common enemy in this war for constitutional liberty and State rights."[25] Eight days later Davis made it official by appointing Randal a First Lieutenant in the provisional army; thereby qualifying him to serve as Smith's aide-de-camp.

If General Smith only had the benefit of a crystal ball, he could have avoided this confrontation with Davis. As soon as General Johnston's army went into camp for the winter, Lieutenant Randal resigned his appointment and returned to his native Texas where he raised a regiment of volunteers and was elected its Colonel. He was assigned to command a brigade in the Trans-Mississippi Department by Edmund Kirby Smith. Randal was fatally wounded at the Battle of Jenkins Ferry in Arkansas in April 1864. Following Randal's departure, Captain Elijah Hawkins of Missouri was appointed aide-de-camp to General Smith.

The fall of 1861 was a time of agony for Smith who was embroiled in one controversy after another though he had not yet fired a single shot at the enemy. In 1861, Smith found himself in competition with General Earl Van Dorn for an assignment in Virginia. In October, Davis ordered Van Dorn to report to Johnston for duty. Van Dorn, who had graduated from West Point in 1842, was an experienced Indian fighter and a veteran of the Mexican War. In January 1861, the Mississippi native had resigned his commission in the United States army and joined the Southern cause. Davis took particular pride in the fact that both he and Van Dorn were from the same state. When Beauregard and Smith became corps commanders, Van Dorn, who outranked Smith by a few days, commanded the First Division in Beauregard's corps. The reorganization angered the proud and ambitious Mississippian who had anticipated the command of the Second Corps for himself.[26] Because Johnston had not requested Van Dorn, he was coldly received and the Mississippian wasted no time in expressing his displeasure to Davis. This protest included an application to be relieved from duty with the Confederate Army of the Potomac. The President warned Van Dorn not to "permit scratches to be mistaken for scar bearing wounds."[27] That Smith was in charge of a corps while Van Dorn was commanding a division caused the latter to leave Johnston's army. Van Dorn confided to Smith that he was too "sensitive and proud" to accept such an embarrassment and humiliation. Before leaving Virginia, Van Dorn apologized to Smith for outranking him. "I am sorry, indeed," he said "that the President did not date your appointment a day or so before mine."[28]

The history of the Confederacy was a never ending story of personality clashes between Davis and his civil and military officials. Fragile egos were as common among Davis' generals as were bayonets at the end of rifles. As egos crumbled, envy and jealousy rose to take their places. In many cases, however, Southern officers were driven more by ambition than ability as they competed for positions in the Confederate army. It was no secret that the Confederate President promoted his favorites and degraded his enemies. And on many occasions his nominees were not capable of handling the leadership positions to which they were assigned. Davis had a propensity for interjecting himself into minor disputes. The Randal case was illustrative of how Davis relegated himself to quarreling over minor military appointments. Some of the President's more memorable controversies centered on the question of promotion. It was this issue that provided the spark for a bitter feud between the rank conscious Smith and his leader a year later. Smith passed the winter of 1862 drilling and instructing his men. As a corps commander, his main duty was trying to ready his soldiers for what he hoped would be an offensive against the enemy. The idle time had made him and his troops anxious for a fight. Smith beamed with confidence, "Let them come in any number they may."[29] He was not alone in his desire to meet the Federals. Brigadier General James Ewell Brown (Jeb) Stuart voiced the same sentiment. In a letter to his wife he said, "The enemy does not seem anxious to fight."[30]

Confidence, however, was no substitute for reality. The army was not in the best condition as evidenced by the hundreds of soldiers who suffered heavily from mumps and measles. Burying the dead became a daily ritual. Another common problem was desertion, which was far more detrimental for the South because of its numerical disadvantage. General Lee believed that the lack of food and non-payment produced dissatisfaction among the soldiers which caused many of them to desert. Governor Zebulon Vance of North Carolina later noted that the hatred of the draft laws, the refusal to grant furloughs, and homesickness were the principal reasons why Southern troops deserted in large numbers. This problem was not limited to enlisted men. Officers were also guilty of walking out of camp without permission. Smith enjoined Captain John Quincy Adams Nadenbousch of the Second Regiment of Virginia Volunteers to arrest all soldiers attempting to leave the Army without legal authority.[31] When not quarreling with Davis, Smith was busy signing orders to reclaim those soldiers who were absent without leave. In early October, Smith ordered Lieutenant Jonathan Pittman of the Thirty-third Regiment of Virginia Volunteers to proceed to Shenandoah City and return "all persons, officers and men, ... absent without leave ... , or [those] who, have ... , overstayed their ... furloughs."[32] Though efforts were made to curb desertion, it remained a serious problem throughout the war.

Another agonizing problem that confronted the Confederate army was the lack of adequate railroad transportation. Smith realized the value of trains to move large bodies of men to the front lines quickly. Under orders from the President, he was assigned to command the Aquia District of Fredericksburg in March 1862. While there, Smith called General Lee's attention to the necessity of having someone there with authority to move the trains at Fredericksburg. Smith suggested that either the president or superintendent of the railroad company should come to Fredericksburg to control the trains or transfer the power to some of their agents there. Smith also informed Lee that he had ordered the railroad not to be interfered with except in an emergency.[33]

As winter slowly gave way to spring, General McClellan, commander of the United States Army of the Potomac, finally opened the Peninsula campaign. The purpose of this campaign was to reduce the Confederate capital and destroy Johnston's army. The reluctant and overcautious Union general commenced his movement by water for Fortress Monroe on March 17, 1862 reaching that place in early April. Fortress Monroe was located between the Chesapeake and James Rivers on the peninsula. McClellan acknowledged that the administration was showing "great impatience" with his slowness in the Peninsula campaign.[34] Lincoln corresponded with McClellan frequently during the first weeks of April to encourage him to take the offensive. On April 6, Lincoln told his Commander: "You now have over 100,000 troops with you ... I think you better break the enemy's line from Yorktown to Warwick River at once." Writing to McClellan three days later, Lincoln said, "I suppose the whole force which has gone forward for you is with you by this time, and, if so, I think it is the precise time for you to strike a blow."[35] From his base of operations at Fortress Monroe, McClellan began his slow and deliberate march up the peninsula, encountering little opposition as he advanced toward Yorktown.

On April 5, Davis learned from Major General John Bankhead Magruder's reports that McClellan had landed a large force at Fortress Monroe. Magruder was an excellent soldier who possessed inexhaustible courage and energy. He was limited only by his fondness for the bottle. Magruder, who occupied the lower peninsula at that time, had a force of a mere 12,000 men with which to oppose the Federal advance. Richmond found itself in a tenuous position. Confronted with this impending crisis, the President directed Johnston to proceed immediately to the peninsula to conduct a careful inspection of the position then occupied by Magruder at Yorktown. Johnston returned to Richmond after his inspection and reported to Davis that the line of defense was too long for the force that occupied it. Particularly disturbing to Davis was the shabby engineering work which caused

Magruder's field fortifications to remain incomplete. Johnston recommended that instead of delaying McClellan's march on Richmond, a force equal to the Federal Army should be assembled there to defend the capital city. Johnston proposed uniting all available forces in the Confederacy from North Carolina and Georgia with those at Norfolk. This would aggregate a number of troops sufficient to repel the inevitable Federal attack. Johnston's pessimistic report and bold recommendation convinced Davis of the importance of Magruder's situation at Yorktown and that it should be discussed at great length with his military leaders.[36]

On April 14, 1862, Jefferson Davis called for a conference to discuss Johnston's report and recommendation.[37] Meanwhile, he directed a continuation of the work on Richmond's fortification. The cold and wet April weather along with poor shelter and inadequate food made life miserable for the Confederate soldiers. Yet they labored along with slaves under difficult conditions to perfect the defenses about Richmond and its vicinity. At the request of Johnston, Generals Smith and Longstreet were invited to attend the conference.

James Longstreet was born in South Carolina in 1821 but moved with his family to Georgia and subsequently to Alabama. He was appointed to West Point from the latter state in 1838 and graduated fifty-fourth out of fifty-six in 1842. He won two brevets for valor during the Mexican War.[38] His trademark was a full beard that covered his lower face and reached down to his chest. Proud and ambitious, Longstreet was a fine soldier and skilled at handling troops.[39] He was appointed a brigadier general in June 1861. Longstreet's slight loss of hearing made him appear reticent. Nonetheless, he could be as strongly vocal as many other Confederate commanders when he felt slighted in matters of personal precedence. Longstreet was outraged when Smith was appointed a major general with no previous service in the Confederate army. General Smith outranked him by about four weeks. Longstreet was not commissioned a major general until October 17, 1861. The usually mild-mannered Alabamian sent a stern letter of protest to Colonel Thomas Jordan, Beauregard's Assistant-Adjutant General. "The placing of persons above me," he said, "whom I have always ranked and who have just joined this service I regard as a great injustice."[40]

General Robert E. Lee and George W. Randolph brought the

number to six who attended the council of war in the office of the President. At the time Lee was Davis' military advisor. Because of his harmonious relations with the President and his knowledge of strategy and tactics, Lee was influential in the planning of wartime policy. Randolph of Virginia had become Secretary of War when Davis shifted Judah P. Benjamin from the War Office to the top position at the State Department in March 1862. The forty-three-year old Randolph assumed his duties on March 24. Prior to the meeting, Johnston had outlined a plan of operation to Smith which included the abandonment of the peninsula. This plan won the support of General Smith and he accepted Johnston's offer to present the proposal at the conference. Johnston had complete confidence in Smith's persuasive abilities. The New York Street Department had served as the school where Smith was tutored in the art of debate. Johnston was convinced that Smith could hold his own against such a prolific debater as the President. Davis called on Johnston to report to the council his examination of the peninsula defenses. Johnston reiterated what he had said earlier that morning to the President. He then produced a memorandum prepared by Smith and given to him just prior to the start of the meeting. President Davis read the memorandum aloud to the group.

The Smith paper contained two plans. The first called for the Confederate forces at Yorktown and Norfolk to be withdrawn and concentrated at Richmond. These soldiers were to be further reinforced by all the troops that could be spared from the Carolinas and Georgia. McClellan would then be lured from the protection of his gunboats and defeated near Richmond with this combined force. The other plan called for the Southern capital to be garrisoned to offer resistance to McClellan while he attempted to besiege it. While he was attacking Richmond, the greater portion of the Confederate army would then cross the Potomac and launch an aggressive campaign to capture Washington and Baltimore or even Philadelphia and New York. The optimistic Smith assured the council that the entire operation could be carried out before Richmond found itself untenable before the Federal army. Of the two plans, Smith preferred the latter.

Both Johnston and Smith argued against a concentration of forces on the peninsula. Longstreet said very little. Randolph was emphatically against abandoning Norfolk, and General Lee, having just returned from Charleston and Savannah, opposed exposing those cities to the possibility of capture. Davis favored the position of Lee and Randolph that called for the sending of an army to the Warwick River on the peninsula. President Davis remained silent during much of the meeting at the Executive Mansion, canvassing the proceedings as if to judge. At 1:00 a.m. on April 15, he handed down his decision by announcing that Yorktown and Norfolk would not be abandoned. Davis subsequently wrote, "Though Gen. J. E. Johnston did not agree with this decision, he did not ask to be relieved, and I had no wish to separate him from the troops with whom he was so intimately acquainted, and whose confidence I believe he deservedly possessed."[41] Johnston found comfort in the belief that "events on the peninsula would soon compel the Confederate government to adopt my method of opposing the Federal army."[42]

Before adjourning the council, Davis directed Johnston to go to the peninsula and take charge. Magruder, who had once occupied the leading role on the peninsula, was now pushed back to fourth, being outranked not only by Johnston, but by Smith and Longstreet as well.[43] He vehemently protested this new arrangement and requested that his command be detached from that of General Smith because they were officers of the same grade. Magruder's request for permission to report directly to Johnston fell on deaf ears at the War Office.

On April 17, Johnston proceeded to the peninsula to assume command. Ten days after his arrival, he informed the War Department of his plans to evacuate the vicinity of Yorktown and Warwick. Magruder, who was anxious for a fight, was greatly disappointed with Johnston's decision to abandon the peninsula. He protested against the move to his superior officer but was reminded that his duty was to obey orders. Johnston deemed it necessary to pull out before the completion of the Union batteries which were being erected in front of Yorktown at that time. In the meantime, Smith had marched down from Richmond to examine the works at Williamsburg. He decided to leave a force there and then continued to Yorktown to be with Johnston. At midnight on May 3, Johnston's army of 56,000 filed out of Yorktown. The next day, the Confederate army had assembled at the old colonial capital of Virginia. Although the march from Yorktown to Williamsburg was short, the soldiers were never to forget how they arrived there. Both men and beasts endured the hardship of marching in deep mud, "that ancestral foe and eternal concomitant of war."[44] The cold and exhausted troops were expecting to rest at Williamsburg, not to fight. In spite of their miserable condition, they were excited and eager to meet the enemy. After several hours of much needed rest, they moved out on the morning of May 5. During this withdrawal, the Blue and Gray met at Williamsburg. The battle raged all day and resulted in heavy casualties on both sides.[45] Johnston stated that the battle of Williamsburg was fought for the purpose of enabling his baggage trains to proceed without interruption and was satisfied that this objective was accomplished. Therefore, he was not disappointed when the Federal army occupied Williamsburg because the action there had slowed the march of the Union army up the peninsula.

General Smith had avoided the action at Williamsburg because he had moved out with his Reserve Division of 15,000 men and baggage trains at dawn on May 5. Marching down the New Kent Road, he bivouacked that night at Barhamsville located midway between Yorktown and Richmond. It was a testimony to the courage and determination of the troops that they were able to march eighteen miles in one day in heavy rain and mud. It was from here that Smith reported to Johnston the landing of a large contingent of Union troops at Eltham on the South side of the York River. Following a personal reconnaissance on May 6, Smith decided not to contest their debarkation. The nature of the ground at Eltham combined with the heavily armed iron clad vessels convinced him that an attack at that time and place would not be prudent. Smith resolved to order an attack once the Federals had come from under the protection of their gunboats. He directed Brigadier General William Henry Chase Whiting to prevent the Union troops from marching on Barhamsville so that the baggage trains could continue to Richmond.

Whiting of Mississippi was blessed with quick perception and courage. He was a student of Smith's during the latter's first tenure as professor at West Point. When Smith was assigned to command the Second Corps in Johnston's army, Whiting assumed command of one of its brigades.[46] Within a few hours after receiving his orders, Whiting had succeeded in forcing the Union troops back to the protection of their naval support. By 2:00 p.m. on May 7, Whiting reported to Smith that he had dislodged the Union skirmishers from the thicket between Eltham Landing and Barhamsville. He was particularly happy to report that his men fought with discipline and courage and that the enemy fired too high which accounted for few casualties.[47] In Smith's official report of the engagement at Barhamsville, he praised his troops and staff officers for their excellent conduct. He was happy to inform the War Office that all the troops engaged fought with perfect control and determination. Motivated by this small victory, Smith was "anxious to meet the invaders at any odds." Perhaps Thomas Vaden captured the mood of the soldiers best by stating, "When we made our fight—All the men were in high spirit."[48] From Crossroads, Smith wrote to his wife in the Confederate capital telling her not to worry about McClellan's army. "I am satisfied that we will keep his gunboats from reaching Richmond," he said, "and give him and his army a good thrashing."[49] The eager Smith, however, would have to wait a few more weeks before he would finally get an opportunity to satisfy his thirst for a good fight.

With the elimination of this minor opposition at Barhamsville, the Confederate army continued its difficult march in the direction of the capital city. With the exception of a few hours respite to feed the horses and to cook rations, the army was constantly on the move. The troops were able to supplement their meagre diet with wild strawberries and cherries found along the way. The action at Barhamsville or Eltham was in reality a skirmish as Smith's command retired from the peninsula. But a reader of Johnston's commendation of Smith and Whiting would never know that the that engagement at Barhamsville was a minor affair. Johnston was especially impressed with the advance in which the troops under Whiting easily forced the Union pickets to return to their landing. Johnston acclaimed Smith and Whiting as indispensable and stated that the Confederate Army needed several more generals of their quality.[50] Concern for the security and protection of the Confederate capital and a lack of provisions forced Johnston to order a withdrawal from Barhamsville on the afternoon of May 7. That the Barhamsville engagement was a minor one should not diminish its importance. The Southern victory there allowed the Confederate army to continue its retreat to the capital. It would then be in a position to offer resistance to McClellan's forces on the outskirts of Richmond. The brief action at Eltham had also provided General Smith with an opportunity to vindicate Johnston's confidence in him as a field commander.

Johnston's devotion to and confidence in Smith was unwavering. While headquartered at the New Kent Courthouse, Johnston turned his attention to a request made by President Davis on May 1. President Davis stated that "necessity" had dictated Johnston send either Longstreet or Smith to command at Fredericksburg. Johnston did not believe that he could part with either general. In his letter to Lee on May 9, Johnston said, "This army cannot be commanded without these two officers [Smith and Longstreet]."[51] More fundamental than Johnston's refusal to order the transfer of Longstreet or Smith was his insistence that Davis commission at least two additional men to the rank of major general. Johnston urged Davis to promote Whiting, but without success. Smith was also a vocal advocate for Whiting's promotion.

Smith championed Whiting's cause in conference with Davis and Randolph on May 21. He argued that Whiting's command and his valor on several battlefields more than qualified him for immediate promotion. Davis startled the persistent Kentuckian when he divulged that Whiting had at a Council of General Officers meeting at Yorktown advocated toppling the civil government and installing Johnston as dictator of the Confederacy. Smith implored the President to name his informant to which Davis retorted, "I am not on the witness stand." Smith denounced the alleged plot to overthrow Davis as preposterous. Smith later concluded that the whole matter was false and that he had never heard of anything so absurd.[52] Whiting was eventually appointed to the rank of major general in April 1863. However, it was his performance on the battlefield and not Smith's intervention which brought him the coveted promotion. In May 1862, Davis appointed Lafayette McLaws and Ambrose P. Hill to the rank of major general. Both officers had distinguished themselves in battle at Williamsburg during the evacuation of Yorktown.[53]

The Federal army had moved up the peninsula in April and May of 1862 with the leaps of a tiger. But once at the gates of Richmond, the steps of McClellan's army had dwindled to those of a kitten. Obviously annoyed by McClellan's slowness, Lincoln issued what amounted to an ultimatum to his field commander. In a telegraphic note to McClellan on May 25, the President said, "I think the time is near when either you must attack Richmond or give up the job and come to the defense of Washington." McClellan replied to his chief that "the time is very near when I shall attack Richmond."[54] By nightfall on May 30, the Union general had partly encircled the Confederate capital from a distance of seven miles. McClellan had ordered the third and fourth corps commanded by Generals Samuel P. Heintzelman and Erasmus D. Keyes respectively to cross to the south or Richmond side of the Chickahominy River. Heintzelman ordered General Philip Kearney's division to defend the Federal position at Bottom's Bridge, and General Joseph Hooker to hold White Oak. General Keyes and his fourth corps continued in the direction of Richmond and halted at Seven Pines. The three other corps of McClellan's army; two, five, and six were under the generalship of Edwin V. Sumner, Henry L. Porter, and William B. Franklin. These soldiers occupied the north bank of the Chickahominy River from Mechanicsville to Grapevine Bridge.[55]

With Richmond becoming more imperiled with the passage of each day, Johnston ordered Longstreet and Smith to his headquarters for a council of war to formulate plans for the anticipated battle at Mechanicsville, five miles north of Richmond. It was decided that Smith would attack the Federals there to prevent McClellan from forming a junction with General Irvin McDowell on the north side of the Chickahominy. The Chickahominy was a stream which flowed from a point northwest of Richmond and united with the James River some forty miles below the capital. It was covered with thick underbrush and forest and, when not flooded, was easily fordable. Though a large Union force had assembled at Mechanicsville, Smith was convinced his troops could easily dislodge them. McDowell was advancing from Fredericksburg with a force of about 40,000 to join McClellan. When Smith learned that McDowell had halted his march, Smith canceled the planned attack. Johnston then directed Smith to order Ambrose P. Hill to withdraw from his position near Mechanicsville. The next day on orders from Johnston, Smith assumed command of the left wing of the Confederate Army of the Potomac. Smith's division was temporarily placed under the command of the Senior Brigadier General, William H. C. Whiting.

Johnston spent the next few days making final preparations for the impending battle. This officer had the respect and confidence of his soldiers. He fought from an advantage; he was not one to take chances. By then Johnston's army had reached its peak efficiency as furloughed troops shortened their leaves and returned in large numbers.[56] The dark clouds looming over the Confederate capital were symbolic of the misfortune about to descend upon the Confederate army. In the late evening of May 30, Johnston wrote to Smith to inform him of his decision to attack early the next morning. Extant records did not indicate whether Johnston had misgivings about the Kentuckian's willingness to shoulder responsibility or to endure the physical strain of battle. Should Smith have fallen sick, General Whiting, whom Johnston admired and respected, would have taken his place.

The records show, however, that Smith's health had been poor prior to the battle of Seven Pines. Writing to Lee on March 20, 1862, Johnston informed him he could not part with Longstreet for the sake of Smith's health. He said, "Major General Smith's health is precarious, it is necessary therefore that there should be in this army at least one other general officer of courage and ability."[57] Two days before the battle of Seven Pines, Smith had been taken to a farmhouse on the Williamsburg road because of illness. In Johnston's correspondence to Smith on May 30, he said, "If nothing prevents, we will fall upon the enemy in front of Major General [Ambrose] Hill ... early in the morning as early as practicable."[58]

Seven Pines was nestled at a junction point where the Williamsburg road intersected the Nine-Mile road. This was seven miles east of the Confederate capital. One mile further was a small railway station called Fair Oaks. Trees, thick underbrush, and heavy rains made the grounds about Seven Pines virtually impassable. Unhealthy swamps, exhaustion, and exposure to rain and mud added to the misery of the soldiers. Union General Erasmus D. Keyes described the rain on the night before the battle:

Through all the night of the 30th of May there was raging a storm, the like of which I cannot remember. Torrents of rain drenched the earth, the thunderbolts rolled and fell without inter-mission, and the heavens flashed with a continuous blaze of lightning. From their beds of mud ... the 4th Corps arose to fight the battle of Seven Pines.[59]

It was at Seven Pines or Fair Oaks that the first major battle between the Confederate and United States Armies of the Potomac occurred. In anticipation of the battle, several hundred men, women, and children occupied the hills about Seven Pines to listen, and hopefully to see the clash of the two great armies.[60]

Because of the heavy rain, a sudden rise in the Chickahominy resulted in the flooding of the swamps, lowlands, and plowed fields in the vicinity of Seven Pines and Fair Oaks. Since the raging river had separated McClellan's army, Johnston was convinced that communications between the Union corps on the south and the main Federal army on the north was impossible. He believed that the division of the Federal army neutralized its superiority and offered an excellent chance for a Confederate victory. Therefore, Johnston had decided to attack Keyes' corps on the Confederate side of the river at daybreak on the last day of May. For success, Johnston's plan would depend heavily on cutting Union communication across the Chickahominy River. The bridges of importance were those between Bottom's Bridge, the lowest downstream to be considered and Meadow Bridge about thirteen miles upstream. The main crossing on the river was at Bottom's Bridge; a mile above that place was the Richmond-York River Railroad. Less than four miles above this point was the Grapevine Bridge, followed by the New Bridge and Mechanicsville Bridge.[61] Johnston intended to attack McClellan at a settlement called Seven Pines on the morning of May 31. While resting at his headquarters on the Brook turnpike about three miles from Richmond, just after midnight on May 31, a courier brought instructions to Smith from Johnston. He was to prepare his forces for an attack early that morning.

The Confederate plan called for Smith and his division along with that of Ambrose P. Hill to march to the junction of New Bridge and the Nine-Mile roads. From there, Smith would be in a position to attack Keyes' right or to provide support for Longstreet's left. Smith's army was held in reserve and was to engage Federal reinforcements should any be sent across the treacherous river. Magruder was to cross the New Bridge road and settle into position between the left wing and the Chickahominy. General Benjamin Huger was to march with his division down the Charles City road and Daniel Harvey Hill was to move by the way of the Williamsburg road. Huger was directed to strike Keyes' left flank and Hill was to attack the Union general's right flank upon hearing Huger's guns. Longstreet, who commanded the right wing of Johnston's army, was to advance down the Nine-Mile road and attack the enemy in the front.[62]

With these dispositions made, Johnston was not only ready to defend

Richmond but also to attack the invaders. Before daybreak on the thirty-first, Smith called on Johnston at his headquarters northeast of the Southern capital, near the Nine-Mile road. Johnston emphasized that Longstreet had specific orders to assault the Federals at Seven Pines, as early as practicable on May 31, with the entire right wing of the Confederate army. Johnston expected nothing less than a complete victory. Furthermore, he hoped that Longstreet's attack would be carried out with alacrity and precision so as to be over before reinforcements from McClellan's army stationed at Bottom's Bridge and on the north bank could reach Keyes'.[63] A driving rain hampered their movements, but Smith and Longstreet were in position by 8:00 a.m. on May 31. The Confederates entered the swamp with excitement and confidence in their ability to either drive the Yankees into the Chickahominy River or capture them.

The field upon which the Confederates met their adversaries was a difficult one. Tangled woods and dark swamps was the scene where most of the close and bloody action took place. Smith noted that the luxuriant foliage of spring made it difficult to distinguish objects even at close range. In spite of these hostile conditions, the Southern troops were nonetheless elated about the chance of meeting the enemy on an open field of battle. The adverse conditions under which they labored was etched in their minds long after the last gun had sounded at the Battle of Seven Pines. It was here that Gustavus Woodson Smith would finally be engaged in a major battle; an aspect of the war which had eluded him for several months. Shortly before 8:00 a.m., an impatient General Whiting called on Smith at the headquarters of Joseph E. Johnston. His advance had been interrupted and delayed by Longstreet's troops who had blocked his line of march. Having heard the request of his divisional commander for assistance to clear his path, Smith ordered his personal aide, Captain Robert F. Beckham, to locate Longstreet to ascertain the reason the soldiers under his command had impeded Whiting's approach to the Nine-Mile road. To expedite the order, Beckham asked Smith to pinpoint Longstreet's location. The Kentuckian promptly referred him to the commander in charge. Johnston informed Smith's staff officer that Longstreet might be found with his division on the Nine-Mile or Williamsburg road.

Shortly after 9:00 a.m., Beckham reported that his search had been futile; that neither Longstreet nor any part of his command were to be found on the Nine-Mile road.[64] Johnston was astonished to learn of Beckham's unsuccessful attempt to find Longstreet. Believing that he had not traveled far enough down the Nine-Mile road, Johnston dispatched his aide-de-camp, Lieutenant James B. Washington, to locate the Southern general. Washington traveled along the same road and was captured near Fair Oaks by a Federal picket under the command of General Silas Casey. His capture was illustrative of inadequate staff preparation and a failure in coordination which contributed to many Confederate blunders at Seven Pines. Washington's arrest was a devastating blow to the Rebels because it alerted the Federals that they were making preparations to launch an offensive. This gave General Keyes, whose corps stretched from Seven Pines to Fair Oaks, time to ready his troops for the anticipated attack. Keyes called his soldiers to arms at 11:00 a.m. Johnston was indirectly responsible for Washington's capture because of his failure to give detailed instructions as to what Longstreet was to do.[65] In the meantime, Captain Beckham who had gone on a second reconnaissance reported to Smith a few minutes past 10:00 a.m. that General Longstreet had been found on the Williamsburg road where he had stopped to allow General Daniel Harvey Hill's men to pass by.

During these unexpected delays, intermittent cannon fire reverberated across the Chickahominy. This was enough, however, to convince the cautious and prudent Johnston to order Smith to take the brigades of Generals Wade Hampton and Robert Hatton to the Chickahominy bluffs to be in a position to check the Federals should they make an attempt to ford the river. Both Hampton of South Carolina and Hatton of Tennessee were known for their distinguished soldierly qualities. After placing the two brigades in position, General Smith saw no need to remain with them on the banks of the river. He then joined Johnston and Whiting at the Confederate headquarters at Old Tavern located about two miles distance from the village of Seven Pines at a junction point on the Nine-Mile road. As the hours passed, nothing was heard from Longstreet since Beckham had returned from the Williamsburg road earlier that morning. At 2:30 p.m., Smith requested permission from Johnston to have his chief of staff, Major Jasper S. Whiting, brother of William Henry Chase, to go and ascertain the state of affairs with General Longstreet.[66] As the afternoon passed, and only occasional cannon shots had been heard, Smith was of the opinion that no serious assault would be assayed against the enemy that day. The mood of the military leaders about Old Tavern was characterized by anxiety and suspense. Ironically, the junction where the officers and men had assembled was scarcely two miles distance from Longstreet's location on the Williamsburg road.

General Longstreet was unwilling to undertake a partial assault and had waited several hours for the arrival of General Huger's division. Finally at 2:00 p.m., Longstreet ordered an attack without the benefit of those troops. Huger's troops were tired when they reached Richmond; having been on garrison duty at Norfolk for several months, they were unaccustomed to marching. Furthermore, his progress was slowed by mud and sheets of water. However, there also seems to have been a lack of discipline in Huger's command. Sergeant D. B. Easley of the 14th Virginia Infantry noted that the soldiers of Huger's division "loafed in the road all day ... that Huger was with us, sitting in our company part of the time, and got on the field at dark by double quick time."[67] Huger was an old soldier who was harshly criticized for his performance at Seven Pines.

General Hill commenced his forward movement through deep water at 2:00 p.m. Since Hill's troops were first in position, he opened the fight on the afternoon of May 31. By three o'clock Hill's entire division became engaged and the fighting was heavy and close. Hill succeeded in driving General Casey steadily backward, forcing the Yankee commander from Rhode Island to abandon his position.[68] To offer resistance to the advancing Confederate States of America right wing, Keyes called up reinforcements. General Samuel Heintzelman arrived on the battlefield shortly after 3:00 p.m. If Longstreet had promptly joined in crushing Keyes, then Heintzelman's advance to help could have been easily thwarted. The late hour of the attack gave the Federals much needed time to be reinforced. The opportunity for victory that the Confederates had hoped for vanished with the passing of each minute.

It was truly amazing that 20,000 Confederate soldiers amassed at Old Tavern on the Nine-Mile road did not move until after 4:00 p.m. although they were ready to begin operations early that morning. A march of a little more than two miles down the Williamsburg road would have brought them in the rear or flank of the Federal troops fighting against Hill. Moreover, a two-and-a-half mile march along the

Chickahominy would have enabled Johnston's army to seize the Grapevine Bridge. Johnston had decided to rely on the sound of musketry to determine the beginning of the action by Longstreet. The wind, however, proved an unreliable messenger. It would have been more practical to have had an aide bring Johnston the news of Hill's offensive movement the instant it got underway. These blunders undoubtedly saved McClellan from total disaster.[69]

The arrival of Major Whiting at the Confederate headquarters in the late afternoon, confirmed that Longstreet was engaged in a fierce battle. Both generals and staff officers impressed upon the soldiers the necessity of moving forward in double-quick time. Smith moved against General Darius N. Couch's right, separating him from the remainder of his division. Couch commanded the second line of defense already, however, the Confederate delays had given McClellan ample time to reinforce Keyes. With extreme caution, John Sedgwick's division of Sumner's corps were the first Union troops to cross the river over the tottering Grapevine Bridge. Sumner's corps reached the battlefield about 5:00 p.m., thereby averting disaster for the Union army.

Realizing that the situation with Longstreet was desperate, Johnston directed Whiting's division and John B. Hood's brigade to move forward without delay. It was obvious that the battle was not going as Johnston had planned, and delays frustrated the Confederate general. When Whiting's lead column reached the vicinity of Fair Oaks Station, Johnston scolded him for being too cautious before crossing the railroad and disposing of a Union force just north of the depot. In the meantime, General Smith had halted about a mile from the railroad crossing at Fair Oaks and had given instructions to Hampton's brigade which had moved from the river bluffs.[70] Smith ordered Hampton to continue marching parallel to the Nine-Mile road which would bring him into the line of battle on Confederate General James J. Pettigrew's left. Smith then enjoined General Robert Hatton to continue his movement down the NineMile road. Hatton's brigade would constitute a reserve to the line of battle formed by Whiting, Pettigrew, and Hampton. After these dispositions, Smith proceeded in the direction of Fair Oaks Station where the action was taking place.

Upon reaching the edge of the woods, Smith sent a courier to notify General Whiting of Hampton's position, but learned from him that several offensive movements had been unsuccessful because of insufficient or improper knowledge of the Federals' position. However, Whiting was optimistic that a combined attack by the Confederate forces would capture the enemy's position in only a matter of minutes. Whiting's hope for success faded when a brigade of Sedgwick's division reached Couch in time to repulse the Confederate attack. Johnston, who was observing the battle from his position just north of Fair Oaks, dispatched an urgent note to Smith at 6:00 p.m. As night was rapidly approaching, Smith was to have all the available soldiers brought up immediately. The only troops available were those of Magruder's and he put them into motion at once. The Rebels had made several uncoordinated attempts to carry the enemy's works, but had been repulsed each time with heavy losses. The Federals did not advance, and the Confederates held their position close to the enemy's line until it was too dark to distinguish the Blue from the Gray.

For two hours before dark, the armies were engaged in a desperate battle at Seven Pines. Deadly and deafening fire echoed through the thick forest and entangled bushes. Bottomless roads and flooded fields forced some of the combatants to stand in water nearly three feet deep. Undoubtedly some of the wounded drowned.[71] Sergeant Easley said many of the wounded were buried in mud "half way [up] their bodies."[72] In spite of the mud, troops on both sides fired with deadly accuracy. Men fell in all directions and the smoke was so dense that visibility was reduced to only a few hundred feet. That so many officers and men were killed and wounded was evidence of the fierceness of the struggle. Henry T. Childs of the Tennessee Brigade, which was commanded by General Hatton, described the battle: "Above us and all around us grape and bombs were falling thick and fast, tearing up the earth in front and rear ... and deadly missiles and treetops were falling around us."[73] Union soldier James J. Marks called the battle a "terrific conflict." He said it appeared to him "that not even a small bird could fly unscathed where fell this storm of bullets."[74] There was certainly no shortage of heroism on the part of the gallant men who fought at the Battle of Seven Pines.

In spite of a Herculean effort, the battle was not going well for the Southerners. General Whiting was being forced backward on the right, and Generals Hampton and Pettigrew were suffering heavy losses a few hundred yards to the north of Fair Oaks. Smith's primary concern at this critical moment was to prevent McClellan's reinforcements from north of the Chickahominy from breaking through the Confederate line and reaching Longstreet's left flank and rear. Smith responded to this emergency by ordering Hatton's brigade and Pettigrew's reserve regiment to move into the woods and support the soldiers engaged there. He went with Hatton's command to the front line where he learned that the chivalric and dauntless Pettigrew had been wounded and taken prisoner. As the soldiers of the Tennessee Brigade approached the field at sunset, they recalled a powerful speech Hatton delivered from atop his horse on May 30. "Boys, before the dawn of another day," he said, "we will be engaged in deadly conflict with the enemy."[75] Inspired by the prophetic words of General Hatton, the Tennesseans were determined to make both their leader and home state proud of them at the Battle of Seven Pines.

As the battle progressed, so did the misfortune that continued to plague the Confederate army. The brave and noble General Robert Hatton was killed at Smith's feet while leading his troops from the extreme front of the line. Childs recorded for posterity the somber mood of the Tennessee Brigade upon learning of Hatton's death. He wrote, "I remember well the tears that were shed the next morning when the boys began to realize that the gallant Hatton would lead us no more."[76] General Hampton was seriously wounded and refused to allow his men to transport him to the rear. Surgeon Edwin S. Gaillard tended to him under a heavy volley from the enemy. As on previous occasions, Hampton was known for his courage and steadiness in perilous circumstances. Smith remembered Hampton as a general who had "few equals and perhaps no superior."

Smith's field commanders were falling like dominoes. The wounding of so many officers of high rank was perhaps an omen of things to come. The rapid depletion of Smith's officers forced him to take control in the woods on the left side. Smith sent word to Whiting to give his full attention to the right side of the line. General Whiting was with his division the entire day until he was wounded just before dark. There in the forests, the opposing armies were at some places less than fifty yards apart.

The Battle of Seven Pines (or Fair Oaks) raged much of the day and was fought with dogged determination on both sides. Smith's left wing numbered about 20,000. The total number in the Confederate Army was 62,000. The Federal forces under McClellan totaled more than

126,000.[77] But the forces actually engaged on either side were about 40,000 apiece. Only darkness prevented the fierce and bloody struggle from continuing. The Confederates had essayed several attempts during the day to rout the Federals, but all ended in failure. General Smith expressed the rather optimistic view that if he had "one more short hour of daylight" with the assistance of Hood's Texas Brigade on the right and other fresh troops, the United States soldiers would have been driven "into the swamps of the Chickahominy." According to Smith, darkness had compelled him to "relinquish an unfinished task."[78] In Smith's official report, he made several references to the strong position of the enemy. But in reality, there was only a semblance of fortification on the part of the line occupied by the fragment of Couch's division. The Union General Alexander S. Webb, who observed Smith in the day's action, was particularly critical of him. In reference to Smith's generalship, Webb said, "The imaginary fortified position which Smith encountered was, in fact, the living wall of brave men who withstood his advance and compelled him finally to retreat."[79]

Once nightfall had halted the fighting, General Smith ordered his men to withdraw from the battlefield. There in the darkness, tired but undaunted, the Confederate troops passed the night in the swamps. The Confederate left had accomplished very little during the first day's fight. It was an interesting twist of history that Smith and McClellan who were friends and had fought side by side in the Mexican War, found themselves representing opposing armies at the Battle of Seven Pines. The first night after the battle was a scene of unbelievable horror. The cries of wounded soldiers punctuated the dark Southern sky. Men with shattered limbs kept the surgeons busy all night performing amputations. Every few minutes, there was an outburst from a sufferer who had undergone the surgeon's knife. Many soldiers prayed for an end to their misery as they waged their final struggle, the battle against death.[80]

Both Davis and Lee had had high expectations for an overwhelming victory at Seven Pines. Once the engagement of May 31 had begun, they rode to the battlefield to observe the action. To avoid a meeting with the anxious President, Johnston mounted his horse and rode swiftly to the front.[81] This was illustrative of how far the feud between Davis and Johnston had gone. Johnston deeply resented Davis' interference with his army. General Johnston's attempt to avoid the

President's entourage would prove to be a disastrous climax to Confederate factionalism. As night covered the battlefield, a messenger informed the President that the superior commander of the Confederate Army had been twice wounded, once in the shoulder and once in the chest.[82] Upon learning of the proud Virginian's misfortune, General Winfield Scott remarked, "There is but one objection to Joseph Johnston as a soldier; he catches too many bullets."[83] The Richmond *Examiner*, in a tribute to the fallen general, stated that Johnston "retained the complete confidence of every officer and soldier ... his wound at this moment is a national disaster."[84] As the severely wounded Johnston was being carried from the field, Davis spoke to him briefly, wishing his field general a quick recovery. Johnston's recuperation would be slow, and he would not return to active duty until November 1862. The Battle of Seven Pines marked the last time that he would command troops in the state of Virginia.

There was no reason for the Confederate commander to have been within range of the enemy's fire. It was not necessary for him to encourage his men as the long period of inactivity had made them anxious for a good fight. It was the duty of junior officers to lead soldiers into battle. Superior officers, who should have been motivated by a higher sense of military intelligence and wisdom, were called upon to formulate strategy.[85] While attending to Johnston, Surgeon Gaillard was hit in the arm resulting in the amputation of that limb.

With the incapacitation of Johnston, command of the Confederate Army devolved upon General Smith, the next ranking officer. Before leaving the battlefield, President Davis located Smith and quizzed him as to what plans he had made for the next day's fight, which was expected to be a fierce one. By then Smith was showing signs of nervousness and fatigue, not confidence. Under intense nervous strain brought on by the excitement of the first day of battle, Smith could not give a concise and conclusive answer. He informed Davis that he was unable to determine what was to be done until he had ascertained the condition of affairs on the right wing under Longstreet and until he knew the strength of the Federal army. This was Smith's way of telling his Commander-in-Chief that he had not yet formulated plans for June 1. Smith's lack of a definitive plan annoyed Davis. The President bade Smith farewell and led his entourage back to Richmond. Along the way, he could see the many slow-moving ambulances transporting the wounded to hospitals. When ambulances proved insufficient, wounded troops were carried upon the shoulders of their comrades. Those who had the strength came into the city on foot. The Battle of Seven Pines had brought the civil war home to the Southern capital. In one day the battle in the suburbs had transformed Richmond from a city of pastoral beauty into one of pain and misery. The wounded veterans of Seven Pines covered the grounds and filled sheds, barns, hotels, and warehouses. Richmond was one huge hospital. The blood-stained streets were evidence that the fight at Seven Pines had been a brutal one. With hospitals filled to capacity, wounded soldiers were taken to the homes of private citizens.

No doubt Davis' conversation with Smith had convinced him of the necessity to make a change in the command structure of the Army. As the President and his military adviser returned to the capital city, a pensive Davis broke the silence of the night when he turned to him and said, "General Lee, I am assigning you to the command of the army. When we get to Richmond, I shall send you the official order."[86] A Southern newspaper expressed the hope that Lee would "prove himself a competent successor" of the wounded General Johnston and "complete his great undertaking" by annihilating McClellan's army.[87] When Davis promoted Lee to the superior command of the Confederate Army, he also designated it the Army of Northern Virginia. Of all the Confederate armies, this would be the most famous. During the next three years, Lee would establish himself as one of the great generals of American history by leading the Army of Northern Virginia in some of the most memorable battles of the war. The rise to command of Lee may have been a mixed blessing because it removed from central command the one competent adviser who had Davis' confidence and confined Lee's talents henceforth to only one army.

Robert E. Lee was born to Henry and Ann Lee of Virginia in 1807. He was commissioned a Second Lieutenant into the elite Engineer Corps upon graduation from West Point in 1829. During the war with Mexico, Lee's work as an engineer won the admiration of Winfield Scott, who valued his advice and accepted him into his inner circle. In April 1861, when it became obvious to Lee that Virginia would leave the Union, he joined the Confederacy and assumed the role of military adviser to the president.[88] Lee combined tact and understanding with character and fortitude to become an outstanding military leader.[89]

Meanwhile, General Smith remained with the Confederate Army at Seven Pines. He had inherited an army beset with chaos and confusion. His army was bewildered and battered and broken bodies were symbolic of broken spirits after the first day's fight. The Confederates were in poor condition as they prepared to renew the battle on the following morning. An atmosphere of consternation rather than conquest surrounded the Southern camp because of the loss of Johnston, the disorganization of the newly-formed commands, and the heavy casualties. In spite of the Army's weakened condition, Smith was expected to achieve victory the next day. In an effort to formulate tactics for the coming battle, it was necessary for Smith to know what had occurred with Longstreet in the right wing of the army on the Williamsburg road.

Dictated by an urgent need to ascertain the state of affairs with Longstreet, Smith ordered several staff officers to locate him. At 11:00 p.m. General Jeb Stuart, the cavalry commander reported to his chief that the Federals had made no advance on the Charles City road during the day and that he had failed to communicate with Longstreet. At approximately the same time, General Lafayette McLaws reported that Union soldiers were constructing a pontoon crossing opposite New Bridge. He added, "If this position is forced, your command will be in great danger, as you are aware."[90] Major Walter H. Stevens, chief engineer of the Confederate Army, returned to Smith's headquarters about midnight and informed him that the position held by the enemy north of Fair Oaks had been strengthened during the evening. Finally, one of the reconnaissance parties succeeded in finding Longstreet shortly after midnight.

In preparation for the next day's battle, General Longstreet visited Smith's headquarters on the Nine-Mile road near Old Tavern at 1:00 a.m. on Sunday morning, June 1, 1862. During the two-hour conference, Smith was surprised to learn that a portion of Longstreet's division had not participated in the fight on Saturday. Perhaps even more astonishing was the revelation that Huger's division had scarcely been engaged at all. The "severest part" of the fighting had been done by General Daniel Harvey Hill whom Longstreet called an officer of "ability, courage, and skill."[91] In the course of the fighting on May 31, the Confederates had succeeded in occupying the small village of Seven Pines and pushed the Federals backward a short distance.

Smith ordered Longstreet to have Huger's division move from the Charles City road to the Williamsburg road and to place one of his brigades on the Nine-Mile road. The detached brigade would support General McLaws at New Bridge. Ambrose P. Hill was directed to guard Meadow Bridge and General David R. Jones to defend the river bluffs from Meadow Bridge to New Bridge.[92] The left wing and center remained in the position occupied on the previous day. Finally, Longstreet was enjoined to push forward at daybreak and build upon the success of the first day. Smith then wrote to Lee in Richmond to inform him of the instructions he had given to Longstreet. Lee attempted to assuage Smith with a friendly letter at 5:00 a.m. on June 1. In it he said, "It will be a glorious thing if you can give a complete victory. Our success on the whole yesterday was good, but not complete."[93]

The command post of the Union army was also buzzing with activity during the night as preparations were made to continue the contest the following day. By dawn on the first day of June, McClellan's forces were in position awaiting the attack. Sedgwick's division had moved into position just east of the Fair Oaks Station. General Israel B. Richardson's division, which had been brought up during the night, was posted on the railroad thus forming a right angle with Sedgwick's line. To Richardson's left was David B. Birney's brigade. On Birney's left came Philip Kearney's brigade, then Casey and Couch's divisions and then Daniel E. Sickles brigade of Joseph Hooker's division.[94] These were the dispositions of the Federal Army with Sumner commanding on the right and Heintzelman on the left. The rising of the sun would be the signal for the competing armies to recommence the fight. It would appear that the Rebels could hardly wait to resume the battle on the second day. Confederate General Cadmus M. Wilcox noted that "the men were eager for the fight, and everything seemed to indicate a success as full and complete as the day previous."[95]

General Daniel H. Hill opened the fighting for the Confederates shortly after daylight by ordering the brigades of Generals William Mahone, Lewis A. Armistead, and George E. Pickett to advance into the woods which intervened between Sedgwick and Richardson. By 6:30 a.m. the firing had become heavy and lasted a few hours. General Smith was unhappy, however, because the attack was not made in full force. Longstreet had ordered the attack with only a small portion of the right wing and his men were steadily being pushed backward. The preponderance of fighting on the second day occurred with the brigades of Armistead and Mahone, both of Huger's division, against Union General William H. French. Just as General French was losing ground, he was reinforced by the brigades of Generals Oliver O. Howard and Thomas Meagher which then formed the front line of Richardson's division. General Pickett, who was positioned to the right of Armistead, sustained heavy losses at the hands of Birney's brigade.[96] The extreme left of Richardson's frontline received a staggering blow from the Southerners, and Howard's brigade was compelled to fall back to the second line of defense. General Howard was knocked out of the action for the remainder of the battle. It was in Richardson's division that the Union army suffered the greatest casualties on June 1.

In the meantime, Major Jasper Whiting, who was watching the enemy across the river reported to Smith the movement of Federal reinforcements along the north bank of the Chickahominy. At 10:30 a.m., Smith received a note from Longstreet which indicated the situation with him was desperate. Longstreet wrote, "The entire army seems to be opposed to me. The ammunition gives out too readily. If I can't get help, I fear I must fall back."[97] Smith responded to the plight of his field general by ordering the 5,000 soldiers from the Chickahominy bluffs to proceed immediately to Longstreet on the Williamsburg road. Furthermore, Smith directed McLaws to go in person to Longstreet to inform him that reinforcements were being rushed to him in double-quick time. It would appear, however, that McLaws' real purpose for visiting Longstreet was to deliver a direct order from Smith. General Smith had instructed McLaws to reassure Longstreet "that the whole army of the enemy was not in his front, and tell him that he must not fall back any further, but drive the enemy; and, if possible, regain the ground he had lost."[98] Smith admitted that he was "completely deceived" by Longstreet's messages with regard to the state of affairs in the right wing on the first day of June, as Johnston had been on the previous afternoon upon receipt of the note from him at 4:00 p.m.

In the early afternoon of June 1, President Davis visited Smith's headquarters to inform him that he had assigned Lee to take command of the Army of Northern Virginia. Smith was obviously stunned. The transfer of power was unpretentious; not the least display of ceremony accompanied it. The bright sun was symbolic of the new found hope of the Confederacy with the elevation of Lee. Davis, who was keenly aware of Smith's fragile ego, employed extreme tact to soften the blow, but he realized that he had made an unforgiving foe by promoting Lee.[99] Doubtless Smith's illness and his comraderie with Generals Johnston and Beauregard were leading reasons why Davis decided not to keep him as commander of the Army. Another major factor, however, was Lee's credentials. A full general was needed to command the Army of Northern Virginia; Lee was qualified and Davis had no intention of promoting Smith to that exalted rank.[100] Though cautious, Lee would not hesitate to press an attack when he deemed it advantageous. Possessing a penchant for details and war strategy, Davis credited Lee with making the Army of Northern Virginia "a rapid, accurate, compact machine, with responsive motion in all parts."[101] While awaiting the arrival of Lee in the headquarters' office, Davis and Smith engaged in pleasant but desultory conversation on a variety of topics. Interestingly, the conversation was void of any mention of the second day's battle. Command of the army had devolved upon Smith and then he had been discarded, all in less than twenty-four hours. The brevity of Smith's tenure did not present him with much of an opportunity to distinguish himself as a military leader. Although Smith had been dropped by the Davis administration, he was not yet ready to pass into oblivion.

When Lee arrived at Smith's headquarters at 2:00 p.m., the dethroned commander told him what had transpired upon the field during the day. The meeting was interrupted by a courier who brought a dispatch from Longstreet dated 1:30 p.m. Longstreet's note read, "The attack this morning was made at an unfortunate time. We had but little ammunition ... I sincerely hope that we may succeed against them in their next effort. Oh, that I had ten thousand men more."[102] General Longstreet's claim of having insufficient ammunition was puzzling. In reality, none of the five Confederate brigades engaged on June 1 had taken part in the battle of the previous day. Therefore, it is highly unlikely that these brigades were in need of ammunition. Furthermore, Smith told Lee that he had ordered 5,000 effectives from the Chickahominy to the Williamsburg road several hours earlier that day.

After reading the note Smith passed it to Lee and then Davis, neither of whom commented upon the terse letter. At 3:00 p.m. Davis departed, leaving Lee and his subordinate in conference alone. Except for the occasional sound of musket and artillery fire, all was quiet on the battlefront. In fact, no firing of any consequence had been heard since 11:00 a.m. Lee did not offer any criticisms of Smith's management of the army during the eighteen hours in which he was the commander. Several minutes later, Lee and his party traveled to the Williamsburg road to join Davis and Longstreet at the front. As they approached their destination, the men from the Chickahominy could be seen leisurely resting in the rear. After the official greetings, Longstreet commenced telling Smith about the state of affairs in the right wing. Smith did not entertain Longstreet's harangue, but instead suggested to him to direct his comments to Lee who was then in command of the army. Shortly after Lee's arrival, Davis' entourage returned to the Southern capital. With Lee's approval, Smith ordered the soldiers who had come to assist Longstreet to return to their position on the Chickahominy River. During the conference, Longstreet did not divulge any special information to his superiors in reference to the battle that morning. At 6:00 p.m. the meeting at the front line adjourned and Generals Lee and Smith went to their respective headquarters on the Nine-Mile road.[103] Both the President and Lee were disappointed when the Rebels withdrew from the field on the afternoon of June 1. The disorganization on the battlefield convinced Lee not to try another assault. The Battle of Seven Pines of the historic Peninsula campaign was over, but not without heavy casualties. Losses for the Confederate army were 6,134 and 5,031 for the Federals.

General Smith had made a faint effort to continue the battle on the second day. Though a man of personal courage, the excitement of the first day had sapped his enthusiasm for a vigorous campaign. His overcautious approach earned him the scorn of many officers who had fought with him at Seven Pines. Responsibility and uncertainty was the combination that wrecked his nerves and shattered his confidence; the responsibility of commanding a large army and the fear that if he did not succeed his reputation would be forever destroyed. Smith's counterpart on the Northern side, General George B. McClellan, was guilty of committing a serious mistake in allowing Keyes' corps to remain garrisoned at Seven Pines within easy reach of the Southern army. Because of illness, McClellan was physically unable to take an active role in the operations of the two-day engagement. Albeit, he was unable to personally direct the details of the fight, it was not a Union disadvantage. Smith acknowledged that they had not "succeeded in crushing" their adversaries. In fact, the Union army had enjoyed a measure of success on the second day by regaining the ground it had lost on May 31. To say that Jefferson Davis was deeply disappointed with the outcome of the battle would be an understatement. In reference to the action on June 1, he noted that "the operations of that day were neither extensive nor important, save in the collection of the arms acquired in the previous day's battle."[104]

On June 1, Smith suffered a mental or physical breakdown brought on by the strain of the fighting on the first day.[105] Smith affirmed that he was completely prostrated by an illness he described as paralysis. Nonetheless, Smith was extremely angry because he had been superseded by Lee. The record shows, however, that Smith was doubtless suffering from an apoplectic condition during the battle and was simply not up to the challenge. Robert W. Barnwell in his sketch of the battle stated as a noteworthy fact that "Smith was on the verge of a stroke of paralysis, which came the day after, and probably was not equal to the situation under such circumstances. His health seems to have been all that kept him from high distinction."[106] Colonel Edward P. Alexander, chief of artillery of Longstreet's division, admired Smith as a soldier and spoke favorably about his generalship at the battle. While observing Smith in action at Seven Pines, Alexander could not help but conclude that illness had drained his strength. He noted that "Smith was a martyr to physical ailments which greatly reduced his energy, [and], especially made riding almost impossible."[107] Further evidence of Smith's physical condition was offered by the opinionated General Longstreet. He said that Smith had become extremely sick and was slow in organizing for the resumption of battle on June 1 and immediately left the Army.[108]

One of the more candid witnesses who observed Smith's leadership at Seven Pines was Major Joseph L. Brent, who served on General Magruder's staff as the chief ordnance officer. Brent was attached to Smith's command at the outset of the engagement by Magruder. This was done so that the latter could receive reliable information concerning any important activities or events that might take place in Smith's division. After the wounding of Johnston, Brent found Smith in complete control of the Army. Brent noted that neither the excitement of actual fire nor the responsibility of commanding the Army affected the pitch of General Smith's voice. Brent made it a habit during the war of recording the voice modulations of officers under fire. Among the many intonations Brent documented, he remembered Smith, who maintained his normal voice in battle. Major Brent recalled that Smith "spoke in so low a voice that it was not easy to hear him if a little distant, and his coolness was perfect."[109]

According to one source, "Smith exhibited a possibly psychosomatic illness that developed whenever pressure or great responsibility was thrust on him."[110] In other words, "Smith's ailments derived more from his mental state than his physical one."[111] The evidence was abundantly clear that Smith's malady had manifested itself during the battle and had prevented him from fighting with vigor. In spite of being quite ill, Smith's pride would not permit him to relinquish command at Seven Pines.

On June 2, Major Whiting wrote to Lee to report on the condition of his chief. "I regret to inform you ... ," Whiting said, "that partial paralysis has already commenced."[112] Undoubtedly one of the major factors which prevented Smith from achieving success as a field commander was illness. It was a universal belief among the authorities in Richmond that the excitement of vigorous and strenuous activity was detrimental to Smith. The Battle of Seven Pines clearly demonstrated that Smith was unable to handle the heavy responsibility of a major command. Smith would in due time rise from his sick bed and continue to support the cause for which he had sacrificed so much. He would be the beneficiary of an impressive and important Confederate victory at the Battle of Honey Hill in South Carolina in November 1864.

In less than forty-eight hours after the start of the battle the two ranking officers of the Confederate Army found themselves out of action. The loss of Johnston because of wounds and Smith to sickness was not as detrimental as might have been expected by the authorities in Richmond. In reality, Johnston's disability was a blessing in disguise. It was on this occasion that President Davis made the most prudent decision of the war by assigning General Lee to take command of the Army. The appointment of Lee was greeted with curiosity by all ranks. The rank and file were unacquainted with Lee, and the senior officers viewed him as a soldier who had established himself as an outstanding engineer.[113] But it was not long before the new commander had transformed their misgivings and distrust of him into respect and admiration. General Longstreet expressed relief that Smith did not retain command of the Army.

It was not surprising that both sides claimed success at Seven Pines. The Union commanders claimed victory because they had reestablished their line and had compelled the Confederate forces to fall back to their camps on Sunday evening. General Daniel E. Sickles proclaimed victory for the Federal army because the "fields were strewn with ... muskets marked "Virginia", thrown away by the enemy in his hurried retreat."[114] General Keyes wrote that the success of Couch and Casey's division on May 31, "was the beginning of the victory which on the following day was so gloriously completed."[115] General Sumner, who emerged from Seven Pines with an exalted reputation acknowledged that the fight on Sunday morning was an "obstinate contest" in which the Confederates attacked with "great fury." He concluded that the United States troops "showed the greatest gallantry and determination, and drove the enemy from the field."[116]

Since the South was defending Richmond, it proclaimed Seven Pines as a Confederate triumph because it had stopped the advance of a numerically superior force. The public was assured of that and the soldiers were eulogized for their valor and heroism. Smith called the troops whom he commanded men of "gallant spirits." General Daniel H. Hill maintained that the rank and file at Seven Pines fought with a gallantry never surpassed. "After this decisive victory, under such disadvantageous circumstances," Hill said, "not a brigade in the ranks seemed to entertain the remotest doubt of our ultimate success over the besieging army of Yankees."[117] General Hill distinguished himself as the most competent commander on the Confederate side at Seven Pines. Several years after the war, a Federal officer addressed a letter to General Johnston asking him to name the intrepid officer who rode a white horse. Johnston replied, General Hill was that officer, "the hero" of Seven Pines.[118]

It was perhaps Davis who was the most exuberant in claiming the trophies for the Confederate nation at the battle on the outskirts of Richmond. On June 2, 1862, President Davis issued a passionate address to his soldiers calling Seven Pines a victory. He stated:

I render to you my grateful acknowledgments for the gallantry and good conduct you displayed in the battles of the 31st of

May and 1st instant, .... On no other occasion have I witnessed more of calmness and good order than you exhibited while advancing into the very jaws of death, and nothing could exceed the prowess with which you closed upon the enemy when a sheet of fire was blazing in your faces ... Defenders of a just cause, may God have you in His holy keeping![119]

Though Johnston's plan had not been carried out, he was still commendatory in his official report of his favorite commander. He wrote, "The skill, energy, and resolution with which Major-General Smith directed his attack would have secured success if it could have been made an hour earlier."[120] Undoubtedly, Johnston felt both vindication and bitterness when the Confederate government adopted the recommendation that he had first intimated to Davis and the conferees at the war meeting in April. No sooner had he lost command of the Army, than the Southern government strengthened its forces at the capital with troops from South Carolina, North Carolina, and Georgia. At least for the immediate future, Richmond, the bastion of Southern independence, was safe. Johnston could also find solace in the fact that he had conducted a successful retreat of the Confederate Army of the Potomac from Yorktown through the peninsula to the Confederate fortifications around the capital city.

A combination of factors prevented the Confederates from striking an effective and decisive blow against the Federals at Seven Pines. Pickett believed that had Johnston not been wounded, the outcome would have been totally different. In his official report, he expressed the opinion that the Army lacked direction following the loss of its leader. "After the fall of the master spirit," Pickett wrote, "there seemed to be no head."[121] General Richard Taylor, son of President Zachary Taylor, voiced a similar point of view. He too believed that the overriding factor which worked against Confederate success was the loss of the commanding general. Confusion ensued and the hope of victory fell precipitously with the fall of Johnston.

Another factor which affected the Seven Pines fight was the weather. The heavy rains on the night before the engagement made the swampy terrain about the battlefield all but impassable. However, it should be noted that the ground was familiar to all the Confederate commanders with the exception of General Huger. The intervention of nature was only one factor which helped to produce unaccountable delays and disappointments. But if Johnston had waited one day before initiating the attack nature would have been a valuable asset. One of the bridges used by Sumner to cross the Chickahominy was completely under water for several hundred yards on June 1. According to McClellan, the left wing of the Federal army would have in probability suffered a devastating defeat had the battle opened a day later. Smith stated unequivocally that it would have been wise to delay the battle for one day when the bridges were not fordable because of the rise of the water. The Rebels permitted the North to fortify prior to the attack thereby throwing away a golden opportunity for victory. President Davis joined the polemics with the belief that it would have been better to have waited another day when the Confederates could have taken advantage of the flood in the river.

A particularly damaging combination was the lack of written instructions and the misunderstanding of verbal ones. As a result misconception brought chaos, and several brigades took the wrong roads and got lost and generally got in each other's way. The result was confusion and the absence of a coordinated assault. On the right wing, only five of the thirteen brigades of Longstreet, Hill, and Huger reached the battlefield while four of the ten brigades of Smith and Magruder were engaged in the action. The Confederate Army lost a brilliant opportunity to achieve a decisive victory by entering the battle in piecemeal fashion and succumbing to faulty leadership and staff work. Smith was certainly a leading example of what went wrong for the Rebel Army.

General Longstreet censured Huger for his failure to cooperate with him. Huger in his defense stated that his orders from Johnston were not explicit, nor was he informed of where the attack was to occur.[122] One point of which there was general agreement was that Johnston's strategy which called for Longstreet's division to crush Keyes' corps was militarily sound. Colonel Alexander stated with certainty that had Johnston's "well devised" plan been "properly carried out" the Confederates would have overwhelmed "all the enemy south of the Chickahominy."[123] But as so often is the case in battle, the best plans of men often go awry. According to Smith, the first great blunder of the battle involved Longstreet. By taking his men from the Nine-Mile road to the Williamsburg road, Longstreet was not in position to attack

Keyes' exposed right flank early in the morning of May 31. Had Longstreet advanced down the Nine-Mile road, Keyes' corps would have been wiped out before the arrival of Heintzelman or Sumner.[124]

Although there was enough blame to go around for the Seven Pines debacle, the ultimate responsibility for the tactical errors must fall upon the shoulders of the Commanding Generals, Johnston and then Smith, neither of whom had had any experience at handling large numbers of troops. Both had won their reputations by bold deeds as the leaders of small bodies of men. Johnston and Smith were on the battlefield and directed the operations during the two days of fighting. Satisfying his hunger for a good fight, Smith had faltered in his first attempt to substantiate his generalship and in the process failed miserably.

After the engagement of Seven Pines, the first major battle of the Peninsula campaign, there was a suspension of active operations in front of the Confederate capital. This was due in part to the weakened and worn condition of both armies as well to the weather which made an advance impossible. This important battle which served as a training ground for the eastern armies revealed that both sides were as yet raw and awkward in maneuvers. It also gave the Southern and Northern armies hope that the same courage and heroism demonstrated at Seven Pines or Fair Oaks would be duplicated on subsequent battlefields. Furthermore, the battle was a testimony to the brave field generals on both sides who taught their troops by personal example how to fight, and if need be, how to die. The Battle of Seven Pines was the first great contest in the East and also the first real attempt to capture Richmond.

The Battle of Seven Pines was an early Confederate turning point in the Civil War. It marked the collapse of the original Confederate States of America command system in the East which rested on President Davis' original appointments. The battle also revealed a major weakness of the Confederate system of appointments which made a sick man of unproven competence second in command. Another way in which Seven Pines represented a turning point was by bringing to command General Lee, a man whose experience with Winfield Scott in Mexico had given him some acquaintance with the management of a large army. Lee's experience would enable him to save Richmond, contrary to the expectations of both sides and prolong the war into one of revolutionary change. Thus the Battle of Seven Pines saved Richmond from capture, though the Confederates lost a chance for a decisive victory over a divided enemy army.

Seven Pines was a turning point in the war not only for the Confederacy, but also in the military life of General Smith. This battle saw the emergence of the Confederacy's most accomplished general, Robert E. Lee and the decline of one of its touted hopefuls, Gustavus Woodson Smith.

# Notes

1. Ezra J. Warner, *Generals in Gray, Lives of the Confederate Commanders* (Baton Rouge: Louisiana State University Press, 1959) 22-23.

2. T. Harry Williams, *P.G.T. Beauregard: Napoleon in Gray* (Baton Rouge: Louisiana State University Press, 1954) 112.

3. Compiled Service Records of Confederate General and Staff Officers, and Nonregimental Enlisted Men. Microcopy No. 331, Roll No. 229. National Archives, Washington, D.C.

4. U.S. War Department, *The War of the Rebellion: A Compilation of the Official Records of the Union and Confederate Armies*, 128 volumes and index (Washington: Government Printing Office, 1880-1901) Part 1, 51:593.

5. Allen Jones and Dumas Malone, *Dictionary of American Biography*, vol. 11, (New York: Charles Scribner's Sons, 1933) 481-84; See also Ezra J. Warner, *Generals in Blue, Lives of the Union Commanders* (Baton Rouge: Louisiana State University Press, 1964) 290-92. Also, Stephen W. Sears, *George B. McClellan: The Young Napoleon* (New York: Ticknor & Fields, 1988).

6. Stephen W. Sears, *To the Gates of Richmond: The Peninsula Campaign* (New York: Ticknor & Fields, 1992) 140. See also Smith to Davis, September 3, 1861, Jefferson Davis Papers, William L. Clements Library, University of Michigan, Ann Arbor.

7. Smith to Davis, September 26, 1861, Gustavus Woodson Smith Collection, William R. Perkins Library, Duke University. In August 1861, Johnston had written to Davis to recommend both Smith and Lovell as two of the best officers whose services could be acquired by the Confederate army. He said, "They are as fit ... as any men in our service." *Official Records*, Series I, Vol. 5, pp. 797-98.

8. Jefferson Davis, *The Rise and Fall of the Confederate Government*, 2 vols. (New York and London: D. Appleton and Company, 1912) 1:230.

9. Douglas Southall Freeman, *Lee's Lieutenants: A Study in Command*, 3 vols. (New York: Charles Scribner's Sons, 1944) 1:111-12. See also Warner, *Generals in Gray*, 161-62. For a detailed but flowery account of Johnston's life, see "In Memoriam: General Joseph Eggleston Johnston," *Southern Historical Society Papers* 18 (January-December 1890): 158-216.

10. Robert Hughes, *General Johnston* (New York: D. Appleton and Company, 1897) 83-84. The generals confirmed in August 1861 were Samuel Cooper, Albert Sidney Johnston, Robert E. Lee, Joseph E. Johnston, and Pierre G. T. Beauregard.

11. Gustavus W. Smith, "Memorandum of the Fairfax Conference," January 31, 1862, Gustavus Woodson Smith Collection, Western Reserve Historical Society, Cleveland.

12. *Official Records*, Series 1, 5, 885.

13. William C. Davis, *Jefferson Davis: The Man and His Hour* (New York: HarperCollins Publishers, 1991) 363, 441.

14. Smith's Memorandum, January 31, 1862, Smith Collection, Western Reserve Historical Society.

15. Davis to John Duncan, November 9, 1861, Jefferson Davis Papers, Louisiana Historical Association Collection, Manuscripts Department, Tulane University Library, New Orleans.

16. Hamilton J. Eckenrode, *Jefferson Davis: President of the South* (New York: The MacMillan Company, 1923) 153-55. See also John C. Stiles, "The Peninusla Campaign," *Confederate Veteran*, 28 (June 1920): 212.

17. *John Cheves Haskell Memoirs*, 7. John Cheves Haskell Collection, William R. Perkins Library, Duke University, Durham.

18. Davis to Smith, October 10, 1861, Davis Papers, Tulane University Library.

19. Gustavus Woodson Smith, *Confederate War Papers* (New York: Atlantic Publishing and Engraving Co., 1884) 318-19. See also the *John Cheves Haskell Memoirs*, 3-5.

20. Smith to Davis, October 14, 1861, Smith Collection, Duke University.

21. Davis to Smith, October 24, 1861, Jefferson Davis Papers, Duke University.

22. Smith to Beauregard, November 14, 1861, Gustavus W. Smith Letters, Dearborn Collection, The Houghton Library, Harvard University, Cambridge.

23. Davis to Smith, October 29, 1861, Davis Papers, Tulane University Library.

24. Smith Memorandum, November 2, 1861, Gustavus W. Smith Papers, Ms 848, Hargrett Rare Book and Manuscript Library, University of Georgia Libraries, Athens.

25. Davis to Smith, November 22, 1861, Smith Papers, University of Georgia Libraries.

26. Robert G. Hartje, *Van Dorn: The Life and Times of a Confederate General* (Nashville: Vanderbilt University Press, 1967) 15, 92.

27. Dunbar Rowland, *Jefferson Davis, Constitutionalist: His Letters, Papers and Speeches*, 10 vols. (Jackson: Mississippi Department of Archives and History, 1923) 5:154.

28. Smith, Confederate War Papers, 317.

29. Smith to Davis, October 14, 1861, Smith Collection, Duke University.

30. Stuart to Wife, March 25, 1862, James Ewell Brown Stuart Collection, Virginia Historical Society, Richmond.

31. Smith to Nadenbousch, October 6, 1861, John Quincy Adams Nadenbousch Papers, 1821-1867, Duke University.

32. Smith to Pittman, October 9, 1861, Smith: BV War 1861-1865, The York-Historical Society, New York. See also Davis to Joseph E. Johnston, March 4, 1862, Davis Papers, Tulane University Library.

33. Smith to Lee, March 31, 1862, RG109 War Department Collection of Confederate Records, Lee Papers, 1862-1865, National Archives, Washington D.

C. See also Smith to Davis October 14, 1861, Smith Collection, Duke University. According to Lash, the military leaders of both Armies "never fully exploited the railroad" because they misunderstood "the complex relationships between field command, the railroad, and logistics." See Jeffrey N. Lash, "Joseph E. Johnston and the Virginia Railways, 1861-62," *Civil War History* 35, No. 1 (March 1989): 5.

34. George B. McClellan, "The Peninsula Campaign," *Battles and Leaders of the Civil War*, eds., Robert Underwood and Clarence Clough Buel, 4 volumes (New York: The Century Company, 1884, reprinted, with an introduction by Roy F. Nichols, New York: Thomas Yoseloff, Inc., 1956) 2:168.

35. *Official Records*, Series 1, Pt. 1, Vol. 11:14-15.

36. Joseph E. Johnston, *Narrative of Military Operations, During the Late War Between the States* (New York: D. Appleton and Company, 1874) 75.

37. Emory M. Thomas, *The Confederate Nation 1861-1865* (New York: Harper and Row Publishers, 1979) 158. See also James Longstreet, *From Manassas to Appomattox: Memoirs of the Civil War in America* (Philadelphia: J. B. Lippincott Company, 1896) 66.

38. Johnson and Malone, *Dictionary of American Biography*, 11: 391-93.

39. Warner, *Generals in Blue*, 192-93. See also Freeman, *Lee's Lieutenants*, 1:164-66.

40. *Official Records*, Part 2, 51:310. It was obvious that Longstreet was referring to Smith and Lovell as the "persons" who outranked him, though they had no prior Confederate military experience.

41. Davis, *Rise and Fall*, 2:88.

42. Johnston, *Narrative*, 115.

43. Freeman, *Lee's Lieutenants*, 1:152.

44. Ibid., 174.

45. The aggregate casualties for the Confederate army was 1565 and 2288 for the Union army. *Official Records*, Pt. 1, 11:568, 450.

46. C.B. Denson, "William Henry Chase Whiting," *Southern Historical Society Papers* 26 (January-December 1898): 149-50.

47. The Confederate army lost forty-eight men at Eltham. General John B. Hood estimated that casualties for the Union side totaled more than 300. This, however, was an exaggeration; Federal casualties numbered 186. *Official Records*, Series 1, Pt. 1, 11:631, 618.

48. Thomas Vaden to wife, May 22, 1862, Letters of Thomas Vaden to Elizabeth Chevaille Heth Vaden, The Heth Papers, Virginia Historical Society, Richmond. Captain Vaden was under the command of Smith during the Army's retreat from Yorktown.

49. Smith to Lucretia, May 14, 1862, Smith Papers, University of Georgia.

50. Freeman, *Lee's Lieutenants*, 1:195, 199; *Official Records*, Series 1, Pt. 3, 11:502-03.

51. *Official Records*, Series 1, Pt. 3, 11:503.

52. Smith, *Confederate War Papers*, 327-29. Whiting had never advocated a conspiracy to depose the President. Davis may have been biased by the false

report when he made his appointments for major general in the spring of 1862.

53. Freeman, *Lee's Lieutenants*, 1:218.

54. Official Records, Series 1, Pt. 1, 11:32.

55. Joseph P. Cullen, *The Peninsula Campaign 1862: McClellan and Lee Struggle for Richmond* (Harrisburg: Stackpole Books, 1973) 52.

56. Richard Taylor, *Destruction and Reconstruction: Personal Experiences of the Late War*, ed. Richard B. Harwell (New York, London, and Toronto: Longmans, Green and Company, 1955) 29. See also Leonne M. Hudson, "Gustavus W. Smith and the Battle of Seven Pines," *Confederate Veteran*, (March-April 1993): 15-23.

57. *Official Records*, Series 1, 12:832. See also Johnston to Smith, May 30, 1862, Schoff Civil War Collection, William L. Clements Library, University of Michigan, Ann Arbor.

58. Ibid., Series 1, Pt. 3, 11:563.

59. Erasmus D. Keyes, "The Battle of Fair Oaks," Autograph Manuscript, 1889, p. 7. William P. Palmer Collection, Western Reserve Historical Society, Cleveland.

60. John B. Jones, *A Rebel War Clerk's Diary*, ed., Earl S. Miers (New York: Sagamore Press, Inc., 1958) 80.

61. Cullen, *The Peninsula Campaign 1862*, 52.

62. *Official Records*, Series 1, Pt. 1, 11:933-35.

63. Smith, *Confederate War Papers*, 163.

64. Smith, "Two Days of Battle at Seven Pines," *Battles and Leaders of the Civil War*, 2:241-42.

65. Gary W. Gallagher, ed., *Fighting for the Confederacy: The Personal Reflections of General Edward Porter Alexander* (Chapel Hill and London: University of North Carolina Press, 1989) 86.

66. Gustavus W. Smith, *The Battle of Seven Pines or Fair Oaks* (New York: C.G. Crawford, Printer and Stationer, 1891) 20.

67. D.B. Easley, "Experiences at Seven Pines," *Confederate Veteran* 37 (April 1929): 130.

68. *Official Records*, Series 1, Pt. 1, 11:940, 943.

69. Alexander S. Webb, *The Peninsula: McClellan's Campaign of 1862* (New York: Charles Scribner's Sons, 1908) 110.

70. Smith, "Two Days of Battle at Seven Pines," 244-45.

71. Eckenrode and Conrad, *George B. McClellan*, 70.

72. Easley, "Experiences at Seven Pines," 131.

73. Henry T. Childs, "The Battle of Seven Pines," *Confederate Veteran* 25 (January 1917): 20.

74. James J. Marks, *The Peninsula Campaign in Virginia or Incidents and Scenes on the Battle-Fields and in Richmond* (Philadelphia: J. B. Lippincott and Co., 1864) 200.

75. Childs, "The Battle of Seven Pines," 20.

76. Ibid.

77. Smith, *Confederate War Papers*, 160-61.

78. *Official Records,* Series 1, Pt. 1, 11:992.

79. Webb, *The Peninsula,* 114.

80. Marks, *The Peninsula Campaign,* 189-91.

81. Clifford Dowdey and Louis H. Manarin, eds., *The Wartime Papers of R. E. Lee* (Boston and Toronto: Little, Brown and Company, 1961) 179.

82. Drury L. Armistead, "The Battle in which General Johnston was Wounded," *Southern Historical Society Papers,* 18 (January-December 1890): 185-88. The best description of the wounding of Johnston is to be found here. *Official Records,* Series 1, Pt. 3, 11:217.

83. John W. DuBose, "Gen. Joseph Eggleston Johnston, C. S. A.," *Confederate Veteran* 22 (April 1914): 176.

84. *Richmond Examiner,* June 4, 1862. Joseph E. Johnston had a propensity for getting wounded. He was wounded eleven times in battle with Indians, the Mexicans, and in the Civil War.

85. Johnston, *Narrative,* 90-91.

86. Hudson Strode, *Jefferson Davis: Confederate President* (New York: Harcourt, Brace and Company, 1959) 254.

87. *Richmond Examiner,* June 4, 1862.

88. Warner, *Generals in Gray,* 179-183.

89. Freeman, *Lee's Lieutenants,* 1: xxv, 5, 713-15. For an interesting account of Lee's life, see "Robert E. Lee," *Southern Historical Society Papers* 18 (January-December 1890): 133-58.

90. Smith, *The Battle of Seven Pines,* 128.

91. *Official Records,* Series 1, Pt. 1, 11: 940.

92. Smith, *Confederate War Papers,* 206.

93. Burke Davis, *Gray Fox: Robert E. Lee and the Civil War* (New York: Holt, Rinehart and Winston, 1956) 75-76.

94. Peter S. Michie, *General McClellan* (New York: D. Appleton and Company, 1901) 310-11.

95. *Official Records,* Series 1, Pt. 1, 11: 988.

96. Michie, *General McClellan,* 311-12.

97. Smith, "Two Days of Battle at Seven Pines," 253.

98. Smith, *The Battle of Seven Pines,* 136.

99. Strode, *Jefferson Davis,* 256.

100. Davis, *Jefferson Davis,* 425.

101. Davis, *Rise and Fall,* 2: 129.

102. Smith, *Confederate War Papers,* 221.

103. Smith, *The Battle of Seven Pines,* 138-39.

104. Davis, *Rise and Fall,* 2: 129.

105. Dowdey and Manarin, *The Wartime Papers,* 179. Years later, Smith said that he "was struck down by disease" at Seven Pines. See Smith to C. G. Jones, November 12, 1875, Schoff Civil War Collection, William L. Clements Library.

106. Barnwell, "The Battle of Seven Pines," 61.

107. Gallagher, *Fighting for the Confederacy,* 88.

108. Longstreet, *From Manassas to Appomattox,* 111.

109. Joseph L. Brent, *Memoirs of the War Between the States* (New Orleans: Fontana Printing Co., 1940) 148.

110. Davis, *Jefferson Davis*, 423.

111. Sears, *To the Gates of Richmond*, 140.

112. *Official Records*, Series 1, Pt. 3, 11: 685-86.

113. Freeman, *Lee's Lieutenants*, 1: 264.

114. *Official Records*, Series 1, Pt. 1, 11: 824.

115. Ibid., 877

116. Ibid., 763.

117. Ibid., 946.

118. James Dinkins, "Lieut. Gen. D. H. Hill," *Confederate Veteran* 38 (June 1930): 218.

119. *Official Records*, Series 1, Pt. 2, 11: 565.

120. Joseph E. Johnston, "Official Report of Seven Pines or Fair Oaks," *Southern Historical Society Papers*, 8 (December 1880): 237.

121. *Official Records*, Series 1, Pt. 1, 11: 983.

122. Webb, *The Peninsula*, 109.

123. Gallagher, *Fighting for the Confederacy*, 85.

124. Smith, *Two Days of Fighting at Seven Pines*, 263.

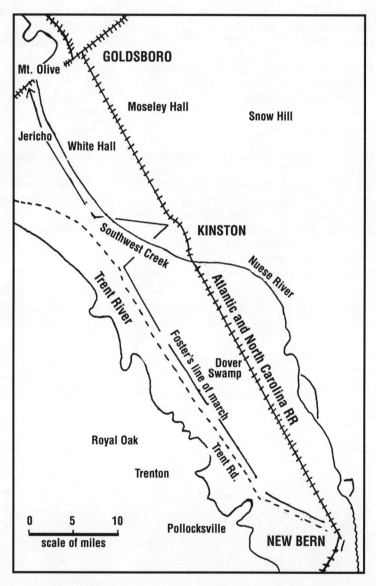

Map 3. General Foster's march from New Bern to Goldsboro in 1862.

# CHAPTER SIX

# A Winter of Discontent

The illness that Smith suffered at the battle of Seven Pines incapacitated him for several weeks. It was not until the summer of 1862 that he resumed active duty. During his recovery, he remained in communication with the War Office and his personal friends. In search of rehabilitation, Smith journeyed to White Sulphur Springs, the famous spa in western Virginia where his recovery was slow. Prior to Smith's return, he was under consideration for the command of the defense of the coast of South Carolina. In early July, Adjutant General Samuel Cooper telegraphed Smith at White Sulphur Springs on behalf of Jefferson Davis to find out whether his health would permit him to take command of the Department of South Carolina and Georgia with headquarters at Charleston.[1] In answering Cooper, Smith said, "My health is not yet sufficiently restored to enable me to return to duty."[2] Writing to Joseph E. Johnston on July 18, Smith revealed, "I do not get straight in brains and nerves as fast as I hoped."[3] He went on to tell Johnston that the general state of his health was quite good and he had been assured by Surgeon Edwin S. Gaillard that a complete recovery was expected.

The forty-year old Kentuckian admitted that he had only partially regained his health when he reported for duty to General Robert E. Lee at Richmond in August 1862. Lee was familiar with Smith having commanded him during a portion of Winfield Scott's march from Vera Cruz to Mexico City during the late war. Lee was also the superintendent of the United States Military Academy when Smith resigned from his teaching position there to join John A. Quitman's filibustering expedition against Cuba in 1854.

On August 14, General Lee issued detailed instructions to Smith outlining the role he was to assume in the Army of Northern Virginia. As the senior officer of the right wing of the Army, Smith's duties included directing its operations in Lee's absence and completing the defenses about Richmond. Smith's knowledge of engineering served him well in this capacity. Lee also assigned Smith the responsibility of defending Richmond and its approaches. Large numbers of undrilled conscripts were arriving daily at the Southern capital to commence their service in the Rebel army. To make certain that these recruits were ready for combat, Lee reminded Smith to pay close attention to the organization, instruction, and discipline of the men under his command.[4] War Secretary George A. Randolph also placed the hospitals in Virginia and North Carolina under Smith and appointed as his medical director Surgeon Gaillard who had remained at Smith's side during his illness in the summer of 1862. Smith was especially impressed with Gaillard, who had lost an arm to amputation on the battlefield of Seven Pines. "With acknowledged skill of the very highest order in his profession," Smith said, "he has few, if any, equals as an administrative and executive officer."[5]

From Smith's headquarters in Richmond, he kept a close watch on the enemy along the coast of Virginia and North Carolina. By assigning Smith this quiet command, it was apparent that the Davis administration had lost faith in him. Smith's new assignment and duties had the full support of the Confederate President.[6] Smith was losing the status he once enjoyed as an important officer in the command structure of the Confederate military. He reflected on the fact that he was slowly being forgotten by the War Office during his convalescence and concluded that, because he was disliked by Davis he had been denied the position of Commanding General of the Army of Northern Virginia. Smith always believed that because he was the next ranking officer to Johnston, he should have assumed command of the Army.[7] Nonetheless, the Davis administration soon gave Smith a new command of at least nominal importance.

By direction of the War Office, General Order No. 69 was issued on September 19, 1862, giving Smith command of the Department of North Carolina and southern Virginia. All of the officers within Smith's command, which extended from the Rappahannock River to the Cape Fear District, were to report to and receive instructions from him.[8] The scope and magnitude of this command was equal to any he held under Johnston. As commander of the state of North Carolina, Smith was again united with one of his favorite officers, General William H. C. Whiting.

Smith developed a close friendship with Governor Zebulon B. Vance of North Carolina. At an early age, Vance had developed a proclivity for stump speaking which endeared him to the public. He had resigned his commission in the Confederate army when he was elected governor of North Carolina in August 1862. Governor Vance implored North Carolinians to work together to rid the state of what he called "foreign" invaders.[9] He held a special place in the hearts of North Carolinians who followed him with unfaltering devotion for many years. The security and defense of the Tarheel State was of utmost importance to the governor. He would not hesitate to protest to Davis when he felt his beloved state was being ignored.

In the fall of 1862 Smith complained to Lee that the large number of conscripts and paroled prisoners contributed to the "confusion and disorder" in Richmond.[10] Evidence of disarray could be seen in the number of stragglers and deserters who roamed the city without fear of punishment. General John H. Winder as commander of the District of Henrico that embraced Richmond controlled these police matters and reported to Smith at this time. Although the condition in the capital city was chaotic, Smith assured Lee that he would see to it that the situation there was ameliorated as quickly as possible. Smith's administrative efforts did not restore him to the favor of his superiors.

On October 15, 1862, Smith learned that seven Lieutenant Generals had been appointed by President Davis under the act enacted by the Confederate Congress on September 18.[11] Smith's performance had not been meritorious; therefore, denial of promotion was justified. It was obvious that "the clear vision with which the president viewed his foes suddenly turned myopic when cast on his friends."[12] Six of the newly promoted officers, Leonidas Polk being the exception, had been Major General Smith's juniors at that rank. The choleric Smith immediately dispatched a terse note to Secretary Randolph to voice his dissatisfaction at being passed over. Having received no formal response from the War Department, Smith called on Randolph for a personal conference. The substance of Randolph's argument was that the command Smith then exercised "in Virginia and North Carolina was not considered one that merited the high grade within the intent of the law."[13] Smith was also informed that the active service of the officers made them eligible for advancement in rank. No doubt this statement was made with reference to the fact that because of Smith's incapacitation he was unable to take to the field. It should be noted, however, that Smith's failure to crush the enemy at Seven Pines had not been forgotten by the Richmond authorities.

Smith was not pleased with Randolph's explanation. He then proceeded to tell the War Secretary of the difficulties under which he labored and the importance of his command to the Confederate army. During the meeting, Smith informed Randolph that he intended to resign his commission. The Secretary asked him to remain in the army until the whole matter could be satisfactorily resolved. At Randolph's insistence, Smith agreed to continue in his post. Randolph did not miss the opportunity to impress upon Smith that both he and the president were satisfied with and appreciative of the service he was providing as an administrative officer and as a commander of troops. Randolph told the Kentuckian that he was passed over because the nominations were made hurriedly and that in due time the situation would be corrected. An angry Smith retorted, "I would rather have been shot dead than to have had my usefulness in so important a command impaired if not destroyed by the recent wholesale overslaughing to which I had been subjected."[14] Once again Smith symbolized the theme of petty quarreling over precedence and rank—a common problem that plagued the Davis government.

The Confederate administration not only had its share of difficulty with military officers but with civil officials as well. Davis' authoritarian personality made it difficult for people to get along with him. The political difficulty between Davis and his cabinet had manifested itself early during his presidency. With the exception of the Naval Office and Post Office, all the departments experienced several changes, the most frequent occurring at the War Department. President Davis himself, once secretary of war for the United States, had a propensity for interjecting himself into the affairs of that department. This may help to explain why a total of six secretaries of war served the Confederacy during its existence. Since Davis virtually administered the department himself with advice from General Lee, the office of war secretary was a sinecure position. The eight-month tenure of Randolph as head of the War Office was contentious.

In Secretary Randolph's humble capacity as a mere clerk, he found himself outside of Davis' inner circle. The president had meetings to which he was not invited and issued orders without his knowledge.

Davis planned campaigns without informing his war secretary and promoted officers without his advice. Randolph's chief made appointments and transferred commanding generals without his consent.[15] In Randolph's reduced role, the President frequently rejected his appointments; even those of a minor and unimportant nature. It was clearly evident that Randolph did not have the power or the dignity that the cabinet position should have commanded. By exercising the functions of the War Office himself, the Confederacy's Chief Executive saw little need to apprise Randolph of its activities.

The squabble between Davis and Randolph over strategy in the western theater reached a climax in the fall of 1862. Exacerbated by the lack of support for more attention to be paid to military operations in the West, Randolph decided to assert his authority. Without the president's consent, he ordered General Theophilus Holmes to move from Arkansas to Mississippi with 10,000 troops to form a junction with General Joseph E. Johnston for the defense of Vicksburg.[16] Such an important decision without approval angered Davis immensely, and he demanded that Randolph rescind the order. By then Randolph was not in a conciliatory mood and rather than obey the president, he resigned from his position on November 15. The Secretary's curt resignation letter hurt Davis deeply. Randolph did not extend the president the courtesy of an interview. Without hesitation, Davis wrote to Randolph, "as you have thus without notice ... retired from the post of a constitutional adviser of the Executive of the Confederacy, nothing remains but to give you this formal notice of the acceptance of your resignation."[17] The *Richmond Dispatch* said that Randolph was "among the most popular men in Virginia ... a man of decided and acknowledged talent."[18] Obviously, Davis preferred a secretary who was obsequious.

Secretary Randolph's unexpected departure forced the President to immediately select someone to maintain the administrative function of the War Department. On November 17, Davis appointed General Smith *ad interim* Secretary of War, although their relationship was already strained. Smith's familiarity with Lee's army, which at that moment appeared threatened by the enemy with a new offensive, at least made the choice seem logical.[19] On the day of Smith's appointment, Lee informed him that the Union army was making preparations for an attack south of the James River. He advised Smith that every effort should be made to oppose the enemy in North Carolina.[20] Having received Lee's letter, Smith called on Governor Vance to muster in the conscripts and to return absent soldiers to their regiments.[21]

Smith's appointment was an interesting one, created out of the necessity to fill the vacancy until a permanent candidate could be found. The only general then available in Richmond, Smith was in the right place at the right time. Therefore, for a short time in November, Davis seemed to have assuaged Smith by appointing him to the top position at the War Department.[22] In any case, Smith's appointment was temporary. It was rumored that Smith would be appointed as the permanent war secretary. An editorial in the *Mobile Advertiser and Register* seemed to have confirmed this. It read:

If the telegraph is to be believed, Pres. Davis has made an admirable appointment of his War Minister in General G. W. Smith. This officer brought into the service a very enviable reputation as a soldier, and those qualified to judge declare that he is possessed of administrative abilities of the highest order. We trust, from all we hear and know, that he is the right man in the right place.[23]

The *Richmond Dispatch* in endorsing Smith called him "an energetic and efficient officer" and hoped that he would carry out the duties of his new position "with the same ability and success that attended the labors of his predecessor."[24] Nevertheless, such speculation proved false.

Though Smith possessed superb administrative skills, he did not have an opportunity to impact upon the office because of the brevity of his tenure. Holding office for only a few days, Smith was replaced by James A. Seddon on November 21. Smith, however, did not vacate the office until a week after Seddon's appointment. During that time Smith cleared his desk of the accumulation of papers by forwarding them to the office of the Adjutant General. Seddon, officially confirmed by the Confederate Senate in January 1863, was a wealthy Virginia lawyer and personal friend of President Davis. The Confederate leader had confidence that Seddon, though sickly, could handle the work load of the War Office.

With the new secretary of war in place, Smith's attention was again directed to the defense of North Carolina. Union soldiers had been invading New Bern since the spring of 1862. New Bern, situated on the Neuse River, was the second largest city in the state and a superb base of operations from which the United States Army could launch an attack against Goldsboro.[25] This small town, located on the coastal plain of North Carolina, was less than fifty miles southeast of the state's capital. At Goldsboro, a vital railroad bridge carried across the Neuse River the Wilmington and Weldon Railroad. This 160-mile line was the major Confederate supply artery along the East Coast. It would have been virtually impossible for either the Confederate or Union army to have maintained large forces on the front line without railroads. The railroads were especially important for the Southerners. While the Confederate railroad system was inferior to that of the North in both mileage and quality, it offered to the Confederates their best opportunity to take advantage of interior lines.[26]

Inadequate transportation was not the only problem facing the Confederate government. In the fall of 1862, the state of North Carolina found itself in peril. The situation in the Tarheel State grew more ominous with the passage of each day. On November 14, 1862, General Whiting, the commander at Wilmington, called Smith's attention to the urgent need for additional troops for the defense of that city. He also asked Smith for permission to destroy the cotton, lumber, and naval stores should it become necessary to prevent them from falling into the possession of the enemy. Wilmington was one of North Carolina's major ports of entry located approximately thirty-five miles above the Cape Fear River. Four days later, Governor Vance delivered a passionate speech to the legislature calling for the raising of a state reserve of at least ten regiments. Vance said the additional units were necessary to defend that part of North Carolina that was threatened by, and partially in possession of the Union army. "The bitter cup that our captured cities and districts have had to drink is cited," Vance concluded, "to show the mercy to be expected if our abolition foes overcome us."[27]

Smith believed that the Federals were making preparations for an offensive south of the James River with Wilmington as the prime target. Confederate forces at Kinston, Goldsboro, and Weldon were not sufficient to defend themselves against a sustained Federal attack. Because of the weak garrisons along the Confederate line, Smith implored Lee to detach units from the Army of Northern Virginia and dispatch them to North Carolina. According to Smith, these detachments would enable the state to be better prepared to deal with an emergency. Although Smith had made a fervent plea for additional men, he did not expect Lee to comply with his request as evidenced by a letter he wrote to General Whiting. "I am satisfied we will not get a man or gun," he said, "from General Lee at present."[28] Lee shared Smith's uneasiness. He too was convinced that the enemy was preparing to strike at Wilmington and other salient points along the coast. In spite of the disparity of numbers, Lee was optimistic that the Rebel soldiers could hold their own against the superior Union army. In response to Smith's concern for the safety of Wilmington, Lee assured him that troops could be brought in from General Beauregard who was commanding the Confederate forces at Charleston.

For several days in December, there was apprehension as a Union army under Major General John G. Foster marched inland from New Bern in the direction of Goldsboro. Foster of New Hampshire was appointed to West Point in 1842 and graduated fourth in the class of 1846. He had served in the Mexican War as an engineer officer and won two brevets for meritorious service. He was the chief engineer of the fortifications at the Charleston Harbor during the bombardment of Fort Sumter in 1861. Foster was assigned to command the Department of North Carolina in July 1862.[29] In preparation for the much anticipated advance against Goldsboro, the Union general strengthened the entrenchments at New Bern, making it one of the most superbly fortified towns in the nation.

General Foster marched out of New Bern with an army consisting of 10,000 infantry, 640 horsemen, and 40 guns on the morning of December 11.[30] It was so cold that the water in the soldiers' canteens had turned to ice. The extreme cold, though, had not chilled the spirits of the Rebels who were in Foster's path and seemed oblivious to their discomforts. Brigadier General Nathan G. Evans of South Carolina, commander of the Confederate force of 2,000 at Kinston, awaited the arrival of the Northern army. Evans promised the War Office that "every step of the enemy's advance shall be through blood."[31] The Union army had as its objective the destruction of the railroad bridge over the Neuse River at Goldsboro. This campaign was planned to coincide with General Ambrose E. Burnside's attack against Lee at Fredericksburg. To impede Foster's expedition, General Lee ordered

Smith to the eastern section of North Carolina. Before leaving Richmond on December 13, Smith issued General Order No. 15 assigning Major General Arnold Elzey to the temporary command of the defenses at the Confederate capital.[32] Smith's priority was an inspection of the fortifications at Wilmington and other important points along the coastal plain.

Smith arrived at Goldsboro on December 15 and was met by Zebulon Vance. The governor informed him that the Confederate troops had "behaved admirably in the engagement" at Kinston on the day before.[33] The relationship between Smith and Vance was one of mutual respect and cordiality. While commanding in North Carolina, Smith was the beneficiary of Governor Vance's willingness to cooperate with him in matters regarding supplies, transportation, and recruiting. In fact, Vance had reorganized the militia of his state and had offered to call them out at Smith's request.[34] In a meeting with Smith, General Evans described the state of affairs in the vicinity of Kinston as gloomy. With exaggeration, Evans informed his superior that the enemy numbered 30,000 and was constantly being reinforced.[35] A day before Smith's arrival at Goldsboro, the Federals had met Evans in battle at Kinston. After a tough fight, Evans was forced to retreat from his position beyond the Neuse River in the direction of Goldsboro. Evans' use of whiskey and his penchant for trepidation placed his men in an unfavorable position before Foster's large army at Kinston.[36] Evans had abandoned Kinston to the United States forces prior to Smith's coming to Goldsboro. The Federal army passed the night after the Kinston fight in an open field on the edge of town.

While bivouacked at Kinston, General Foster was informed that Lee had repelled Burnside's attack at Fredericksburg. Smith, however, could not know that the Union general would be defeated in time for General Lee to dispatch soldiers from his Army to him in the Tarheel State. Neither Burnside's defeat nor the pouring of Confederate reinforcements into the State was enough to discourage Foster. On December 15, he ordered his exhausted troops to take up the march on the river road for the railroad bridge at Goldsboro.[37]

Writing to Secretary Seddon two days after the Kinston battle, Smith reported that the enemy had abandoned Kinston but not before ransacking the town. Smith also told Seddon that he was awaiting the arrival of troops, including cavalry, from Richmond. Smith impressed upon the war secretary that reconnaissance had confirmed that Foster's army was moving up the south side of the Neuse River toward Goldsboro. Smith was confident that with the arrival of troops from Richmond he would be able to strike a decisive blow against the enemy. Smith acknowledged laboring under difficulties including slow railroad transportation. He lamented, "Railroads are an uncertain reliance. They will worry me out of my life, yet, I think."[38] In spite of adversities, Smith's men were in good spirits.

Late in the afternoon of December 16, reinforcements were hurried to Goldsboro on the Wilmington and Weldon Railroad. Smith was happy to receive a regiment from Wilmington and another from Petersburg. It was rumored that General Beauregard was coming from Charleston to command at Goldsboro. The thought of the Louisiana general leading the Rebels in battle gave them a renewed sense of hope and enthusiasm. But instead, it was Beauregard's comrade Smith who came in person to take charge there. Colonel John G. Pressley of the Twenty-fifth South Carolina Volunteers remembered that the men gave Smith a cordial welcome. "The knowledge that [Smith] was at the front," he said, "gave confidence here."[39]

Smith sent the regiments which had come from Wilmington and Petersburg to the right bank of the Neuse and placed them under General Thomas L. Clingman of North Carolina. During the day Clingman was reinforced by the Eighth, Fifty-first, and Fifty-second North Carolina Regiments. Smith ordered Colonel William Allen, commander of the Fifty-first to, be held in reserve between the Eighth and Fifty-second Regiments. Colonel Stephen D. Pool's Tenth North Carolina Artillery and a section of J. B. Starr's battery were positioned on the north side of the Neuse River, with orders to guard the immediate approaches to the Wilmington and Weldon Railroad.[40]

Early on December 17, Smith enjoined Evans and Clingman to make a reconnaissance to determine the strength of the Federal army. Moments after receiving this order, Clingman was given a note from a staff officer stating that the Union army was only a few miles from the position occupied by his three weak regiments near the railroad bridges. Clingman read the dispatch to Evans and Smith. The latter directed the North Carolinian to advance his brigade across the river and engage Foster's army. Upon returning to his command, Clingman found the Union line completely formed and heavily fortified with both infantry and artillery. Surrounded at his headquarters by staff officers, Smith awaited the start of the fight. Although confronted by a superior army, he was certain the Confederates would carry the day at the battle of Goldsboro.

Emboldened by the victory at Kinston, the high spirited Federals triumphantly marched into Goldsboro on December 17. By then the additional troops Smith had ordered from Petersburg and Richmond had arrived. Much to his disappointment though, no cavalry were among them. The Confederate force at Goldsboro numbered about 15,000 and Foster's army 20,000. The Union commander ordered a detachment of cavalry and several regiments forward with instructions to destroy the bridge over the river.

The fighting immediately became heavy as musketry and cannon fire ran up and down both lines. When the contest started, Colonel Walter H. Stevens, chief engineer of Smith's army accompanied his superior to where the action was taking place. Positioned to the right of Clingman's command, Smith could see the entire battlefield. Superior Union fire power caused the Rebel troops to withdraw. Although there were other Confederate troops in the vicinity they did not participate in the Goldsboro engagement because of a lack of transportation. Doubtless dissatisfied with the manner in which Clingman was conducting the battle, Smith ordered Evans to proceed to the front and assume command.[41] The change of leadership, however, made little difference. A few hours after the battle had commenced, Lieutenant George W. Graham of the Twenty-third New York Battery torched the railroad bridge. Satisfied that "the fire was doing its work" Foster ordered his men to return to the protection of their gunboats.

During the countermarch to New Bern the Union soldiers laid waste to the countryside by destroying homes, factories, and several miles of tracks. "Never did an army professing civilization," stated the *Richmond Examiner*, "commit such wanton destruction of property."[42] Smith reported seventy-one killed, 268 wounded, and 400 taken as prisoners.[43] The purpose of Foster's march was to destroy not merely damage the bridge and railroad in the vicinity of Goldsboro. Although a *New York Times* editorial called Foster's victories in North Carolina "gleams of light and glory in a dark hour," it was also extremely critical of his expedition. The editorial concluded that the damage to the bridge, railroad, and telegraph lines was a "rather small fruit" compared with the heavy losses sustained by the Union army.[44] Foster's loss in killed, wounded, captured, and missing during his march from New Bern to Goldsboro totaled 591.[45] There was, however, disagreement among Foster's soldiers concerning the operations at Goldsboro, many believing it was a total failure.

One of Smith's major problems at Goldsboro was that he was slow in the deployment of troops. Therefore, the Confederates were unable to save the bridge. Foster's strengthening of his base at New Bern should have alerted Smith to fortify the Neuse River crossings and railroad. Foster sent a telegraphic note to Henry W. Halleck, general-in-chief of the United States Armies on December 24 calling his expedition a "perfect success." Although Foster's demonstration against Goldsboro was no more than a raid, it produced displeasure in Richmond and apprehension in North Carolina. Lee believed that the attack at Goldsboro was a diversionary tactic, with the real destination being the important port city of Wilmington. The operations at Goldsboro, however, raised questions about the competence of Smith's command in North Carolina.

One Confederate officer who was critical of General Smith's action at Goldsboro was General Samuel G. French who later claimed that for reasons unknown, Clingman's brigade did not move until the Union soldiers had attacked the bridge. French noted that Clingman's failure to advance as directed paved the way for Union success and concluded that the Confederate troops under Smith "were not properly handled at Goldsboro."[46]

Smith, as on other occasions, found himself on the defensive. When he submitted his official report of the operations at Goldsboro to the War Office, he placed blame for the lack of success on factors beyond his control. He claimed that his foremost difficulties were the lack of artillery, reinforcements, and cavalry. Smith intimated to Whiting the day after the Goldsboro raid that he was at a disadvantage because of a lack of cavalry. Smith was familiar with the ground and should have strengthened the fortifications at Goldsboro before the inevitable attack. At no time did he order his men to pursue their adversaries but was content to let the Federals retreat without a fight. According to Smith, the lateness of the hour and the want of cavalry rendered a pursuit useless. Finally, Smith offered a somewhat puzzling view of the Federal raid on Goldsboro. He seemed disappointed that Foster's army did not remain inland for a few more days before returning to New Bern. "I regret that this grand army of invasion," Smith said, "did not remain in the interior long enough for us to get at them."[47] It should be noted that the Union army had marched from New Bern to Goldsboro and had countermarched to its base with little opposition. It was also a fact that the Federal army had already advanced deep within the Tarheel State prior to Smith's arrival.

Although the Federal army had succeeded in reaching Goldsboro, the victory was not complete. It was marred by its failure to take advantage of its superior numbers to strike a decisive blow at the Wilmington and Weldon line. The damage to the bridge and tracks was superficial at best. The temporary interruption was more of a Confederate inconvenience than a Union victory. A permanent lodgement by the Federals would have effectively severed the artery of communication between Richmond and points further south. By December 23, Smith could report to the War Office that all was quiet in the direction of New Bern and railroad cars were once again crossing the Neuse River at Goldsboro.

Smith opened the new year by requesting additional troops from the Army of Northern Virginia. After an inspection of the various defensive positions in North Carolina, Smith informed Lee of the inability of those forces to protect the long line from Richmond to Wilmington. In a letter to Smith on January 4, Lee rejected so bleak an outlook of the situation in the Tarheel State. He did not believe the Federal army had the capability of deploying a large force in the vicinity of Wilmington and Goldsboro. He also noted that many of the Union troops were new recruits and therefore were undrilled and unreliable. Lee, the consummate general, was aware of how difficult it was for the enemy to attack "evey [sic] assailable point" along the eastern seaboard as well as how difficult it was for the Confederates to defend them. Finally, Lee told Smith that "Wilmington should be defended at all hazards."[48]

The many stragglers who filled southern towns and communities presented a major problem for General Smith in North Carolina. It was obvious that the loss of morale and lax discipline was a fact of life in the Confederate army. Rebel leaders recognized that an appeal to southern patriotism alone was insufficient to halt this particular vexation. Smith also knew that the possibility of each straggler becoming a deserter was an unpleasant reality. To counter the problem, Smith issued the following order on January 15, 1863. "Our victories have with few exceptions been rendered fruitless ... and thousands of lives sacrificed," he said, "by the disgraceful and cowardly habit of straggling." To Smith a straggler was a traitor, "an enemy to his country more deadly and despicable than the vilest among the hordes of the invader." Smith decreed that no soldiers would be allowed to fall out of line on the march or in battle except for sickness as certified by a physician. And each brigade should have a provost guard of at least one-hundred men to follow the army and to return them to the line.[49]

Writing to Governor Vance from Goldsboro on January 21, Smith informed him of his order against straggling and sought his support in encouraging officers and men absent without leave to return to duty. Smith believed that Vance's influence with the people of his state was a valuable asset in rallying troops to the southern cause. Smith asked Vance to make a special appeal to the ladies of the Tarheel State for them to exhort their husbands and men to take their places on the field of battle. Smith also implored Vance to issue a proclamation to his fellow North Carolinians. Vance agreed and his proclamation of January 26 was an appeal "to deserters to stand by their country yet a little longer and not to sully by desertion the bright and glorious reputation of the State which they have helped to win on a hundred hard fought fields."[50]

The outcome at Goldsboro had given Foster's men a feeling of invincibility. The ease with which they had marched along the Atlantic and North Carolina Railroad had caused North Carolinians to view the protection of their state as problematical. The Federal fleet that was organizing in Hampton Roads in late December 1862 added to the state of anxiety there. General Beauregard advised Smith to keep a close watch on the fleet because once deployed it could land anywhere on the coast. However, it was universally believed among the Confederate leaders that Wilmington was the destination of the fleet. Smith knew it was imperative that the Confederate government hold Wilmington to prevent the tightening of the Union blockade. Both Smith and Vance agreed it would be far easier to hold Wilmington than to retake it.

Because of the heavy concentration of soldiers at New Bern, Smith believed that the Federal army was making preparations for an expedition against Wilmington. He estimated the enemy force at New Bern and Beaufort at between 20,000 and 40,000. He deemed it necessary to have North Carolina reinforced at once with experienced troops. He appealed to Lee to detach 20,000 men from his command at Fredericksburg and send them to him. But instead of sending troops, Lee sent advice. He instructed Smith to arrange judiciously and concentrate his soldiers to defend and protect the frontier line in the Tarheel State. Lee also suggested a more vigorous effort at motivating North Carolinians to enlist in the Confederate army. In the meantime, Beauregard had responded to the Federal threat by sending 5,000 infantry troops to General Whiting at Wilmington.

Reacting to Smith's lack of confidence in his ability to defend his command, the Confederate authorities in Richmond realized the time had come to make a change in North Carolina. In an effort to find someone who could provide organizational structure while boosting Confederate troop morale, authorities canvassed the general officers corps. When Governor Vance learned the President was considering removing Smith from his state he voiced his opposition and called upon the North Carolina delegation in the Confederate Congress to do the same. Davis remained adamant and Vance's intervention was to no avail. Secretary Seddon sent a telegraphic note to Major General Daniel H. Hill to ascertain his willingness to accept command of North Carolina. Hill expressed his preference to serve under Smith, his West Point classmate. But as commander of the forces in his native state, Hill would remain under Smith whose departmental command included the Tarheel State. General Hill reluctantly accepted the responsibility of commanding the Confederate forces in his home state.[51]

In February 1863, on orders from General Lee, Daniel H. Hill assumed command there. Though sickly, he was a fine soldier and a courageous fighter as demonstrated at Seven Pines. However, the success that had characterized Hill at Seven Pines would not be duplicated in his native state. Lee had given the North Carolinian orders to keep the Federal forces confined to their bases of operations. In March, Hill made a feeble demonstration against Foster's army at New Bern. At the time of the attack, the Southern commander was suffering from an illness. "I started out," wrote Hill, "with my throat in a terrible fix and thought it might cost me my life."[52] General Foster's subsequent reporting of Hill's movement against him was no exaggeration when he said, "The whole affair, meant to be effective and strong, was ineffective and weak, inflicting no damage and accomplishing no object."[53]

Although a man of honor and dauntless spirit, Hill did very little with his new command in North Carolina. The command of the grand department that included lower Virginia and North Carolina, however, remained with Smith. Meandering from place to place without showing any sign of brilliance as a field commander, Smith continued to besiege the War Office with requests for reinforcements from the Army of Northern Virginia.

The passage of time had not softened his bitterness at not having received promotion to the rank of Lieutenant General. On January 14 Smith told Seddon, "Before I was reduced in relative rank in this army it was a question whether General Lee or myself should command the active forces in Northern Virginia, the other to command in Richmond."[54] A few days later, he wrote with a bit more assurance, "My health is not as good as I would wish, but I won't break down if [the enemy] will only come."[55] Smith's poor health and the lack of promotion weighed heavily on him during the early weeks of 1863. That he believed Lee kept him in the dark contributed to his state of depression. However, Smith's claim of being ignored by Lee was untrue. The relationship between Smith and his commanding officer was outwardly harmonious and civil; and Lee held him in high esteem. Ever since Smith's commission in the Confederate army, the state of his health had been a frequent topic of discussion not only in the President's Office but in the field as well. Lee told Davis that Smith's poor health made him "apprehensive of exertion or excitement."[56] Despite that, Lee had placed Smith in charge of the defense of Richmond and had assigned many duties to him. Lee trusted Smith and recommended that he be returned to his position at Richmond.

Lee had sent Major General Robert Ransom with his half-division to North Carolina at the time he dispatched Daniel Hill. Once there, Ransom had an opportunity to observe Smith's leadership as a command officer. He was dissatisfied with Smith's ineffectiveness and was determined not to let his state remain in Smith's hands. Ransom wrote to General Robert H. Chilton of Lee's personal staff in which he articulated his displeasure with Smith's lack of energy and vitality.[57] As expected, Chilton immediately shared the contents of the letter with Lee. Believing the situation in North Carolina was serious enough to merit the attention of the President, Lee promptly forwarded the letter to him.[58] Davis concurred with Lee, and Smith was recalled to

Richmond.

Though Smith's poor health was the pretext for his removal from active command in North Carolina, it was also a convenient opportunity to place him in a position in which he could do the least amount of harm. Davis ordered Major General Samuel G. French from Southside Virginia to Goldsboro to fill the vacancy created by Smith's departure until a permanent commander could be found. Governor Vance was not one to remain reticent when he believed his beloved North Carolina was being neglected by the Davis administration. When Smith was relieved, Vance protested that the change of command would result in the loss of valuable time as the new commander familiarized himself with the military affairs of his state.

When Smith arrived in Richmond in late January, rumors were rampant that he would be ordered to Louisiana or Texas. He was much relieved when the suppositions proved false. In an effort to assuage Smith's fragile ego, Davis invited him to the Executive Mansion for a personal interview on January 28, 1863. During the desultory meeting, Davis attempted to placate Smith with a few insignificant questions about details in North Carolina. But Smith left the meeting both disappointed and perturbed because the vacillating President had not given him instructions as to what was expected of him in terms of the command structure of the Confederate army. Once in Richmond, Smith wrote a long letter to Governor Vance hailing him as a man of lofty character and integrity. He thanked the governor for his support during a difficult time and told him that he would always cherish deeply the personal and official relations that existed between them. Smith also mentioned that the intentions of the Confederate government concerning himself seemed nebulous. Concluding his letter on an optimistic note, he said, "I take a deep interest in all that concerns the welfare of the people of North Carolina . . . and hope that soon under a better leader than I am, the invaders may be driven from her soil, and that we may all enjoy peace, freed from connection with the intermeddling fanatical Yankee."[59]

General Smith, a proud and perceptive man, had seen the handwriting on the wall since the fall of 1862. Within the bureaucratic departmentalization of the Confederate military, he was relegated to that of a nominal commander. His value and importance as a field commander had diminished with the passage of time. And the celebrated status that accompanied Smith into service eighteen months earlier was a fading memory. For several days during the winter of 1863, the Kentucky general contemplated leaving the army. Smith devoted a substantial amount of time on February 7 penning letters to his friends and the War Department. Writing to Samuel French at Goldsboro, Smith intimated that he was totally dissatisfied with the organization of his command and disappointed that the Davis administration had not made him the permanent commander in charge of Richmond and its immediate defenses. Smith was determined not to serve under any of the Lieutenant Generals whom he had once ranked at the grade of Major General. In fact, Smith had protested being overslaughed to Lee in October 1862. "I feel that government has not helped me in the cause," Smith said, "by placing six Major Generals who were my juniors over me in the army."[60] Smith, who was in a melancholy mood, confided to French his plans to submit his resignation to the War Office on that day. On the same day he also addressed a letter to Beauregard at Charleston, asking his friend not to pass judgment on his action until he had a chance to peruse the relevant letters. He then outlined his plans for the immediate future noting that he probably would remain in Richmond for a short time and proceed to Charleston. He told the Louisiana general, "I shall come on and be your Vol. aid [sic] if you will have me."[61] This was Smith's way of inviting himself to join Beauregard in South Carolina.

On February 7, 1863, Smith submitted his official letter of resignation to Secretary Seddon and urged him to accept it without delay. He also attached the letter which he had addressed to George W. Randolph on October 21, 1862, detailing his disatisfaction at being passed over.[62] The February letter was as much a protest memorandum as it was an announcement of the resigning of his commission in the Confederate army. Smith wrote:

> The nature and amount of my duties in this city during the last summer and fall, and the annoyance consequent upon the action of the Government in reference to myself, have prevented the thorough reestablishment of my health. I cannot consent to remain here and be responsible at this time for operations in North Carolina. Neither am I willing to serve under the orders of those who were recently my juniors. I

hereby tender my resignation as Major General in the Provisional Army of the Confederate States.[63]

A concluding statement was added in which Smith indicated his willingness to continue working for the cause of Southern independence. He was appreciative to Secretary Seddon and his predecessor for their support of him as a field commander. Davis in a letter to Seddon three days after Smith's resignation revealed his position on the matter. Without equivocation he wrote, "If the alternative of resignation or appointment as Lieut. Genl. be presented ... it will only be proper to accept the resignation."[64] Smith's quitting took Lee by surprise. Writing to his wife on February 23, Lee expressed regret for having lost him. He said, "I am very sorry to hear of the resignation of Genl. Smith. No one ought to resign now, from any cause, if able to duty. Nor do I know what he is going to do."[65] After a few days of contemplation, the Secretary of War sent a terse letter to Adjutant General Cooper recommending that Smith's wish be granted and that he be notified at once of the acceptance of his resignation.[66] Smith always believed that he was a victim of unnecessary interferences who was treated with contempt and indifference by the Davis administration.

On the afternoon of February 16, President Davis returned the resignation letters and spared no invectives in his response to Smith's letter of October 21, 1862, that Davis called a "remarkable paper." Since that letter was originally addressed to Randolph and involved matters unfamiliar to Seddon, Davis felt obligated to respond to it. According to the President, commitment was more important than rank if Smith's only purpose was to provide assistance to the Confederacy in its effort to maintain a separate government. In no uncertain terms, Davis was suggesting that Smith's personal ambition had superseded his southern patriotism. In refuting Smith's assertion that he should have been given command of the Confederates forces after Johnston went down at Seven Pines, Davis noted that he had fallen ill and was therefore unable to lead the Army of the Potomac. Davis continued his vitriolic attack against Smith by stating, "When a General of Division ... leaves his command ... he should expect another officer to be selected to succeed him, the public interest rather than personal wishes being the proper rule of conduct."[67]

On February 17, 1863, the Adjutant and Inspector General's Office issued Special Order No. 49 confirming Davis' acceptance of Smith's resignation effective that day.[68] Smith did not originally intend to respond to the President, but Davis' endorsements were of such an opprobrious nature that he felt compelled to do so. Smith stated that his letter of resignation was endorsed by the President in his worst vein and was both unfair and full of insinuations. Smith, who was tutored as a politician in New York, had learned that the pen was mightier than the sword. He took his time and with the precision of a surgeon set out to dissect Davis' letter point by point. The main thesis of Smith's lengthy letter of February 23, was that he had not been recommended for the rank of Lieutenant General.

The promotions of several of Smith's juniors had convinced him that he had no choice but to leave the army. Smith affirmed that he had never applied to Davis for a promotion. In response to Davis' contention that Smith complained about being supplanted by Lee at Seven Pines, Smith claimed that he "had been actually superseded by General Lee for more than eighteen hours" before the manifestation of his illness.[69] Lee's promotion as commanding general of the Army was the source of much resentment by General Smith. Finally, Smith entered into a discourse concerning his initial appointment in the army. "You appointed me Major General," an arrogant Smith said, and "I was ordered to the Army of the Potomac, was assigned to General J. E. Johnston's corps, and placed in command of it."[70] Thus Smith unconsciously called attention to the weakness of the Confederate appointment system that resulted in the elevation to high rank of an untested junior officer.

General Smith's letter to President Davis was filled with bitterness and conceit. In the process of refuting Davis, Smith never failed to call attention to himself. He reminded Davis that he had been a corps commander and had participated in several important conferences with him. This letter was written for self-satisfaction as much as it was an instrument to take issue with Davis. This was the kind of memorandum that an egotist would be proud to display for all to see. If nothing else, Smith could find comfort in knowing that one day in February 1863, he called upon all of his skills as a debater and took on the President of the Confederacy. Davis never took the time to answer Smith. Realizing that Smith was obstinate, Davis undoubtedly allowed the controversy between himself and the General to subside. But in actuality both Davis and Lee treated Smith rather well although he did not make Lieutenant General.

Smith had many supporters during this controversy with Davis. Among those who lamented his departure was Daniel H. Hill who called Smith one of the Confederacy's "very best officers."[71] Governor Hawes encouraged Smith to return to his native state. Because of Smith's "fitness and capacity" for command, the governor assured him of an important position in the Kentucky regiments when the military forces of that state were organized.[72] Smith confided to Hawes that it was a "source of much comfort" that so many of his friends while expressing regret, approved of his resignation.[73] Indeed it was intriguing that so many high ranking officers continued to believe in him.

Smith's departure created a vacancy within the command structure of the Army of Northern Virginia that led to the appointment of Longstreet. The instructions Longstreet received from the War Office on February 25, read, "You are by special orders, this day assigned to the command of the department recently made vacant by the resignation of Maj. Gen. G. W. Smith."[74] The new commander was an ambitious fighter who possessed incredible energy and admirable administrative skills. With headquarters at Petersburg, the total number of troops ready for duty under Longstreet numbered about 42,000. By the end of February, Smith had departed from Richmond for South Carolina. Once in Charleston he volunteered to serve as an aide to Beauregard who also disliked President Davis. A year had passed since Smith and Beauregard had served together in the same army. The War Office had ordered Beauregard from Manassas to the Mississippi Valley in February 1862. In September of that year, Beauregard had relieved General John C. Pemberton as the commander of the Department of South Carolina and Georgia.

General Smith's resignation marked the end of his affiliation with the Army of Northern Virginia. In actuality, Smith was abandoning a major part of his effort to establish Southern independence, a cause that he had espoused for years. He had entered the Confederate army with a fine reputation, amidst great expectations, only to end in an unceremonious exit. He had failed, however, to achieve any spectacular results as a field commander. Gustavus Woodson Smith departed from the Confederate army in February 1863, an embittered man, a singular symbol of the disillusionment that had begun to hobble the Southern cause during his winter of discontent.

# Notes

1. Cooper to Smith, July 5, 1862, Gustavus W. Smith Papers, Ms 848, Hargrett Rare Book and Manuscript Library, University of Georgia Libraries, Athens.

2. U.S. War Department, *The War of the Rebellion: A Compilation of the Official Records of the Union and Confederate Armies*, 128 volumes and index (Washington: Government Printing Office, 1880-1901) Pt. 2. 51: 593.

3. Ibid., 594.

4. Ibid., Series 1, Pt. 3, Vol 11: 677.

5. Horace H. Cunningham, *Doctors in Gray: The Confederate Medical Service* (Baton Rouge: Louisiana State University Press, 1958) 261.

6. Davis to Lee, August 21, 1862, Jefferson Davis Papers, Louisiana Historical Association Collection, Manuscripts Department, Tulane University Library, New Orleans.

7. *Official Records*, Pt. 2, 51: 593-94.

8. Mark Mayo Boatner, *The Civil War Dictionary* (New York: David McKay Company, Inc., 1959) 772.

9. Beth G. Grabtree, *North Carolina Governors, 1585-1958: Brief Sketches* (Raleigh: State Department of Archives and History, 1958) 96-97; Richard Yates, *The Confederacy and Zeb Vance, Confederate Centennial Studies Number Eight* (Tuscaloosa: Confederate Publishing Company, Inc., 1958) 18. See also Allen Jones and Dumas Malone, *Dictionary of American Biography* (New York: Charles Scribner's Sons, 1933) 19: 158-61.

10. Smith to Lee, October 16, 1862, Civil War Miscellaneous Collection, United States Army Military History Institute (Here after cited as the USAMHI) Carlisle Barracks, Pennsylvania.

11. The Act stated that "each army corps shall be commanded by a lieutenant general, to be appointed by the President with the advice and consent of the Senate ...." See Marcus J. Wright, *General Officers of the Confederate Army* (New York: The Neale Publishing Company, 1911) 14. The following officers were promoted to the rank of Lieutenant General: William J. Hardee, James Longstreet, Theophilus H. Holmes, Edmund K. Smith, Thomas Jackson, John C. Pemberton, and Leonidas Polk.

12. William C. Davis, *Jefferson Davis: The Man and His Hour* (New York: Harper Collins Publishers, 1991) 441.

13. Douglas Southall Freeman, *Lee's Lieutenants: A Study in Command*, 3 vols. (New York: Charles Scribner's Sons, 1944) 2: 420.

14. Memorandum attached to the letter from Smith to Randolph on October 21, 1862, Civil War Miscellaneous Collection, USAMHI, Carlisle Barracks.

15. Edward Younger, ed., *Inside the Confederate Government: The Diary of Robert Garlick Hill Kean* (New York: Oxford University Press, 1957) 30-31. See also John B. Jones, *A Rebel War Clerk's Diary*, ed. Earl Schenck Miers, (New York:

Sagamore Press Inc., 1958) 120.

16. Burton J. Hendrick, *Statesmen of the Lost Cause: Jefferson Davis and His Cabinet* (New York: The Literary Guild of America, Inc., 1939) 325.

17. Dunbar Rowland, *Jefferson Davis, Constitutionalist: His Letters, Papers and Speeches*, 10 vols. (Jackson: Mississippi Department of Archives and History, 1923) 5: 374.

18. *Richmond Dispatch,* November 17, 1862.

19. Davis, *Jefferson Davis,* 479.

20. Lee to Smith, November 17, 1862, Vance Papers, North Carolina Department of Archives and History, Raleigh.

21. Smith to Vance, November 20, 1862, Vance Papers, North Carolina Department of Archives and History.

22. Freeman, *Lee's Lieutenants,* 2: 420.

23. *Mobile Advertiser and Register,* November 19, 1862.

24. *Richmond Dispatch,* November 17, 1862.

25. Freeman, *Lee's Lieutenants,* 2: 473.

26. Charles W. Ramsdell, "The Confederate Government and the Railroads," *American Historical Review* 22 (July 1917): 794-95.

27. *Richmond Dispatch,* November 21, 1862.

28. Gustavus Woodson Smith, *Confederate War Papers* (NewYork: Atlantic Engraving and Publishing Co., 1884) 266.

29. Ezra J. Warner, *Generals in Blue, Lives of the Union Commanders* (Baton Rouge: Louisiana State University Press, 1964) 157-58.

30. *Official Records,* Series 1, 18: 54.

31. *Richmond Examiner,* December 15, 1862.

32. General Order No. 15, December 12, 1862, Hankins Family Papers, Virginia Historical Society, Richmond.

33. Smith to Seddon, December 15, 1862, The Murray J. Smith Collection, USAMHI, Carlisle Barracks.

34. Smith, *Confederate War Papers,* 294.

35. Smith to Whiting, December 15, 1862, The Murray J. Smith Collection, USAMHI, Carlisle Barracks.

36. William R. Trotter, *The Civil War in North Carolina,* 3vols. (Winston-Salem: John F. Blair Publisher, 1989) 3: 178. See also *Official Records,* Series 1, 18: 113.

37. John G. Barrett, *The Civil War in North Carolina* (Chapel Hill: University of North Carolina Press, 1963) 144.

38. Robert C. Black, *The Railroads of the Confederacy* (Chapel Hill: University of North Carolina Press, 1952) 144.

39. John G. Pressley, "Diary of Lieutenant-Colonel John G. Pressley of the Twenty-Fifth South Carolina Volunteers," *Southern Historical Society Papers* 14 (January-December, 1886): 44-45.

40. Walter E. Clark, ed., *Histories of the Several Regiments and Batallions from North Carolina in the Great War 1861-65,* 5 vols. (Raleigh: Published by the State, 1901) 1: 493-94. See also Barrett, *The Civil War,* 146-47.

41. Barrett, *The Civil War*, 147.

42. *Richmond Examiner*, December 22, 1862.

43. *Official Records*, Series 1, Vol. 18, 110.

44. *New York Times*, December 24, 1862.

45. *Official Records*, Series 1, Vol. 18, 60.

46. Samuel G. French, *Two Wars: An Autobiography* (Nashville: Confederate Veteran, 1901) 154.

47. *Official Records*, Series 1, 18: 110. See also Smith, *Confederate War Papers*, 281.

48. Lee to Smith, January 4, 1863, The Murray J. Smith Collection, USAMHI, Carlisle Barracks.

49. General Order No. 3, January 15, 1863, Thomas L. Clingman Papers, Southern Historical Collection, University of North Carolina, Chapel Hill.

50. *Official Records*, Series 1, Vol. 18, 861, 928.

51. Smith, *Confederate War Papers*, 302.

52. *Official Records*, Series 1, 18: 189.

53. Ibid., 184.

54. Ibid., 847.

55. Ibid., 855.

56. Ibid., 856.

57. Freeman, *Lee's Lieutenants*, 2: 423.

58. Lee requested Davis to destroy the letter after his perusal because Ransom did not know that it would be seen by the President. Davis destroyed Ransom's letter. Official Records, Series 1, 18: 856.

59. Smith to Vance, February 5, 1863, Vance Papers, North Carolina Department of Archives and History.

60. Smith to Lee, October 16, 1862, Civil War Miscellaneous Collection, USAMHI, Carlisle Barracks.

61. Smith to Beauregard, February 7, 1863, P. G. T. Beauregard Papers, Rare Book and Manuscript Library, Columbia University, New York.

62. For a copy of that letter see Smith to Randolph, October 21, 1862, Civil War Miscellaneous Collection, USAMHI, Carlisle Barracks.

63. Smith to Seddon, February 7, 1863, Compiled Service Records of Confederate General and Staff Officers, and Nonregimental Enlisted Men. Microcopy No. 331, Roll No. 229. National Archives, Washington, D.C.

64. Davis to Smith, February 10, 1863, Smith Papers, University of Georgia Libraries.

65. Dowdey and Manarin, eds., *The Wartime Papers of R. Lee*, 408.

66. Seddon to Cooper, February 16, 1863, Compiled Service Records.

67. Smith, *Confederate War Papers*, 306.

68. Special Order No. 49, February 17, 1863, Smith Papers, University of Georgia Libraries.

69. Smith, *Confederate War Papers*, 313.

70. Smith to Davis, February 23, 1863, Smith Papers, University of Georgia Libraries.

71. Smith, *Confederate War Papers,* 338.

72. Ibid., 342.

73. Smith to Richard Hawes, July 25, 1863, Richard Hawes Papers, Special Collections and Archives, Margaret I. King Library, University of Kentucky, Lexington.

74. *Official Records,* Series 1, 18: 895.

# CHAPTER SEVEN

# From Atlanta to the Atlantic

With the passing of Gustavus Woodson Smith's winter of discontent, the embattled general looked for an escape. The many unpleasant memories of the Confederate capital had made him eager to establish a new residence. On the occasion of being passed over, Smith remarked, "Richmond in itself is enough to run you d___d crazy."[1] His life up to this point was characterized by constant change and frequent moves. However, Smith's enthusiasm for the southern cause did not abate with his resignation. He promptly left for Charleston where he volunteered to serve as aide-de-camp to Beauregard who was in charge of the department headquartered there. Beauregard was willing to find a place for his friend and fellow opponent of the Davis administration.

General Smith's most valuable asset was his engineering expertise. He was charged with inspecting the various defensive points in the vicinity of Charleston. While Smith was conducting an inspection of Fort Sumter, it came under attack by the Federal fleet on April 7, 1863. The Union ironclad *Keokuk* had penetrated within a thousand yards of the fort when its guns opened fire. The Confederate gunners fired with superb accuracy in repelling this attack. The *Keokuk* was hit several times and sunk the next day in the Charleston harbor. The fort survived the Federal bombardment unscathed.

General Smith rendered valuable service to the Southern commander during his brief stay in Charleston. As the vicissitudes of Smith's life dictated, he soon found himself on the move again. Shortly after the *Keokuk* incident, he accepted the invitation of Joseph E. Brown, governor of Georgia to serve as his aide-de-camp. In this capacity, Smith superintended the construction of fortifications at salient locations in north Georgia.[2] Smith's training and practical experience made a favorable impression on the governor. However, when Smith's services were needed in a capacity that would benefit the Confederate cause as a whole, Brown did not hesitate to facilitate such a move. Based on the recommendation of the governor, Smith was offered the presidency of the Etowah Manufacturing and Mining Company by its owners, William L. Quinby and William Robinson. The Kentucky native accepted the position in May 1863.[3]

According to the by-laws of the company, all the business of the Etowah iron works was to be transacted under the direction of its president. In addition to negotiating contracts, Smith was also responsible for supervising a large staff with authority to remove any officer whose performance was unsatisfactory. The president of Etowah reported to its Board of Directors.[4] The industrialists Quinby and Robinson, along with Brown, wielded tremendous influence in the state of Georgia. Brown was an ardent defender of states' rights and slavery. Blessed with a gregarious personality, political acumen, and great perception, he dominated the Democratic party in his state and was elected governor four times beginning in 1857. The pugnacious governor constantly found himself at odds with President Davis.[5] Brown and Davis, both intoxicated with pride and power, possessed unconquerable egos. Governor Brown hated the Confederate administration as much as did Smith. General Smith's dislike for Davis and his reputation as a capable industrial manager had preceded him to Georgia.

Smith was one of only a few Southerners with superb qualifications in iron manufacturing. He had demonstrated his ability for such work at the Cooper and Hewitt Company in Trenton several years earlier. His practical engineering experience and industrial knowledge along with his administrative talents made him an ideal choice to oversee the operations of the Etowah facility. Located on the Etowah River in north Georgia a few miles northeast of the Allatoona Railroad station, the Etowah iron works was built in 1844. The property of the Etowah Manufacturing Company amounted to 10,000 acres of land and several individual facilities and pieces of machinery. The company works consisted of three furnaces for pig iron, a rolling mill, and a nail factory. Etowah also included works of a smaller nature such as two grist mills, flour and saw mills. A supply store, boarding houses, private dwellings, and stables dotted the manufacturing site. The labor force of 800 included many Negroes. The Etowah Railroad that was constructed in 1859 was also the property of the industrial company.

The company was laden with problems. Sickness, broken down equipment, and the nonfulfillment of government contracts were among the difficulties awaiting the new president. Doubtless, these problems impacted upon the financial status of the company. Upon his arrival, Smith found the company in trouble with the Confederate government. In September 1862, the Davis administration had advanced Etowah a million dollars for the manufacture of shell castings and ammunition. Because of an inability to honor its contracts, the company was the subject of a contemplated seizure by the authorities at Richmond. The Etowah company had also issued bonds in the amount of $500,000. Smith lamented to Governor Richard Hawes of Kentucky that there were enough problems at the Etowah works to make him "nearly crazy." In July 1863, Smith returned to Etowah from Savannah to find one vice president and several other employees incapacitated due to illness. He was also greeted with the disappointing news that two of the three furnaces had been shut down for repairs.[6] Although faced with problems, Smith's confidence in his ability to ameliorate the situation never faltered. He confided to Hawes that in a short period of time he would get the "vexations, entanglements, and misunderstandings" all straightened out.[7] Rescuing Etowah from its unstable financial condition was Smith's primary concern. The desperate state of financial affairs attracted the attention of Governor Brown who recommended state assistance as a way of maintaining and developing this private firm.[8] No doubt his generous offer was motivated by a need to prevent the company from falling into the hands of the Davis government.

The need to procure coal and to hold meetings with shareholders required that Smith travel extensively throughout the South. He intimated to Beauregard that he disliked explaining to shareholders the need for them to raise money to keep the company operative. In spite of his difficulties, Smith found consolation in the belief that he was doing some good at Etowah. Although Smith had established an impressive record in heavy manufacturing, he could not reconcile the fact that perhaps he was a better manager of industry than of soldiers. General Smith believed that he was more valuable to the Confederacy as a field commander.[9]

Although Smith had enjoyed only meager success as a field general, he longed to return to the battlefield. Writing to Governor Hawes on

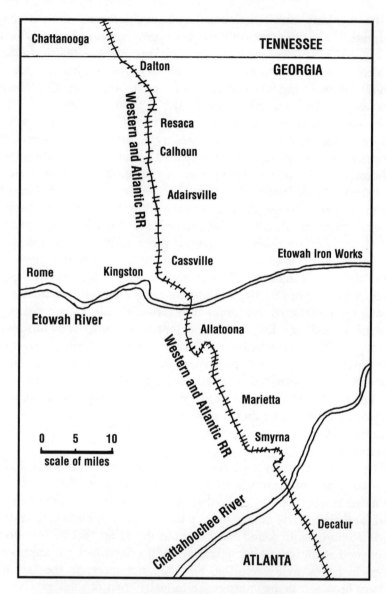

Map 4. Positions on the Western and Atlantic Railroad
from Dalton to Atlanta.

July 25, 1863, from Georgia, Smith expressed his eagerness to fight with the state of his "first and great love" should Kentucky "rise against yankee despotism." He wrote, "I am now a citizen of this state ... but will when that time comes gladly accept at your hands any position you may wish me to occupy, and will serve the state to the utmost of my ability."[10] Smith told Hawes of the antagonism that existed between he and the president. In Smith's letters to Beauregard, he also articulated a willingness to serve at the side of the Louisianian. But as a detached spectator, Smith could only offer encouragement to Beauregard in the latter's efforts to repel Federal attacks against Charleston. "I hope ... the bodies of dead yankees will fertilize Morris Island," Smith said, "until the sand hills of that famous locality may blossom as a rose."[11]

The fertile lands of the South blossomed but not with the corpses of Union soldiers. The South was an agricultural region dependent on the cultivation of staples for export. Industry and transportation were relegated to second place in its economy.[12] Because of the subordinate position of manufacturing industries, the South lacked the technological ability to compete with the North. The absence of initial capital and skilled workers made the industrial sector of the southern economy weak.[13] Despite the South's ambitious efforts at manufacturing, the dearth of iron and steel production would prove crucial to its military efforts. The Confederacy's lack of capacity to produce heavy guns was equaled by the paucity of facilities for the manufacturing of railroad iron. The Tredegar iron works of Richmond was unquestionably the most productive industrial facility in the Confederacy. The Etowah works, one of only a few other rolling mills in the South, was the only facility south of Richmond capable of manufacturing railroad car axles during the war.[14] At the beginning of the war, the tremendous burden of heavy cannon production fell to the Tredegar plant. The Davis administration attempted to ease the burden on the Richmond facility by granting ordnance contracts to industrialists at other places in the South who agreed to begin the production of weapons.

In the spring of 1861, Secretary of War Judah P. Benjamin had contracted with Mark A. Cooper for columbiads, field artillery, and ammunition.[15] The lack of ore and minerals for production made it difficult for the company to fill the orders for the War Department. General Smith compensated for the lack of coal by using wood, though it was hardly an adequate substitute. He complained that wood was impracticable for making iron because it was "slow, troublesome, and expensive."[16] On October 29, 1863, Beauregard wrote to Smith to express concern for the difficulty he was encountering in his efforts to procure coal. However, Beauregard was happy to inform his friend that Charleston was still firmly in the hands of the Confederates despite repeated attacks by the enemy's land and naval batteries.[17] By the winter of 1864, the prospect of Etowah's becoming one of the leading industrial centers of the South was not promising. Writing to Colonel Moses H. Wright, commander of the Confederate Arsenal at Atlanta on February 22, Smith admitted that he was no longer able to fill large orders and that iron was being manufactured "under great disadvantage and at a heavy cost."[18] In spite of difficulties, Smith, through frugal management, was rescuing the company from financial chaos. In fact, in March 1864, Smith proffered $249,300 to the Confederate treasury as partial payment of the advance made to the company by the government.

The year 1864 was a memorable one in the life of Georgians as their state became the focal point of the desperate struggle. The historic Atlanta campaign began in May 1864. A straw in the wind was General Sherman's immediate threat to Smith's iron works. On May 20, he removed the most valuable machinery, teams, wagons, and Negroes from Etowah to prevent them from falling to Sherman's army. When the Union army reached the abandoned industrial facility, Sherman ordered its destruction. Smith traveled by rail from Etowah to Macon where he intended to rebuild the facility. While making preparations to resume production, Smith received a bit of delightful news.[19]

It was in Macon that the Smith learned the Georgia militia had selected him to command them in the field. A surprised Smith stated, "Unsolicited by me ... the civil and military officers of the State of Georgia, when called up to take up arms in defense of their homes, almost unanimously elected me their leader."[20] The prevailing view regarding the Georgia militia is that it was comprised of soldiers whose incompetence provided rich material for humorists. The militiamen were considered misfits who made no significant contributions to the military effort of the South or to the Confederate Army of Tennessee. Furthermore, this motley collection of inexperienced volunteers was satirized in the familiar Civil War song, "Eatin Goober Peas." Although not a paragon of excellence, the militia provided valuable service to the

Confederate army during the siege of Atlanta and General William T. Sherman's march to the sea.

The Georgia militia were subject to the legal authority of Governor Brown. Brown confirmed Smith as commander of the Georgia militia on June 1, 1864, and ordered him to Atlanta to assume leadership of those civil and military officers who were exempted from Confederate service.[21] General Henry C. Wayne gladly relinquished command of the militia to Smith so he could resume his duties as Adjutant and Inspector General of the state. In a letter to William Robinson, president of the Board of Directors on June 3, Smith resigned his position with the Etowah Company. "I have been called to Atlanta by the Governor of the State for Military Service," Smith said, "the length of the time for which I will be absent is uncertain. You will please take control of the business of the Co. during my absence as provided for by the By Laws of the Company."[22]

The *Daily Constitutionalist* on the occasion of Smith's appointment called him a "master of the art of war in all its details of engineering, artillery, cavalry and infantry service."[23] A few days after assuming command, General Robert Toombs, who had also resigned his commission in the Confederate army and who also hated President Davis joined the forty-two year old Smith at Atlanta where he served as his Inspector General.[24] Smith immediately began to prepare the militia for a regimen of drilling and instruction. The militia was organized into two brigades of three regiments and a battalion of artillery which totaled a little more than 3,000 men.[25] Many of the regular troops were critical of the militia and referred to them as "Joe Brown's Pets." Captain Tom Key found them amusing. "It is laughable to see their awkward motions," he said, "and blunders at simple military evolutions."[26] Private Sam R. Watkins offered this humorous description of the militia, "the dwarf and the giant were marching side by side; the knock-kneed by the side of the bow-legged; ..." he said, "and whose diet was goobers and sweet potatoes ...."[27]

As a collection of men, the Georgia militia were not well-drilled but they compensated for the lack of preparation with dogged determination. In late June 1864, engineers assisted by a large force of Negroes and a contingent from the militia worked diligently to fortify the north shore of the Chattahoochee River a few miles northwest of Atlanta.[28] The city's foundries, munitions factories, and railroad connections made Atlanta extremely vital to the Confederacy. In anticipation of the Federal attack on Atlanta, Smith informed General Wayne that the fortifications there had been strengthened.[29] General Joseph E. Johnston, then commander of the Army of Tennessee was aware of the militia's shortcomings including its inability to endure prolonged hardship; therefore, he ordered them to protect the bridges and ferries of the Chattahoochee River from Westpoint to Rosewell.[30]

Early on the morning of July 4, Smith received an order from Johnston to take up a defensive position on the crest of Nickajack ridge which covered an important route to the city of Atlanta. This ridge was located about three miles North of Turner's Ferry. When Smith occupied this position, he was unaware at the time that the armies of Union Generals James B. McPherson and John M. Schofield were in his immediate front. Although facing superior numbers, the Confederate commander had resolved to make a stand at Nickajack ridge. "I intended to hold the position ... and was determined to sacrifice the command, if necessary," Smith said, "in an earnest effort to prevent the Federals from crossing the ridge that afternoon."[31] Protected by breastworks, Smith awaited the inevitable attack. As anticipated, the Federals essayed a movement against Smith's position on the afternoon of July 4th.

Supported by a strong skirmish line, the Northerners prepared to attack Smith in force. Smith had deployed his men to protect his flanks against enemy attacks. The fighting became heavy and lasted until dark. Despite having penetrated within a few hundred yards of Smith's line, the enemy made no attempt to carry the Confederate stronghold by assault. A confident Smith assured General Johnston that his small garrison would continue to resist the advance of the Federals with determination and vigor. According to Smith, the Georgia militia "behaved well" and "thoroughly executed the part assigned them in this engagement."[32]

Shortly after nightfall Smith informed Johnston that he was unable to hold the Federals back and would have to relinquish his position. Smith received a dispatch from Johnston during the night ordering him to withdraw from Nickajack at sunrise to the fortified works on the north bank of the Chattahoochee. When the Georgians arrived at that location, they found the main body of the Confederate army already there. Earl J. Hess concluded in his analysis of Smith's performance in the action on July 4, that "the militia could not be blamed for failing to hold back portions of two Federal armies ... neither can its stand that day be credited with saving the Army of Tennessee .... "[33] Johnston paid a handsome compliment to the small militia force in a letter punctuated with praise for Smith to Governor Brown on July 7. In reference to the action on July 4 he wrote, "You know that distinguished officer at their head is competent to high command."[34]

Smith's reunion with Johnston was brief. On July 17, Samuel Cooper notified Johnston that he had been relieved of command of the Army of Tennessee and replaced by General John Bell Hood. Hood, however, was not an innocent bystander in Johnston's demise. A clandestine campaign by Hood in which he labeled General Johnston as "ineffective" influenced Davis' decision to remove the General.[35] Upon assuming command, Hood instructed Smith to report to him directly instead of through a corps commander. The Union army by this time had set up camp between the Chattahoochee and Atlanta. Hood inherited an army of 48,750 disciplined and seasoned soldiers. He was convinced that organization, spirit, and confidence were on the side of the Army of Tennessee.

The justification for Johnston's removal was that he had failed to halt the advance of the Northerners in their approach to the gates of Atlanta. The Davis administration was of the opinion that he could neither defeat nor repel the invading army. The *Georgia Journal and Messenger* of Macon expressed disappointment at this decision noting that "such changes are much to be regretted, as the army and the public generally seem to have entire confidence in the military capacity and management of Gen. Johnston during the time he has been in command."[36] Throughout the war Davis placed too high a value on his own ability while at the same time underestimating the military genius of his field commanders. Of course, the relationship between Davis and Johnston was not a cordial or harmonious one. They had quarreled incessantly from the beginning to the end. Johnston was regarded with suspicion and frequently transferred by the authorities in Richmond. The spark for the animosity between Davis and Johnston included both personal matters and questions of military strategy.[37] When superseded by Hood at sunset on July 18, Johnston had been fighting an opposing army of a tremendous numerical advantage for more than seventy consecutive days. Johnston remained inactive until February 1865, when General Robert E. Lee assigned him to command the Department of the South.[38]

Hood was born in Owingsville, Kentucky in 1831. He entered the Military Academy at West Point from his home state and graduated in 1853. An aggressive, courageous, and judicious man, perhaps Hood's major weakness was that he was a bit too sanguine. General Hood lost a leg at Chickamauga and the use of an arm at Gettysburg. In spite of his physical disabilities, he was an excellent horseman. Hood was promoted to the rank of full general in July 1864.[39] The *Weekly Chronicle and Sentinel* of Augusta called Hood "a fighting General, of the Napoleonic cast, full of dash and courage ... and with the advantage of a wide experience, in fighting battles."[40] Smith was a distant cousin of John B. Hood. Smith was also involved in defending General Hood after the Nashville campaign.[41]

By the summer of 1864, General Sherman stood poised on the outskirts of Atlanta. The lack of provisions, stores, and ammunition made it difficult for the Confederates to resist siege by the Northern general. On July 20, the Union General George H. Thomas forded Peach Tree Creek and established his army on the south side of that stream, a distance of five miles east of Atlanta. General Smith's forces occupied the line of defense south of the Augusta road on the edge of the city. Smith was confronted by the strong forces of General McPherson. General Hood set about the task of preventing McPherson from reaching the railroad leading to Macon.

On July 21, Hood summoned his three corps commanders to his headquarters for a meeting to discuss plans for the upcoming battle that would take place just east of Atlanta. General Hood believed it was advantageous to give instructions in a general officers' meeting in order to eliminate the possibility of confusion and delay once the battle had commenced. In preparation for the battle, Hood made the following dispositions in the Confederate line: General Alexander P. Stewart was ordered to the left nearest to the Chattahoochee River, General William J. Hardee occupied the center, and General Benjamin F. Cheatham assumed the position to the right.[42] As Hardee maneuvered his corps into position on the night of July 21, word circulated that Hood was evacuating Atlanta. This premature announcement led to a brief period of public disorder as Atlantans resorted to looting. The civil unrest was quickly brought under control by the Georgia militia.

Unlike Johnston, who took a cautious approach to using Smith's unit in an offensive campaign, Hood included the militia in his plans for an assault on the left wing of Sherman's army at the battle of Atlanta.[43] According to Hood's plans, the militia were positioned to the right of Cheatham and to the left of Hardee. By dawn on July 22, the Confederate forces were in their respective positions along the strongly fortified line on the outskirts of Atlanta. They waited behind entrenchments for the battle to be initiated by General Hardee. While Hardee was attacking the enemy, Hood ordered Cheatham's troops to advance. Realizing the potential danger on his left, Smith enjoined his men to close the interval in the line and ordered the militia forward in support of Cheatham's attack. Though facing superior numbers, the Georgians scaled over the parapet and advanced more than a mile against McPherson. With the assistance of Captain Ruel W. Anderson's battery, Smith advanced within 400 yards of a Union embrasure and silenced it in a matter of minutes. The militiamen were eager to press the fight, but Smith considered it imprudent to continue the offensive with a force of only 2,000 men.[44] Smith held his position for two hours while awaiting orders from General Hood, and just before dark Hood instructed Smith to withdraw his soldiers to the trenches of Atlanta.

The battle of Atlanta was fierce. The Union and Confederate soldiers fought not only with guns but with fists, bayonets, and swords. Hardee called the fight "one of the most desperate and bloody of the war ...."[45] Hardee's capture of 1,500 Union prisoners was overshadowed by his casualty list which included 3,000 killed, wounded, and missing. Smith reported fifty casualties. Of equal importance to him as the few casualties was the surprising revelation that not a single straggler could be found.[46] Hood's failure to defeat Sherman's left wing cost the Army of Tennessee a chance to change the fortune of the war in the Georgia campaign.

Although the battle of Atlanta was a disappointing defeat for the Confederates, the city remained in their possession. According to Albert Castel, "the fundamental reason for Hood's failure on July 22 is that he tried too much with too little in too short a time."[47] Another major criticism of Hood's handling of the Confederate army was his lack of supervision during the battle. An obvious example of this deficiency was his failure to order the militia forward once the action had commenced, thereby denying them the chance to prove their mettle in a major engagement. Writing to Governor Brown on July 23, Hood said, "The State Troops under Major General Smith fought with great gallantry in the action of yesterday."[48]

General Smith hardly had a chance to reflect on his success of July 22 before Hood enjoined him to proceed to Poplar Springs, a southwestern suburb near the Atlanta and West Point Railroad. Before Smith had completed the encampment there, he was ordered to the trenches on the left of the Marietta road. As Smith and the Georgia militia moved from one portion of the line to another, they became involved in some of the hottest fighting of the Atlanta siege. The intrepid Confederate soldiers had helped to maintain the defense around Atlanta for several weeks, but the continuous fighting against superior numbers finally rendered the city untenable.

On August 30, 1864, Secretary of War James A. Seddon, on President Davis' orders, requested Governor Brown to hand over the militia to the Confederate government. Davis hoped to use these troops to help repel the Union invasion of Virginia. Brown surmised that this was a calculated scheme on the part of Davis to gain control of the militia and dismiss those officers who were under the jurisdiction of Georgia law. It was obvious that Brown had Smith and Toombs in mind, both of whom had left the Confederate army because of disagreements with Davis. Admittedly, the tentacles of Confederate politics easily reached from Richmond to Milledgeville, but Brown remain unshaken.

On the last day of August the Union army succeeded in isolating Atlanta, however, and by then Hood had decided to abandon the city. He ordered Generals Stewart and Smith to prepare their soldiers for the exodus. The next night General Hood led a processional through the streets he had zealously defended for several weeks. The evacuation was carried out with so little confusion that by midnight most of the troops were out of Atlanta. General Stewart's corps had the distinction of being the last soldiers to leave the city. With the fall of Atlanta, the morale of the troops fell as well. The Georgia campaign was the death knell of the Confederate cause, and the recollection of heroism did not soften the reality that so much blood had been shed in a futile effort.

Although the evacuation of Atlanta was discouraging to Southerners, the Georgia militia could find some comfort in knowing they had done their best there. In spite of suffering from imperfect organization and inadequate training, the militia gave a good account of themselves during the arduous defense of the southern city. According to Hood, the militia "rendered excellent and gallant service during the siege of Atlanta."[49] On September 5, Smith summarized the performance of his men in a letter to Brown. He wrote, "upon the battlefield, on the line of march, in laboring upon fortifications, and defence [sic] of entrenchments, ... the militia of Georgia have won the respect and esteem of the gallant officers and men composing the regular army under Gen. Hood."[50] Following the capitulation of Atlanta, Hood ordered the militia to Griffin to protect the Confederate communications in that vicinity.

The march to that location convinced Smith that soldiers over the age of fifty were physically unable to endure the rigors of military life and he advised Brown to withdraw them from service. Responding to Smith's recommendation and with Hood's concurrence, the governor discharged men over that age and gave the remaining men a much needed respite by furloughing them for thirty days to return home to attend to domestic affairs. Sherman was convinced that the militia were "dispersed to their homes, to gather the corn and sorghum, then ripe and ready for the harvesters."[51] Commenting on the furlough, T. Conn Bryan maintains that it "was for the purpose of gathering the autumn crops, but was in reality to prevent the state troops from being enrolled in Confederate service."[52] It would appear that Brown who was a champion of states' rights, had outmaneuvered Davis while defending the sovereignty of Georgia at the same time. Upon Smith's return to service, he received a telegram from Hood ordering him to assemble the militia at Lovejoy's Station just south of Atlanta to provide support to the small Rebel cavalry observing the Union army there.[53] The militia did not form a part of Hood's operating army but remained in their home state and offered opposition to the Union army in its march to the sea.

On the night of November 15, 1864, Smith withdrew from Lovejoy's to the entrenchments at Griffin. The Federals made a few demonstrations against that Confederate position, but no real effort was made to capture the town. The next day, Smith marched from Griffin to Forsyth, a distance of less than forty miles in about twenty-four hours. On November 17, the Georgians clashed with the advance of the Federal cavalry at the latter place and saved a large quantity of supplies there. The next day Smith left Forsyth for Macon. He arrived at

East Macon in time to help repel a strong Federal demonstration against that town. It should be noted that Sherman's intention was not to occupy the fortified Confederate positions in the interior of Georgia but was merely passing through them en route to the sea.

While in Macon, Smith's superior, General Hardee, directed him to go to Augusta. By then, Hood had taken his army into Tennessee believing he could change Sherman's direction by attacking the Union army from the rear. Realizing that he would be detained in Macon to procure supplies and transportation, Smith ordered his men to proceed under the command of Brigadier General Pleasant J. Phillips. They were instructed to stop at the village of Griswoldville, a distance of about ten miles north of Macon and wait for Smith to join them. If attacked, the Georgians were to fall back to the fortifications at East Macon. Phillips, who had been drinking, disobeyed Smith's orders and marched past Griswoldville. Phillips having received reports that the Union force there was small, ordered the men to attack, the results of which were disastrous.[54] On November 22, about one mile beyond the village, the Georgia militia became engaged with Sherman's rear guard. Charging up a small hill, the Confederates suffered heavy casualties in a desperate fight but were unable to dislodge the Federals who were protected by temporary works. Smith reported a loss of fifty-one killed and 472 wounded.[55] The Union army suffered about 100 casualties. After dark, the militia pulled back to Macon, and the enemy made no attempt to pursue them.

The battle of Griswoldville was a wasted effort; it failed to slow the advance of the Federals. Sherman marched inexorably past Macon on to Milledgeville and finally to Savannah. An important factor which may help to explain Phillip's decision to take the offensive at Griswoldville was that many of the troops under his command were from there as well as nearby communities. The sight of Union soldiers ravaging the countryside produced anger among the militiamen, thereby justifying the attack to avenge what they had seen. Although Smith's absence from Griswoldville was legitimate, William Harris Bragg did not hesitate to point out that he had a reputation for avoiding "responsibility and danger."[56] Though Smith had missed the Griswoldville debacle, Sherman's plans would soon put him at the center of action at the battle of Honey Hill.

This battle had its origin in a telegraphic note of November 11 from

Sherman to General Henry W. Halleck, chief of staff of the United States Armies. "I would like to have General Foster," he said, "break the Charleston and Savannah Railroad about Pocataligo about December lst."[57] Shortly after the war had commenced, General Beauregard had warned Confederate authorities in South Carolina that the enemy would attempt to destroy the railroad between Charleston and Savannah.[58] John G. Foster, commander of the South Atlantic fleet and army at Hilton Head, informed Halleck that he was making preparations to cut the railroad at the Grahamville depot, a distance of thirty-six miles northeast of Savannah.

The battle of Honey Hill was the culmination of previous attacks against the railroad which occurred in conjunction with General Sherman's epic march to the sea. The Charleston and Savannah Railroad had become the major lifeline for the two ports since the Federal blockade had brought water commerce to a trickle. Cutting the railroad would have penned General William J. Hardee, commander of the Confederate garrison in Savannah, leaving him without an avenue of retreat. Moreover, a successful lodgement on the Charleston and Savannah would have provided Sherman with a base from which to operate before risking his troops in battle at either of the well-defended port cities. In compliance with General Halleck's orders, General Foster designated 6,000 soldiers, including several units of United States Colored troops, six gunboats, and ten pieces of artillery for the purpose of securing for Sherman a foothold on the mainland in the Palmetto State.[59] Every precaution was to be used to conceal from the Rebels the movement of the transports as the vessels departed from Hilton Head on November 28 for a place called Boyd's Landing on the south shore of Broad River in Beaufort County. West of Boyd's Landing, nine miles inland, was situated the village of Grahamville with the railroad one mile farther. General Foster, before returning to Hilton Head, placed General John P. Hatch in command of the Coastal Division with orders to cut the railroad at Grahamville.[60] Hatch's army consisted of largely inexperienced soldiers.

As the Union army bivouacked in the vicinity of Grahamville, the Confederates were busy making preparations to offer resistance in both Georgia and South Carolina. Smith, who had departed from Macon on November 25 with his Georgia troops, was headed for Savannah. He could not proceed directly there because the Union army had destroyed

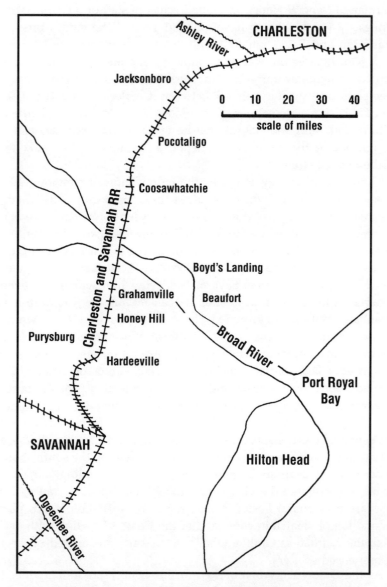

Map 5. Positions on the Charleston and Savannah Railroad including the location of Honey Hill.

the Georgia Central Railroad line. The destruction forced him to take an alternate route from Macon to Thomasville via Albany. Smith had moved from Macon to Albany by train but was forced to go by foot on to Thomasville. His tired troops arrived on November 28, having marched about sixty miles in little more than fifty hours. Because of insufficient rail transportation at Thomasville, Smith did not reach Savannah until about 2:00 a.m. on November 30 and then with only a portion of his militia. Upon his arrival, Smith was ordered by Hardee to continue to Grahamville to assist the South Carolinians who were being threatened by Hatch's army. Smith was furious; not only because his troops were in need of rest, but also because he felt they were needed in the state of Georgia. The angry militia commander demanded a personal interview with General Hardee who had established his headquarters at a private house in the city. Getting his superior out of bed, Smith said, "If you can satisfy me that it is absolutely necessary that my command shall go into South Carolina, I will endeavor to carry out your orders."[61]

General Hardee's order, however, was in contradiction to state law which stipulated that the Georgia militia were not to serve beyond the state line during the war without the authorization of the governor. Hardee explained to Smith that the advancing Union army had interrupted Governor Brown's communication with eastern Georgia; therefore, he had been temporarily superseded by Ambrose R. Wright, the presiding officer of the Georgia Senate. Hardee had secured permission from Wright for Smith to take the Georgia troops across the state line. Smith was specifically ordered to return them to their native state once the battle in South Carolina had ended. The mood of Smith's men changed from excitement to consternation when they learned that they would be going to the neighboring state. However, when General Smith announced to them that their actual purpose for going to South Carolina was not so much to defend the state as it was to keep open a railroad by which reinforcements would be brought in for the defense of Savannah, the troops agreed to leave their state. The available part of the Georgia militia, heavy with fatigue, departed from Savannah for Grahamville early in the morning of November 30, 1864.[62]

The foresight of General Lee had made it possible for the Georgia militia to occupy prepared defensive positions at Honey Hill near Grahamville. It was one of the important stations along the Charleston and Savannah line he had fortified in 1862. Honey Hill was perfectly situated for the defensive battle that the Confederates would wage against the Union army. About ten feet above water level, Honey Hill was nestled on the north bank of a small stream.⁶³ The entrenchments commanded the road as it made its way through the swamp at the bottom of the hill. The terrain about Honey Hill was characterized by almost impenetrable thickets of vines and underbrush.

The Confederate officer in command of the third military district of South Carolina was Colonel Charles J. Colcock who was headquartered at Grahamville. A planter before the war, he had done extensive cotton business in several southeastern states. Colcock had also been a railroad entrepreneur and had taken the lead in having constructed the Charleston and Savannah line which he was now defending. The colonel had scheduled his third marriage for November 30, but the exigency of the battle forced him to postpone his wedding for a few days.⁶⁴ The outcome at Grahamville might have been different had duty not prevailed over romance. At 7:00 a.m. Colcock was informed by the telegraph operator that General Smith was momentarily expected at the Grahamville station. The Georgia state troops pulled up to the depot at 8:00 a.m.⁶⁵ Smith was greeted by Major John J. Jenkins, commander of the Third South Carolina cavalry. When Smith divulged his illness of two years earlier to the Major, the two men exchanged horses. Jenkins' inactive horse was more to Smith's liking. This pleased Smith very much, and they rode out to the battlefield to meet the district commander.

After making the dispositions for the coming battle, Colcock tendered his resignation from further direction of the battle to Smith, the only general officer present at Honey Hill. In refusing to accept the management of affairs, Smith said, "No Colonel, you have prepared so fine an entertainment that you must receive your guests; retain charge, and if you wish at any time to consult with me you will find me a little to the rear."⁶⁶ The Rebel army at Honey Hill numbered about 1,500 effectives. There behind the Honey Hill fortifications, beneath the bright South Carolina sun, the Rebel soldiers waited patiently but confidently to defend the state that had the distinction of being the first to leave the Union four years earlier. The silence around Honey Hill was abruptly disturbed by the eruption of artillery and musketry fire. During the height of the battle, a Confederate officer later wrote, "The noise of the battle at this time was terrific, the artillery crashing away in the center, while volley after volley of musketry ran down both lines and were reverberated from the surrounding forests."[67]

Having ordered several attacks, General Hatch decided that he could not dislodge the well-entrenched Confederates. He was now faced with the reality that his only alternative was to retreat and as darkness covered the battlefield the retrograde movement got underway. Smith deemed it prudent not to pursue the Yankees with exhausted and hungry troops. Late in the afternoon, General Hardee in Savannah received a welcome dispatch from Smith.[68] With determination and courage the Union soldiers had been repulsed at Honey Hill. The small entrenched rebel army had decisively defeated the United States troops and had saved the valuable railroad from capture.

For the Union army, the battle of Honey Hill was fought without a plan, without commanding officers near enough to give intelligent orders, and without regimental leaders possessing the wherewithal to use good judgment in the heat of conflict. The piecemeal commitment of units threw away the Union's numerical advantage. The Herculean effort by the soldiers at the engagement was wasted because of inferior generalship. The Union general, Jacob D. Cox, was particularly critical of the performance of the Northern commanders. "It was a fresh instance of the manner in which irresolute leadership in war," he said, "wastes the lives of men by alternating between an ill- timed caution and an equally ill-timed rashness."[69] In the final analysis the Union army had simply "launched a poorly planned attack on the railroad that led from Charleston to Savannah."[70]

The Confederate leadership proved excellent from the beginning to end. As a result of good management, seasoned with good luck, the Confederates brought a force from western Georgia to the coast of South Carolina so opportunely that it moved into position only a few minutes before the start of the battle. In a report of the battle to General Hardee, Smith said, "I have never seen or known a battlefield upon which there was so little confusion ... and where a small number of men, for so long a time successfully resisted the determination and oft-repeated efforts of largely superior attacking forces."[71] General Smith paid a handsome tribute to Colonel Colcock, remembering him as the gallant South Carolinian who was "entitled to the honors" of victory.[72] Governor Brown called the Confederate triumph at Grahamville "one of the most significant victories of the war in proportion to the number engaged."[73]

If casualties are used as a yardstick for determining a winner at the Honey Hill fight, the Southern army overwhelmingly would be declared victorious. Smith reported a Confederate loss of eight killed and forty-two wounded. Having been on the attack against entrenchments, the United States bore the brunt of the casualties. Foster reported eighty-eight killed, 623 wounded, and forty-three missing.[74] In describing the battleground, the Confederate General James Chesnut said, "It was the bloodiest of fights—a carnage. Before the dead were buried the next day, the battlefield was awful to see."[75] According to a Savannah newspaper, "some sixty or seventy bodies were counted in a space of an acre many of which were horribly mutilated by shells, some with half their heads torn off."[76] Captain John J. Abercrombie of the Union army recalled seeing wounded soldiers creeping "aimlessly about on their hands and knees; some crawled on their bellies, dragging useless limbs behind them."[77]

The battles of Griswoldville and Honey Hill are especially revealing in that they serve as evidence that the militia were at their best when defending rather than assaulting a fortified position. Furthermore, the Honey Hill victory took on added significance for the Confederates because it came late in the war, thereby providing them with the then rare opportunity of scavenging the personal baggage and haversacks of the dead Union soldiers.[78] The work of the Georgia militia did not go unnoticed by the legislature of the state of Georgia. On March 9, 1865, that body passed a commendatory resolution in acknowledgment of their service. It read:

> Resolved by the Senate and House of Representatives, in General Assembly met, that the thanks of the State are due and are hereby tendered to General G. W. Smith, and to the officers and men composing the First Division of Georgia Militia, and to the Officers and men of the Georgia State Line, for their conspicuous gallantry at Griswoldville in this state; and especially for their unselfish patriotism in leaving their state and meeting the enemy on the memorable and well fought battlefield at Honey Hill in South Carolina.[79]

On December 1, General Hardee came to survey the site of the

Confederate victory at Grahamville. Smith, feeling that the necessity to detain the Georgia militia in South Carolina no longer existed, obtained permission from Hardee to return his weary but victorious troops to their own state.[80] Smith's men fell in with the Savannah garrison as they awaited the arrival of Sherman who began to siege the city about the middle of December. Hardee was in a perilous position.

On December 16, General Hardee called his generals together for a meeting to discuss the deterioration of the situation in Savannah. Hardee's intention was not to hold Savannah but rather to delay Sherman's army as long as possible, then evacuate in steamboats. Upon learning of Hardee's plan, Smith advised him of the need to erect a pontoon bridge over the Savannah River. After urgent appeals by Smith, Hardee reluctantly gave him permission to try his hands at bridge building. The construction of the bridge was an important contribution to the Savannah campaign and evidence of Smith's ability to improvise. With Savannah invested, Hardee informed President Davis that "Unless assured that a force sufficient to keep open my communications can be sent me, I shall be compelled to evacuate Savannah."[81]

With no assistance coming from Richmond, Hardee took the most prudent course and on December 20 ordered the evacuation of Savannah. The Georgia militia were the last rebel troops to leave the city. They proceeded through South Carolina en route to Augusta. Once there, the militia went into camp for the winter. The Georgians were later transferred to Macon, where they remained for the duration of the war. Hardee would later acknowledge that if he had relied upon the slow moving steamboats his entire command would have been captured. The retreat was a solemn moment, as many of the Savannah soldiers were leaving not only their long-held military post, but their homes as well.[82] However, the Confederates could still find comfort in knowing that their victory at Honey Hill had preserved the Charleston and Savannah Railroad which had made possible the evacuation of the Georgia city by the sea. Sherman got Savannah, but not Hardee's army. These men could now offer resistance to the Union general as he made his trek through the two Carolinas during the early weeks of 1865.

The success of the militia was due in no small measure to Smith's leadership and was evidence that he was more effective with small units. He instilled in his men a sense of confidence and they willingly followed him into battle. As a collection of soldiers, the militia were inadequately drilled but they compensated for their lack of preparation with courage. Despite many limitations, they contributed to the Confederate cause by participating in active military operations and performing duties of a noncombat nature as well. The story of the militia was that of dedicated soldiers who endured the hardships of war like veterans. Smith was satisfied that the militia had done their part to help maintain the Confederacy and in the process had made the state of Georgia proud. The fact that the militia did not alter the Atlanta campaign or the course of the war should not diminish their record of success.

The war produced many ironies. One involved a request by Generals Hardee, Smith, and LaFayette Mclaws for Sherman to protect their wives. These officers were forced by the exigency of the war to leave their families in Savannah. Not only were they enemies of the Union general, but they had also propagandized Sherman's reputation as an ogre. General Sherman honored Smith's request and visited his home in Savannah to make sure his wife was receiving proper treatment. Smith was appreciative to Sherman for the expression of kindness extended to his wife during the Federal occupation of the beleaguered city.[83] Surprisingly, Sherman's civility was sometimes extended to families other than those of high ranking officers. With the Confederate troops firmly planted on South Carolina's soil, they anxiously awaited the arrival of their uninvited guests.

The Union soldiers, who had demoralized Georgia were excited at the prospect that after many years of fighting they would finally march on South Carolina. Because of the state's lead role in the secession crisis, Sherman was determined to make South Carolinians pay for bringing upon the nation the most devastating war in its history. Writing to General Halleck on December 24, he said, "the truth is, the whole army is burning with an insatiable desire to wreak vengeance upon S.C. I almost tremble at her fate, but feel that she deserves all that seems in store for her."[84]

Simultaneously with the Union general's withdrawal from Savannah, a meeting of several Confederate officers was held near Augusta on February 2, 1865. Beauregard called the conference to formulate a plan of defense for the Palmetto State. At that time, General

Daniel H. Hill was commanding the subdistrict of Augusta with Smith occupying the defensive line of Briar Creek several miles south of Augusta. They were headquartered at Green's Cut Station, on the Augusta and Savannah Railroad. Beauregard wished to have both Hill and Smith in conference with him. Since they could not leave their commands, it was decided that Beauregard and Hardee should go to their headquarters at Green's Cut Station. The meeting lasted several hours with the views of Beauregard being accepted with little opposition.

General Beauregard estimated that a total of 33,450 effectives could be procured by February 5. This meager force was faced with the colossal challenge of stopping Sherman's army which seemed to gain momentum with each victory. From Augusta, Beauregard informed the Confederate President that a force of less than 34,000 was not sufficient to halt Sherman's march. Davis, however, could not provide Beauregard with additional troops because of the heavy fighting in Virginia and North Carolina. Moreover, the Confederate commander had exaggerated the strength of his projected force. Only about two-thirds of that number ever reported for duty. The reduction of forces was made worse because desertions outnumbered new recruits. An addition to Beauregard's disappointment was the fact that the Georgia state militia under Smith were prohibited by law from crossing the state line; therefore, they were not available for duty in the Carolinas.[85]

On February 14, General Hardee received orders from Beauregard to abandon Charleston, and three days later the Confederate garrison began leaving the city. The army retreated in a northward direction eventually moving into North Carolina. In a period of a little less than two months Hardee had successfully evacuated the most important port cities in Georgia and South Carolina. By then the collapse of the Confederacy was imminent, and it was only a matter of time before its leaders would see the wisdom of surrender.

On April 2, 1865, General Lee informed the Confederate administration that his position at Petersburg had become untenable. The four years of misery and carnage began to come to an end when Richmond was evacuated that night. The day after the official surrender at the Appomattox Court House, Lee issued what he considered a fitting tribute to his men. Lee's General Order No. 9 read:

The Army of Northern Virginia has been compelled to yield to overwhelming numbers and resources. But feeling that valor and devotion could accomplish nothing ... I determined to avoid the useless sacrifice of those whose past services have endeared them to their countrymen. With an increasing admiration of your constancy and devotion to your country .... I bid you all an affectionate farewell.[86]

Smith spent the last two months of the war on garrison duty at Macon. The end for Smith came on April 20, 1865, when he was captured there by Union cavalrymen.

For the Confederate States of America the four years of arduous fighting was a time of crisis and sacrifice. The Rebel troops were not the only ones who endured the hardships of war. The civilian population was called upon to make the war effort a priority. One of the more remarkable aspects of the desperate struggle for independence was the willingness of Southerners to accept severe measures with little opposition. There was always the problem of balancing the needs of soldiers against those of the people. Soldiers had to be provisioned, and civilians convinced that defeat would be tantamount to death were willing to forego their needs accordingly. But in the final analysis the military and political leaders of the Confederacy failed to sustain the morale of the men and women behind the front lines. Of course, the North was not flawless; it too made mistakes but had resources enough to recover. The South was simply too weak to afford the luxury of errors. President Davis in his first Inaugural Address had prepared his people for what would lay ahead. From the Confederate capital at Montgomery, he had issued a prophetic statement: "You will have many errors to forgive, many deficiencies to tolerate ...."[87]

One of the more obvious internal weaknesses of the Confederacy involved petty rivalries, disputes, and jealousies. Ambitious officers competed and argued about rank and assignments before they had proved their worth on the battlefield. Among Davis' most apparent shortcomings were his persistent feuding with subordinates and his penchant for making bad appointments. Davis had the awesome challenge of trying to appease officers and politicians brought together by the phenomenon of secession. The clash of personalities between Davis and Generals Johnston and Beauregard produced a litany of quarrels during the war. Davis would have done well to have feuded less and allowed his field commanders to carry out campaigns with minimal interference from Richmond. Davis always believed that Johnston and Beauregard were determined to undermine the Confederate government in an effort to further their political ambitions. Writing many years after the war, "there was so much credit given where so little was due," Davis said, "as in the case of Beauregard at Charleston."[88]

The factional differences between the Confederate President and his generals manifested themselves early during the war. General Smith's military career was an anomaly. Because of his West Point training, prewar experience, and circle of influential friends, he began his Confederate service almost at the top with a commission as major general. Although he was relegated by the Confederate authorities almost from the beginning, he was respected by his fellow officers. Davis was notorious for his contentious encounters with General Smith. Their differences were many and varied. The question of promotion provided the ammunition for Smith to engage in an acrimonious dispute with Davis. The anti-administration bloc believed that Davis' treatment of Smith was unfair, malicious, and vindictive. Smith's military career was punctuated with controversy but void of any significant achievements which may help to explain why he was not promoted.

Perhaps a leading factor that prevented Smith from achieving notable success was illness. Smith's paralysis was a major contributor to his inability to fulfill the expectations of his friends and the Confederate administration. He had a history of sickness dating back to his days as Street Commissioner of New York City. General Smith reported ill several times during the war. It was a common belief among the authorities in Richmond that the excitement of vigorous service was detrimental to Smith. The symptoms of Smith's malady were believed to have been of an apoplectic nature. Smith's recurrent attacks of paralysis should have qualified him for retirement. At any rate, Smith's incapability to undertake active command should have consigned him to an administrative position.

Although the war had created many heroes, it had also produced an equal number of failures and Smith's military career was a record of unfulfilled promises. Successful generals were measured by their victories. By applying this definition to Smith, he was a failure. He never enjoyed the thrill of leading a Confederate army to victory. At Seven Pines, he took part in the loss of one of the Confederates' best chances for a decisive victory. Like many other generals of the Confederacy, he failed to live up to expectations because he would not accept the uncertainty of danger and the responsibility that went with it.

The fear of failure was Smith's Achilles' heel. He distinguished himself during the war as an engineer of outstanding ability. Smith enjoyed his greatest triumph of the war during the Georgia campaign. The battle of Seven Pines had clearly illustrated that Smith was unable to handle the heavy responsibility of a major command. His leadership of the Georgia militia was evidence that he was more effective with small units. Although General Smith enjoyed some success in several engagements they were overshadowed by the loss of the war. He survived the Civil War, but his reputation was forever shattered.

# Notes

1. RG 109, Smith to Beauregard, November 2, 1862, War Department Collection of Confederate Records, "CitizensFile," 1861-1865 National Archives, Washington, D.C.

2. *Encyclopaedia of Contemporary Biography of New York*, 11 vols. (New York: Atlantic Publishing and Engraving Co., 1882) 2: 63.

3. Smith to Richard Hawes, July 25, 1863, Richard Hawes Papers, Special Collections and Archives, Margaret I. King Library, University of Kentucky, Lexington.

4. Corporation By-Laws, Confederate Papers Relating to Citizens or Business Firms (Hereafter cited as Confederate Papers) Microcopy No. 346, Roll No. 287. National Archives: Washington, D.C.

5. Allen Jones and Dumas Malone, *Dictionary of American Biography* (New York: Charles Scribner's Sons, 1930) 3: 141-43. See also W. Buck Yearns, ed. *The Confederate Governors* (Athens: University of Georgia Press, 1985) 69-83.

6. RG 109, Smith to Beauregard, July 24, 1863, "Citizens File."

7. Smith to Hawes, July 25, 1863, Hawes Papers.

8. Joseph H. Parks, *Joseph E. Brown of Georgia*, Southern Biography Series, (Baton Rouge: Louisiana State University Press, 1977) 110.

9. RG 109, Smith to Beauregard, July 24, 1863, "Citizens File."

10. Smith to Hawes, July 25, 1863, Hawes Papers.

11. RG 109, Smith to Beauregard, July 24, 1863, "Citizens File."

12. Raimondo Luraghi, "The Civil War and the Modernization of American Society: Social Structure and Industrial Revolution in the Old South Before and During the War," *Civil War History* 18 (September 1972): 234.

13. Charles W. Ramsdell, *Behind the Lines in the Southern Confederacy* (Baton Rouge: Louisiana State University Press, 1944) 4, 100. See also Raimondo, Luraghi, *The Rise and Fall of the Plantation South* (New York: New Viewpoints, 1978) 106-07, 111.

14. Robert C. Black, *The Railroads of the Confederacy* (Chapel Hill: University of North Carolina Press, 1952[rpt. 1998]) 23.

15. Charles R. Dew, *Ironmaker to the Confederacy: Joseph R. Anderson and the Tredegar Iron Works* (New Haven: Yale University Press, 1966) 86. Mark A. Cooper, who was the original owner of the Etowah company sold it to Quinby and Robinson in 1862.

16. RG 109, Smith to Beauregard, October 20, 1863, "Citizens File." The shortage of coal resulted in unemployed workers enlisting in the army; therefore, the want of laborers added to the problems at Etowah.

17. U.S. Department, *The War of the Rebellion: A Compilation of the Official Records of the Union and Confederate Armies*, 128 volumes and Index (Washington: Government Printing Office, 1880-1901), Series 1, pt. 2, 28: 456.

18. RG 109, Smith to Wright, February 22, 1864, "Citizens File."

19. Gustavus Woodson Smith, "The Georgia Militia About Atlanta," *Battles and Leaders of the Civil War*, eds., Robert Underwood and Clarence Clough Buel, 4 Volumes (New York: The Century Company, 1884, reprinted with an introduction by Roy F. Nichols, New York: Thomas Yoselloff, Inc., 1956) 4: 332.

20. *Official Records*, Series 1, Pt. 3, 38: 971. The records of the Georgia state militia were destroyed by fire shortly after the surrender of Macon to the Union cavalry leader General James H. Wilson in April 1865. See Gustavus W. Smith to Charles Colcock Jones, Jr., October 3, 1867, Charles Colcock Jones, Jr., Papers, William R. Perkins Library, Duke University, Durham.

21. *Encyclopaedia of Contemporary Biography of New York*, 2: 63. The militiamen ranged in age from sixteen to fifty-five.

22. Smith to Robinson, June 3, 1864, Confederate Papers.

23. *Daily Constitutionalist*, (Augusta), June 3, 1864. *The Southern Confederacy*, (Atlanta), on June 9, 1864, assured its readers that the militia were in good hands "under the brave leadership of the gallant Maj. Gen. G. W. Smith."

24. *The Southern Confederacy*, (Atlanta), June 18, 1864,

25. *Official Records*, Series 1, Pt. 3, 38: 970. According to Smith the militia did not number more than 5,000 effectives.

26. James L. McDonough and James P. Jones, *War So Terrible: Sherman and Atlanta* (New York: W. W. Norton and Company, 1987) 278.

27. Sam R. Watkins, "CO. Aytch," *A Side Show of the Big Show*, with a New Introduction by Roy P. Basler, (New York: Collier Books, 1962) 197.

28. William Key, *The Battle of Atlanta and the Georgia Campaign* (New York: Twayne Publishers, 1958) 43.

29. Smith to Henry C. Wayne, July 15, 1864, Incoming Correspondence to Georgia's Adjutant and Inspector General, Henry C. Wayne, Georgia Department of Archives and History, Atlanta, Georgia.

30. Earl J. Hess, "Civilians at War: The Georgia Militia in the Atlanta Campaign," *The Georgia Historical Quarterly* 66 No. 3, (Fall 1982): 335. According to Isaac W. Avery, it was commonly known that the militia "were unable to stand much hardship." See Avery, *The History of the State of Georgia from 1850 to 1881* (New York: Brown and Derby Publishers, 1881; reprinted, New York: AMS Press Inc., 1972) 286.

31. Smith "The Georgia Militia About Atlanta," 333.

32. *Official Records*, Series 1, Pt. 3, 38: 970.

33. Hess, "Civilians at War," 336.

34. Avery, *The History of the State of Georgia*, 286.

35. Walter Brian Cisco, *States Rights Gist: A South Carolina General of the Civil War* (Shippensburg: White Mane Publishing Company, 1991) 125.

36. *Georgia Journal and Messenger*, (Macon), July 20, 1864.

37. Richard M. McMurry, *John Bell Hood and the War for Southern Independence* (Lexington: University Press of Kentucky, 1982) 94, 121-23.

38. Special Order No. 3, February 22, 1865, William P. Palmer Collection, Western Reserve Historical Society, Cleveland. The Department of the South included the two military departments known as the Department of Tennessee

and the Department of South Carolina, Georgia, and Florida.

39. Ezra J. Warner, *Generals in Gray: Lives of the Confederate Commanders* (Baton Rouge: Louisiana State University Press, 1959) 142-43. See also Smith, "The Georgia Militia About Atlanta," 335.

40. *Weekly Chronicle and Sentinel*, (Augusta), August 3, 1864.

41. Mcmurry, *John Bell Hood*, 10, 185.

42. John Bell Hood, "The Defense of Atlanta," *Battles and Leaders of the Civil War*, 4: 339.

43. Hess, "Civilians at War," 336.

44. *Official Records*, Series 1, Pt. 3, 38: 970.

45. Ibid., 970-71.

46. Nathaniel Cheairs Hughes, Jr., *General William Hardee: Old Reliable*, Southern Biography Series, (Baton Rouge: Louisiana State University Press, 1965) 230.

47. Albert Castel, *Decision In The West: The Atlanta Campaign of 1864* (Topeka: University Press of Kansas, 1992) 413.

48. Avery, *The History of the State of Georgia*, 286.

49. *Official Records*, Series 1, Pt. 3, 38: 633.

50. *The Macon Daily Telegraph*, September 13, 1864.

51. William T. Sherman, *Memoirs of William T. Sherman*, 2 vols. (New York: Charles L. Webster and Co., 1891) 2: 227-28.

52. T. Conn Bryan, *Confederate Georgia* (Athens: The University of Georgia Press, 1953) 163.

53. Smith, "The Georgia Militia During Sherman's March to the Sea," *Battles and Leaders of the Civil War*, 4: 667.

54. William Harris Bragg, *Joe Brown's Army: The Georgia State Line, 1862-1865* (Macon: Mercer University Press, 1987) 103.

55. Smith to Hardee, December [6], 1864, Smith Collection, Duke University, Durham.

56. William Harris Bragg, "A Little Battle At Griswoldville: A Rough Stop on the March to the Sea," *Civil War Times Illustrated* 19 (November 1980): 45. Also, see Gary Livingston, *Fields of Gray: The Battle of Griswoldville* (Macon: Mercer University Press, forthcoming 1998).

57. *Official Records*, Series 1, Pt. 3, 39: 740. See also the article by the author, "A Confederate Victory at Grahamville: Fighting At Honey Hill," *South Carolina Historical Magazine* 94 No. 1, (January 1993): 19-33.

58. Beauregard to John A. Calhoun, January 9, 1862, Beauregard Papers, South Caroliniana Library, Columbia, South Carolina.

59. *Sunday News* (Charleston), December 10, 1899.

60. *Official Records*, Series 1, 44: 420.

61. Hughes, *General William J. Hardee*, 256.

62. *Official Record*, Series 1, 44: 906.

63. *Sunday News* (Charleston), December 10, 1899.

64. A. S. Salley, Jr., "Captain John Colcock and Some of His Descendants," *South Carolina Historical and Genealogical Magazine* 3 (October 1902) 230-31. See

also William H.Courtenay, "Tribute to Charles Jones Colcock," 1898, Colcock Family Miscellaneous Papers, South Carolina Historical Society, Charleston, S.C.

65. *Official Records*, Series 1, 44: 415.

66. *Sunday News* (Charleston), December 10, 1899.

67. The *Savannah Republican*, December 3, 1864. The Union army's losing more than one hundred men in only a matter ofminutes further illustrated the fierceness of the battle. See Luis F. Emilio, History of the Fifty-Fourth Regiment of Massachusetts Volunteer Infantry, 1863-1865 (Boston: The Boston Book Company, 1894) 243.

68. Hughes, *General William J. Hardee*, 256.

69. Jacob D. Cox, *The March to the Sea* (New York: Charles Scribner and Sons, 1906) 49.

70. Edwin S. Redkey, ed., *A Grand Army of Black Men: Letters from African-American Soldiers in the Union Army, 1861-1865* (New York: Cambridge University Press, 1992) 32.

71. Smith to Hardee, December [6], 1864, Smith Collection.

72. Courtenay, "Tribute to Charles Jones Colcock."

73. Herbert Fielder, *A Sketch of the Life and Times and Speeches of Joseph E. Brown* (Springfield: Press of Springfield Printing Company, 1883) 353.

74. *Official Records*, Series 1, 44: 420.

75. C. Vann Woodward, ed., *Mary Chesnut's Civil War* (New Haven and London: Yale University Press, 1981) 684.

76. *The Savannah Republican*, December 3, 1864.

77. John J. Abercrombie, "Battle of Honey Hill," *Confederate Veteran* 22 (October 1914): 453.

78. Bragg, *Joe Brown's Army*, 104.

79. Charles C. Jones, Jr., *The Battle of Honey Hill* (Augusta: Chronicle Printing Establishment, 1885) 16.

80. *Official Records*, Series 1, 44: 417.

81. Ibid., 44: 960.

82. Hughes, *General William J. Hardee*, 269.

83. John G. Barrett, *Sherman's March Through the Carolinas* (Chapel Hill: University of North Carolina Press, 1956) 28. See also Edward Robins, *William T. Sherman*, American Crisis Biographies (Philadelphia: George W. Jacobs and Company, 1905) 261-62.

84. Sherman, *Memoirs of William T. Sherman*, 2: 227-228.

85. Alfred Roman, *The Military Operations of General Beauregard in the War Between the States, 1861 to 1865*, 2 vols. (New York: Harper and Brothers, 1884) 2: 336-41.

86. General Order No. 9, April 10, 1865, Lee Papers, Western Reserve Historical Society, Cleveland.

87. "Inaugural Address of President Davis at Montgomery, Alabama February 1861," *Southern Historical Society Papers* 1 (January 1876): 22.

88. Davis to Lucius B. Northrop, April 24, 1879, William P. Palmer Collection, Western Reserve Historical Society, Cleveland.

# CHAPTER EIGHT

# Reformer of the Insurance Industry

Smith, like many other military and political leaders of the former Confederate States of America, found his world turned upside down with the collapse of his beloved country. Smith and his comrades could no longer escape the harsh reality that their attempt to create a sovereign nation through rebellion was a lost cause. Families had been shattered, and tens of thousands of men had gone off to war never to return home. The scars of war were a constant reminder to Southerners of their futile effort to establish independence through armed conflict. Widespread destruction, a concomitant of civil war, suggested that rebuilding would be both slow and costly. Cities that once stood as proud testimonies to the best of Southern culture lay in ruins. It was in the prostrated Deep South that many high ranking leaders of the fallen Confederate government sought refuge prior to Robert E. Lee's surrender.

The peace truce of April 9, 1865, had taken Lee's army out of the war. Since this truce applied only to the Army of Northern Virginia, all others were still free to fight if they wished. Union General James H. Wilson continued to occupy towns and take prisoners for several days after Lee's surrender to Ulysses S. Grant. Wilson, a West Point graduate, was an engineer of exceptional skills. The industrious Illinoian distinguished himself as a brilliant cavalry leader during the war. Wilson's talent for organization and strategy earned him the rank of major general by the age of twenty-seven.[1] He was as ruthless and courageous as Smith was controversial.

General Wilson's memorable cavalry campaign terminated in Macon. He marched through Alabama and focused on Georgia with the single mission of destroying the Confederacy's last stronghold. The chief targets of the enemy were railroads, iron establishments, and military supplies. Wilson and his Raiders attacked Selma on April 2, destroying three rolling mills, several railroad cars and capturing thirty-two guns and 2,700 prisoners.[2] Building on the momentum of the Selma engagement and the reality that the war was nearing an end, the imperious cavalry leader marched victoriously into Montgomery ten days later. The destruction of 85,000 bales of cotton, several steamboats, and a paucity of railroad cars was evidence that he had done his job well in what was once the Confederate capital.[3] Next, Wilson and his men made an incredible march from Montgomery to Macon via Columbus, a distance of 235 miles in only six days. The end of the war found Smith with his Georgia militia camped at Macon awaiting their fate at the hands of·the victorious Yankees.

On April 20, 1865, Wilson's cavalry reached Macon. Faced with the inevitability of capture, Confederate Generals Howell Cobb and Smith realized that the final curtain had descended upon their stage. Cobb was the commanding officer at Macon, the most important city in central Georgia. He was a former governor of Georgia and an outspoken proponent of secession. Without offering resistance, Cobb and Smith surrendered to Colonel Frank White and the Seventeenth Indiana Regiment at 6:00 p.m. on the twentieth. The Southern generals knew there was no way they could have successfully resisted the invasion by the superior Northern army. General Cobb protested vigorously to Colonel White the occupation of Macon by the Union cavalrymen. The basis of his argument was that an armistice had been agreed upon between Generals Sherman and Johnston. When Cobb's complaint was divulged to Wilson, who did not arrive at the Georgia town until 8:30 that night, he refused to acknowledge the reported armistice for fear it was untrue.[4]

General Wilson's occupation of Macon resulted in the capture of five field guns and the destruction of two cotton factories. Also, about 350 commissioned officers were arrested. In addition to Major Generals Cobb and Smith, Brigadier Generals William W. Mackall, Hugh W. Mercer, and Felix H. Robertson were among the officers apprehended.[5] The fortune of Smith's military life had changed drastically since his entry into the Confederate army. He had embarked upon his noble cause in 1861 amidst great expectations only to find himself reduced to a prisoner of war four years later. Although Smith had been the veteran of several battles during the rebellion, he was not taken prisoner until the very end. However, his wife Lucretia was not as fortunate. She fell into Union hands when Savannah fell to Sherman in December 1864. The Illinois general who was not on hand during the initial surrender of the Georgia town, found Cobb and Smith with their staff officers nervously awaiting his arrival at the Macon City Hall. It was here that Wilson convened a conference with them. After speaking to the recalcitrant commanding officer, Wilson turned to the Kentuckian and said, "General Smith, I am going to ask you the question I have just asked Cobb and hope you feel at liberty to answer it fully and frankly. Have General Lee and his army surrendered?" Without delay Smith straightened himself up and answered, "Yes, sir, Lee and his army have surrendered."[6] General Wilson affirmed that Smith's candid response "was the first trustworthy information" he had received on the subject of the reported armistice. For a man who had a reputation for harshness, Wilson treated his captives with surprising civility. He gave the general officers permission to return to their quarters with instructions to report to him daily. Smith and his fellow officers were satisfied with the lenient terms imposed upon them during their lengthy interview with the Union cavalry leader.

Late in the evening of April 20, Wilson telegraphed Sherman to inform him of the capitulation of Macon which included the capture of the Confederate garrison numbering 3,000.[7] Perhaps it was ironic that the captured Rebel soldiers had barricaded themselves in the very stockade at Macon's Camp Oglethorpe that had been constructed to house Union prisoners of war.[8] Upon receiving Wilson's dispatch, General Sherman sent him a terse note over the enemy's wire from Raleigh. Sherman's telegram confirmed the validity of the armistice and ordered Wilson to cease all military operations in Georgia. Wilson's cavalry campaign had covered 500 miles in thirty-five days and had resulted in the capture of more than 6,000 Confederates and almost 160 guns.[9] On May 8, 1865, General Wilson informed Sherman of his decision to dispose of his prisoners "including the generals on simple paroles."[10] According to his parole certification the soldiers were permitted to return home without fear of being harassed by Federal troops as long as they did not violate their parole. Therefore, General Smith was released soon after his capture.[11]

With the military aspect of the rebellion over, the nation focused its attention on the Johnson administration in Washington. The United States government was now faced with the enormous challenge of restoring the divided country. When Andrew Johnson became president after the murder of Abraham Lincoln, he inherited the complex problem of reconstruction. Following Appomattox, the task which lay ahead was that of bringing the defeated South back into political fellowship and harmony with the United States. There were no provisions in the Constitution for reunion. Inextricably bound with reconstruction was the question of amnesty.

Johnson's amnesty proclamation of May 29, 1865, excluded Confederate generals, other high ranking officials, and those whose taxable property totaled more than $20,000. Driven by vengeance, President Johnson was determined to punish wealthy Southerners whom he was convinced had brought upon the nation the spectacle of secession and the horrors of war. Johnson's proclamation, however, contained an important provision allowing the excepted classes to petition him for a pardon. The result was that he was overwhelmed with applications from both Confederate generals and civilian officials requesting amnesty. Petitions for amnesty were documents in which the authors accepted military defeat as the end result of secession and admitted that the Civil War was a lost cause. Immediate restoration of their civil and political privileges were their aim. Political considerations, however, were not the only factors which motivated them to seek presidential clemency. There was an economic factor as well. The former Confederates could not reclaim their property until they had been paroled.

Pardons became a lucrative business, a consequent result of which was widespread corruption. A common feature of amnesty applications were letters of support from relatives, loved ones, and other interested persons who championed a pardon for the ex-Rebel. Such filing papers usually included the petitioner's oath of allegiance.[12] Before being paroled, Smith pledged his loyalty to the federal government. He said:

> I Gustavus W. Smith ... do solemnly swear that I will faithfully support, protect, and defend the Constitution of the United States ... and faithfully support all laws and proclamations which have been made during the existing rebellion with reference to the emancipation of slaves.[13]

Eager to obtain amnesty, Smith submitted his application in June 1865.

His petition was championed by Wilson.

Writing to General George H. Thomas, commander of the Department of the Cumberland, Wilson informed him of Smith's application for a pardon that included his oath of allegiance and a letter to President Johnson. Wilson noted that Smith had behaved in strict accordance with the terms of his parole. He praised Smith for his influence in "restoring good order" at Macon. Finally, Wilson said that Smith was "easy and pleasant" and if allowed the privileges of a pardon would be "governed in good faith" by whatever restrictions the government imposed.[14]

Smith's letter to the President was an appeal for the restoration of his privileges as a loyal citizen. Smith made it a point of telling Johnson that he had nothing to do with the secession of any of the Southern states during the winter of 1860 and 1861. He concluded by stating that "every man who willingly remains in the United States must acquiesce in the emancipation of the slaves ... and be governed by the constitution of the United States."[15]

Both Wilson and Thomas considered their fellow West Pointer's case worthy of Johnson's attention and could see no reason why the President would refuse to grant him clemency. Thomas endorsed Smith's amnesty papers and forwarded them to Washington.[16] Smith wished to return to the remnants of the Etowah iron works as quickly as possible. It was Smith who had abandoned that facility in the spring of 1864 before General Sherman's army came through. Neither Wilson nor Thomas could find any reason that would have prevented him from resuming the business of the Etowah enterprise.

Following his release, Smith returned to Etowah to begin rebuilding the company. His talents for engineering and management were all the more valuable because of the extensive destruction to the facility. Because of Smith's technical and managerial experience, it was not surprising that he would play a vital role in foundry operations of the southern economy in the old Confederacy during the postwar era.

While at Etowah, Smith called on his friends and acquaintances to write letters to support his amnesty application. The response was overwhelming, and, during the fall of 1865, letters from influential men poured into Washington on his behalf. A common theme of the letters was a summary of Smith's civil and military career down to the outbreak of the War of the Rebellion. Writing from Louisville to the

United States Attorney General James Speed, former treasury secretary James Guthrie made a passionate plea for his one-time construction engineer. Guthrie remembered Smith as an "excellent worker" while employed at the Treasury Department in the 1850s. Guthrie stated that Smith was "an intelligent gentleman of high qualities who I should be gratified to see pardoned and made a useful citizen."[17] The Union general John T. Croxton, who was with Wilson when Smith was captured, also wrote a recommendation to aid the cause of his fellow Kentuckian. In his letter to President Johnson, Croxton said, "I am convinced that the restoration of his rights as a citizen would be a judicious exercise of Executive clemency." Croxton went on to tell the President that by granting clemency to Smith the country would benefit from the service of "a man whose abilities and attainments render him exceedingly useful."[18]

On November 30, M. C. Johnson of the Northern Bank of Kentucky at Lexington wrote to the President to support Smith's case for a pardon. He assured Johnson that Smith was in favor of the "most speedy restoration of the Union" and the "peaceful submission" of the South to the Federal government. "It would be very gratifying," he said, "if a full pardon would be extended to him."[19] Finally, Governor Thomas E. Bramlette of Kentucky wrote to Andrew Johnson to assist Smith in his effort to obtain amnesty. Speaking of Smith, the governor stated, "he now cheerfully accepts the results of the war and desires to be pardoned and to be restored" to full citizenship. Bramlette concluded that Smith was "an honorable man" and therefore deserving of Executive clemency.[20] In spite of the strong recommendations, Smith would have to wait before receiving a presidential pardon.

In the meantime, Smith's stay at Etowah was short. In early 1866, the forty-four-year old ex-Confederate general departed from Georgia for Chattanooga where he accepted the position of general manager of the Southwestern Iron Company at the request of the New York ironmaster, Abram S. Hewitt. Once again, a past acquaintance had helped Smith to land on his feet. There were several reasons for Hewitt's investment in the Chattanooga works; among them humanitarian concerns. Hewitt believed he had a moral obligation to assist the war-torn states of the South. Furthermore, he hoped that other Northern manufacturers would follow his lead and invest capital in that region as a way of stimulating economic recovery. Hewitt also desired to do something to promote a sense of comraderie between the two regions. This may also help to explain why Hewitt selected Smith to oversee the operations at Southwestern. Finally, Hewitt believed that the Chattanooga company was a sound economic investment, one that would prove profitable.[21] Hewitt's business ventures made his name well-known in the South during the postbellum years.

The almost total destruction of southern foundries caused iron manufacturing to resume only on a small scale. Rebuilding was slow because it had to be done in an area that was impoverished by the war. Capital with which to build up the industrial economy of the region was not available in sufficient amount.[22] However, the most promising effort toward the resumption of iron manufacturing was in the former Confederate states of Alabama and Tennessee.[23] The growth of the iron industry around Chattanooga, the largest town in Hamilton County, was phenomenal. This Tennessee city had the advantage of an abundance of cheap labor, raw materials, and excellent transportation facilities. Chattanooga is located about 140 miles north of Atlanta on the Tennessee River at the foot of Lookout Mountain. This beautiful city developed rapidly as a leading manufacturer of iron and steel after the war.[24] Although other business opportunities existed in Chattanooga, it was the iron industry which seized the imaginations of newcomers and became the foundation for the future growth of the city.[25] In a small way, Smith was contributing to the rebuilding of the defeated South through his position at Southwestern. One explanation for the rapid growth of the iron industry was the realization that minerals had barely begun to be exploited before the war.

During the Civil War, the Southwestern Iron Company had been operated by Union soldiers but was sold by the Federal government at the end of the conflict. The moving force behind the purchase of the Southwestern works was Hewitt who organized and dominated the corporation that paid the War Department $300,000 for the company. Hewitt contributed $60,000 of his personal money to this enterprise. When the time had come to select a general manager of Southwestern, he turned to someone with whom he was familiar. The New York industrialist called on his friend, Gustavus Woodson Smith, who had served as chief engineer of the Cooper and Hewitt company of Trenton during the mid-1850s. Smith's appointment was evidence of Hewitt's influence in the corporation.

At first the Southwestern plant proved more profitable than Smith or its owners had anticipated. The optimism faded when business started to take a downward spiral in 1868. The Chattanooga works was equipped only to rework old twisted rails. This was a crucial weakness of the company because its survival depended totally on scrap iron. Enough scrap could not be procured to operate the mill at its capacity of 300 tons a week. A sudden drop in the price of iron from $80.00 to $35.00 per ton and the prohibitive costs of operation forced the owners to explore other possibilities in an effort to remain solvent.[26] One consequence of the economic slump was the merger of the Southwestern facility with the Roane Iron Company in 1870. The Roane Company was incorporated by the ex-Federal general John T. Wilder of Ohio at Rockwood, near Nashville in 1867.[27] The juxtaposition of the Southwestern and Roane companies less than seventy miles apart, one a rolling mill without a furnace, and the other a furnace without a rolling mill also facilitated the merger.[28] Roane operated Southwestern until the latter went out of business in 1877.

While at Southwestern, an agonizing incident caused Smith to double his efforts to win a presidential pardon. On October 15, 1867, he received an unexpected visit from the United States Marshall for the East District of Tennessee. The officer had come to Chattanooga for the purpose of arresting Smith on the charge of treason. Believing the order to have him apprehended was issued by Chief Justice Salmon Chase, Smith wrote to General Ulysses S. Grant for advice. Smith told Grant that he was of the opinion that his parole had exempted him from being arrested. Obviously angered by the whole episode, Smith closed his letter on a sardonic note. "Is it impossible to obtain favorable action upon my application for pardon made to the President," Smith said, "and recommended by yourself and other military commanders in 1865."[29] Smith also used the occasion to tell Grant about the state of his health. Smith intimated to him that he had suffered an "attack of congestion of the brain" earlier that year. Smith admitted that his health had improved but, he had not fully recovered.

Immediately upon receiving Smith's correspondence, Grant transmitted all the papers pertaining to his case to Chase. In response to Smith's threatened arrest, Grant told the Chief Justice that the paroles granted to Confederate officers and soldiers at the end of the rebellion, "so long as they were faithfully observed" exempted them from arrest for treason. Therefore, it would appear that Smith was protected from punishment for any military offenses committed during the war. General Grant also completely denied supporting Smith in his quest for a pardon. Grant said that "no application for the pardon of General Smith has been recommended by me."[30] Following Chase's review of Smith's application papers, he returned them to Grant with an explanation regarding Smith's belief that he had authorized his arrest. According to Chase, the writ was issued to Smith by direction of the District Attorney for the Eastern District of Tennessee. It was a procedural matter that required all writs from United States Courts to be issued in the name of the Chief Justice. Chase intimated to Grant that he was "seldom-almost never consulted in relation to the issuing" of writs. The jurist affirmed he had no knowledge of the writ issued to Smith.[31] There was no evidence that Smith was ever taken into custody. The writ contained a technical error; the name Augustus Smith appeared on the form, although the Marshall informed Gustavus that it was intended for him.

Legal problems and illness weighed heavily on Smith in the fall of 1867. Writing to Michael Burns, president of the Nashville and Chattanooga Railroad Company on October 28, a distraught Smith revealed that he was in poor health and had grown tired of waiting for a decision on his application from the president. Moreover, the question of Smith's proposed arrest was a constant source of aggravation to him. "The East Tennessee authorities," Smith confided to Burns, "are worrying me upon a charge of treason to the U.S. Govt. during the war."[32] Doubtless feeling a sense of urgency, he called on his old friend and former boss, Edward Cooper to write to Johnson on his behalf. Cooper's letter to the President on November 4, emphasized that Smith had complied with the terms of his parole and his deportment was exemplary. Cooper concluded by informing President Johnson he wished to see Smith "restored to the right and privileges of a loyal citizen."[33] A little more than two weeks later, Smith was rewarded for his persistence with a pardon by order of President Andrew Johnson on November 21, 1867. Finally, a burden had been lifted from the Kentucky general who had only a few years earlier fought desperately in an attempt to create a separate and independent government.

Following Smith's work in Chattanooga, he was appointed the first Insurance Commissioner of Kentucky by Governor John W. Stevenson in June 1870. The death of Governor John L. Helm three years earlier had elevated Stevenson to the governorship of the Blue Grass state.[34] A number of ex-generals and prominent Confederates found employment with insurance companies after the war. Smith had been recommended for the executive appointment by Colonel D. Howard Smith of Georgetown. Before being elected Auditor of Kentucky in 1867, Colonel Smith had served in the Confederate army and in the state legislature as a representative from Scott County.[35] On March 10, 1870, the Kentucky legislature passed a law that established the Insurance Bureau authorizing the appointment of an Insurance Commissioner at an annual salary of $4,000. It was a universal characteristic of the insurance enterprise that once sworn in, the commissioner was virtually safe from removal for the duration of his term in office. Although the chance of dismissal was remote, incompetence, breach of trust, and malfeasance were causes for removal.

The concept of political appointment was in keeping with the belief that ordinary citizens were capable of handling any American government job. This idea became popular during the presidency of Andrew Jackson.[36] One weakness of the appointment process was that the commissioner or superintendent was not a permanent official, which mitigated against continuity in office. The administrative regulation of the insurance industry suffered as a result of frequent personnel changes. Each new commissioner lost valuable time as he acquainted himself with the voluminous records and many duties of his office.[37] In most states the commissioner was appointed by the governor, in others elected by popular vote. The term of a commissioner ranged from two to six years in the various states. The Democrats were in power in Kentucky, and Smith was a Democrat of some prominence. Although Smith was a man of character it did not hurt that he was also a native son of Kentucky.

Smith's new position required him to move to Frankfort, the capital city, located in the heart of the blue grass district only a few miles from Georgetown. Smith was not one to stand still when a chance for advancement presented itself. Moving, it would appear was endemic to him. Smith's proven administrative talents gave him confidence to move into his new position. The life insurance industry necessarily involved detailed and technical work which Smith's mathematical competence enabled him to handle with little difficulty. Among the state administrative offices which required a high degree of technical knowledge was the Insurance Bureau.

The post Civil War era was an interesting period in the history of American life insurance. Like other businesses at that time, it was enjoying phenomenal growth throughout the nation, an expansion accompanied by many problems. Dishonesty, unfair policy stipulations, and inadequate reserve funds often led to bankruptcy. Reckless investments and managerial incompetence also caused many companies to become insolvent. Corrupt insurance businessmen frequently considered premium payments their personal treasuries and often refused to pay policyholders' claims. The popularity of life insurance made it clear that citizens needed the greater protection from such corruption that a full-time person with special training could afford them. Therefore, the administration and supervision of life insurance companies on the state level was entrusted to a commissioner or superintendent of insurance. No doubt Smith's transition from industry to insurance was made easier because of his propensity for mathematics which came as natural to him as engineering. After his appointment as Insurance Commissioner, Smith had published a 136-page hardbound book detailing the theoretical and practical aspects of the business of life insurance.[38]

As head of the Insurance Bureau of Kentucky, Smith's duties were varied and many. One of his primary functions was to enforce the insurance laws of the state. The Kentucky legislature passed the first Life Insurance Law in March of 1870 which required companies doing business in that state to deposit $30,000 in Kentucky bonds with the commissioner's office.[39] The provision of this law was unpopular but necessary to assure the solvency of insurance companies as well as to protect policyholders from unscrupulous carriers. If needed, these securities could be used to pay claims of policyholders. Section 39 of the law mandated that agents pay a $20.00 license fee to the state.[40]

Perhaps Commissioner Smith's most important duty was the supervision of insurance companies. The inquisitorial powers of the commissioner were enormous. This included conducting periodic examinations of companies to ensure their adherence to the insurance laws of Kentucky. Smith also could demand the right to examine a company's records at its home office. Without this authorization, he would have no way of knowing whether the annual financial report submitted by a company was an accurate assessment of its operations and transactions.[41] He also could revoke or suspend an insurer's license if found to be in violation of its charter or any provision of the Kentucky law. Smith also had to supervise a large staff consisting of attorneys, auditors, clerks, accountants, and examiners. Insurance companies were prohibited by law from functioning at a deficit. Should the net cash value[42] of a company fall below its liabilities, it was the duty of the commissioner to advise the company to discontinue issuing new policies. In order for money to be available for the prompt payment of the amounts insured, a sufficient amount of the premium over and above expenses had to be set aside in a requisite reserve fund.[43]

As Insurance Commissioner, Smith was the liaison between the companies and the public with the expressed purpose of protecting the interests of policyholders. This was particularly beneficial to lay persons since many of them possessed only limited knowledge about the complex calculations used by insurance companies. In case of a dispute or discrepancy involving a company, a policyholder could appeal to the Insurance Bureau for resolution. Smith, however, implored the public to use "judgement and discretion" in choosing an insurance company with which to place funds for the benefit of their families and heirs. According to Smith, companies should be regulated by "wise and stringent laws, rigidly enforced."[44] As part of the regulatory machinery, Smith required companies to submit an annual financial statement (called the convention blank) to the Insurance Bureau. The annual statement was a detailed financial summary of the company for the reporting year. It included information on assets, net worth, reserves, liabilities, expenditures, and investments. In his important work on insurance, Edwin W. Patterson gave this description of an insurance commissioner. He wrote:

> Sometimes the insurance commissioner is an official clerk, sometimes he is a judge, sometimes he is a law-giver, and sometimes he is both prosecuting attorney and hangman. He is partly executive partly judicial and partly legislative; and yet he is not confined within any of these categories.[45]

To maintain the solvency of life insurance companies in Kentucky was of utmost importance to Smith. He understood that only when a company was financially sound could it serve the needs of the people. Smith's prescription for the successful management of an insurance company included skill, good judgment, and integrity.[46] Smith's work was not lost on Auditor Howard Smith when he proffered his first report of the Insurance Bureau to the legislature in January 1871. He called Gustavus W. Smith "an eminent and distinguished Kentuckian" who was superbly qualified to carry out the duties of his office. "I think I may prudently and safely say," concluded Howard Smith, "that he has already made the Bureau a success, indeed, that the friends of insurance reform in Kentucky could hope to accomplish in so short a period of time."[47]

To bring uniformity to the insurance industry of Kentucky was also one of Smith's objectives. To achieve this goal, he enforced the provision of the Insurance Law that required companies to make a valuation of their policies. To facilitate this process, Smith required that all companies file a registry and valuation form with his office. This form provided information on the number of policies issued or changed during a given period. Without an accurate registry of policyholders, no computation could be made of the accrued liability of a company. It was not unusual for companies to appeal to Smith for an extension of time to submit valuation blanks. Such an appeal was made by Edward B. Smith, actuary of the Kentucky Branch of the Pennsylvania Life Insurance Company, headquartered at Lexington. He informed Smith that as of December 31, 1869, his company had more than 7,000 policies in force. He wrote, "There has not been made a valuation of the policies of this company .... The work required to make up one will be laborious and necessarily slow."[48]

Though competent, Smith's dogmatic personality often propelled him into contentious encounters. Not long after becoming commissioner, Smith found himself embroiled in a memorable controversy with Pliny Freeman, president of the Globe Mutual Life Insurance Company of New York. On August 12, 1872, Smith told the Globe company of his dissatisfaction with its annual report for the year 1871. The report showed that a large number of policies had expired before the time in which a legal claim could be made on the company for the payment of insurance benefits.[49] The Kentucky Insurance Bureau was convinced that Globe was attempting to evade the terms of its charter by permitting an inordinate amount of its policies to lapse. The inability of policyholders to pay their premiums often resulted in policies being terminated. And in many cases regardless of how many years a contract had been in force, a missed premium payment meant the immediate cancellation of the policy. Smith noted that it was incumbent upon life insurance companies to deal fairly with policyholders. He expected them to give thorough and accurate information to insurers before issuing policies. Only then, Smith said, could companies diminish the number of lapsed policies.

In the fall of 1872, Smith traveled to New York City to commence an investigation into the affairs of the Globe company under the jurisdiction of Kentucky law. Believing he had nothing to conceal, Freeman expressed gratification when Smith told him of his intention to examine the records of the company.[50] Freeman communicated to the Kentucky Commissioner that the company would welcome a rigid examination into every detail connected with its business. Freeman was certain that an examination would reveal no irregularities and would therefore elevate the public trust of the company. He also assured Smith that his officers would cooperate with him and his assistants in the investigation.

Smith informed Freeman that he had selected William A. Smith an officer of the Insurance Bureau of Kentucky and William Peck of New York to assist him in the investigation. Freeman immediately rejected Peck as one of Smith's examiners. Writing to Smith on October 16, Freeman disclosed that Peck was employed for many years as the head bookkeeper of the company but was "discharged for cause." Because of Peck's dismissal, Freeman believed he would lack objectivity. He appealed to Smith to employ another person to replace Peck.[51] Smith honored Freeman's request and selected another investigator to assist him. The review of the Globe company began in October 1872 at its headquarters in the city. During the investigation, Smith requested to see the cash books of the company. Freeman balked and postponed all further proceedings. Freeman intimated to Smith that he had no right to do anything more than to examine the liabilities and assets to determine the solvency of the Globe company. An angry Freeman wrote to Smith:

If you find the assets less than required to meet the liabilities on the legal standard, revoke the authority for the company, to do business in your state and if the assets are greater than the liabilities you have nothing further to do with it.[52]

On October 17, Freeman asked Smith to return all the books, papers, and minutes of the examination. Smith refused to honor Freeman's request.

Smith responded to Freeman's intransigence by penning a prolix letter to the Board of Trustees of the Globe Company on October 19, 1872. "Mr. Freeman himself and family own a majority of the stocks in this company," he said, "but this does not constitute him as the Board of Trustees." Smith then reminded the Board of a prior meeting in which it had agreed to permit him to have access to all the records of the company.[53]

Having received no satisfaction from Freeman or the Board of Trustees, Smith wrote to George B. Church, Superintendent of the Insurance Department of New York to seek his assistance in the stalled investigation. Smith's letter of November 5 detailed the difficulty he had encountered at the Globe headquarters. Smith told Superintendent Church that he had "good reason to suspect" that a thorough examination of the company would have revealed that the liabilities had increased while the assets had diminished. The Kentucky Commissioner lamented to his New York counterpart that irregularities would continue if companies were "permitted to go unchecked by the state officers." Smith concluded that State Superintendents and Commissioners could not effectively carry out their duties if companies could not be forced to submit to complete examinations of their books.[54]

The withdrawal of the Globe company from Kentucky during the investigation prevented Church from having to intervene in the controversy between Smith and Freeman. Smith indicated to Church in a subsequent letter that he had been notified by Freeman that the Globe company was no longer under the jurisdiction of the Kentucky Insurance Bureau. The Board of Trustees concluded that the information regarding the business of the company for 1871 was not needed by Smith "for any legitimate purposes."[55] It was obvious that the company had withdrawn from Smith's jurisdiction to avoid an examination of its transactions for the year in question. Smith was perplexed as to the legality of the action taken by Freeman and the Board. After consulting an attorney, Smith was advised that the company could not under New

York state law be compelled to submit to an examination once it had withdrawn from the state of Kentucky.

Before leaving the city, Smith deposited the information he had in his possession relating to the investigation with the Insurance Department of New York. A disenchanted Smith returned to Kentucky with the memory of an examination gone sour. During the protracted controversy with the Globe company, Smith was supported by the Kentucky state legislature. On January 13, 1874, the House Committee on Insurance passed a resolution "declaring the action of Insurance Commissioner Smith in investigating the affairs of the Globe Insurance Company of New York in perfect accordance with his sworn duties."[56]

The confrontation with the Globe company was evidence that the insurance industry was in disarray. One apparent problem was the lack of uniformity in state insurance supervision. Confusion existed because each state had a different set of insurance laws that were interpreted and enforced by an assortment of officials from commissioners to clerks. The states could not agree upon a uniform method of determining the valuation of policies and the computation of reserves. No two states in the country required the same form or blank to obtain financial information from its companies. The rapid growth of the life insurance industry witnessed a proliferation of mismanagement and unscrupulous business practices. The leader among the states in the passage of regulatory legislation was New York. Therefore, it was not surprising that the Empire State would take the lead in calling for a National Convention of Insurance Commissioners (NCIC). In February of 1871, George Miller,[57] Superintendent of the Insurance Department of New York invited, the superintendents and commissioners from thirty-five other states to meet in New York City. Smith of Kentucky was one of twenty-nine state representatives at the first National Insurance Convention that convened in May 1871.

The delegates gathered in New York to discuss the flaws in existing methods of insurance supervision and to adopt uniform regulations to maintain the solvency of insurance companies throughout the nation. The creation of uniform blanks for the submission of annual reports was a priority of the convention. The convention also sought to establish a uniform standard for determining premiums. The *New York Times* editorialized that if the convention could bring about such uniformity "it would be well repaid for its labors."[58]

The National Convention of Insurance Commissioners[59] was the most influential organization of its kind in the country and a landmark achievement toward the effective administration of the insurance industry. By the end of its first year of existence, the NCIC had established an impressive record of success. The acceptance by most of the states of a certificate of solvency, the preparation of a new standard mortality table, and the creation of a new reserve valuation standard were listed among its accomplishment. The Convention's crowning achievement in its first year was the adoption by all states of a uniform blank for the annual financial statements that were filed with the commissioner or superintendent of insurance. Because the NCIC had recommended its acceptance, it was commonly called the convention blank and was used by the states for the first time in 1872.

During Smith's tenure as Insurance Commissioner, he was an important fixture at the annual meetings. Because of his knowledge on the subject of life insurance, he was highly respected by his contemporaries. Smith understood the principles upon which the net values in life insurance were calculated. He was one of only a few people in the nation who had a solid understanding of the esoteric language of the insurance industry. This special knowledge combined with his insistence on fairness gave him the tremendous influence he wielded in the insurance community. Smith believed that the business transactions between the insurer and the insured should always be conducted in an atmosphere of honesty. Smith's *Notes* did much to enlighten the public, executives, and professional actuaries in regard to the principles upon which calculations of legal net values in life insurance were based.[60]

Smith was a forceful and erudite writer on the subject of life insurance. The appearance of an abundance of literature on the subject before the turn of the century was an indication of the rising significance of life insurance in the United States. Smith's book was considered an important addition to this literature. In regard to Smith's book, William H. Bartlett, Actuary of the Mutual Life Insurance Company of New York stated, "It gives me great pleasure to say that Notes on Life Insurance, by General G.W. Smith, is a very valuable contribution ... and I very heartily commend the work to public favor." Professor David Murray of Rutgers College commented, "I am free to say that I consider it the best popular explanation of the theory and practice of Life Insurance I know."[61] William Alexander called Smith's treatise on the subject of life insurance "an excellent book."[62]

Smith's influence extended far beyond the boundary of Kentucky. He was well-known in insurance circles nationally as a reform advocate whose opinions carried weight with both companies and commissioners. Careful not to abuse his almost autocratic power, he conducted the business of the Insurance Bureau competently and judiciously. In spite of Smith's influence, intelligence, and experience, he never held an elected office in the National Convention of Insurance Commissioners. He was, however, elected to its executive committee in 1875. Having served six years as Insurance Commissioner, Smith departed from Kentucky in 1876 and returned to New York City.

Chapter Eight

# Notes

1. S. Nye, "James H. Wilson-A Profile," *Civil War Times Illustrated* 1 (May 1962): 40-41; Ezra J. Warner, *Generals in Blue, Lives of the Union Commanders* (Baton Rouge: Louisiana State University Press, 1964) 566-68. See also Edward G. Longacre, *From Union Stars to Top Hat: A Biography of the Extraordinary James H. Wilson* (Harrisburg: Stackpole Books, 1972) 13-14.

2. Longacre, *From Union Stars to Top Hat*, 209.

3. U.S. War Department, *The War of the Rebellion: A Compilation of the Official Records of the Union and Confederate Armies*, 128 volumes and index (Washington: Government Printing Office, 1880-1901), Series 1, Pt. 3, 47: 357.

4. James Pickett Jones, *Yankee Blitzkrieg: Wilson's Raid through Alabama and Georgia* (Athens: University of Georgia Press, 1976) 167. In early 1865 the Confederate President placed Cobb in charge of the subdistrict which included Macon"so that he would rank Smith and could prevent any recurrences of the problems that the general had created on the Peninsula—and, no doubt, to deny his old antagonist any real authority." See also William C. Davis, *Jefferson Davis: The Man and His Hour* (HarperCollins Publishers, 1991) 587.

5. Frank Moore, ed., *The Rebellion Record*, 12 vols. (New York: D. Van Nostrand, 1868) 11: 506.

6. James H. Wilson, *Under the Old Flag*, 2 vols. (New York and London: D. Appleton and Company, 1912) 2: 280-81.

7. *Official Records*, Series 1, Pt. 1, 49: 425; Series 1, Pt. 3, 47: 263.

8. William Harris Bragg, *Joe Brown's Army: The Georgia State Line, 1861-1865* (Macon: Mercer University Press, 1987) 108.

9. *Official Records*, Series 1, Pt. 1, 49: 344,663.

10. Ibid., Series 1, Pt. 2, Vol. 49, 663.

11. Rembert W. Patrick, *Jefferson Davis and his Cabinet* (Baton Rouge: Louisiana State University Press, 1944) 132. See also *New York Times*, July 7, 1865.

12. Jonathan T. Doris, "Pardoning the Leaders of the Confederacy," *Mississippi Valley Historical Review*, 15 (June 1928): 3.

13. RG109: Oath of Allegiance, Amnesty Papers of Gustavus Woodson Smith, National Archives, Washington, D.C.

14. RG109: Wilson to Thomas, June 19, 1865, Smith's Amnesty Papers.

15. Ibid., Smith to Johnson, June 19, 1865, Smith's Amnesty Papers.

16. *Official Records*, Series 1, Pt. 2, 49: 1058, 1059, 1064, 1069.

17. RG109: Guthrie to Speed, October 11, 1865, Smith's Amnesty Papers.

18. Ibid., Croxton to Johnson, November 8, 1865, Smith's Amnesty Papers.

19. Ibid., Johnson to Andrew Johnson, November 30, 1865, Smith's Amnesty Papers.

205

20. Ibid., Bramlette to Johnson, December 16, 1865, Smith's Amnesty Papers.

21. Allen Nevins, *Abram S. Hewitt: With Some Account of Peter Cooper* (New York: Octagon Books, Inc., 1935; reprinted1967) 252-53.

22. Herman H. Chapman, *The Iron and Steel Industries of the South* (Birmingham: University of Alabama Press, 1953) 109.

23. Victor S. Clark, *History of Manufacturers in the United States, 1860-1893*, 3 vols. (New York: McGraw-Hill Book Company, 1929) 2: 68.

24. Archer Anderson, "Campaign and Battle of Chickamauga," *Southern Historical Society Papers*, 9 (September 1881): 393-94.

25. Gilbert E. Govan and James W. Livingood, *The Chattanooga Country, 1540-1976: From Tomahawks to TVA* (Knoxville: University of Tennessee Press, 1977) 295.

26. Morrow Chamberlain, *A Brief History of the Pig Iron Industry of East Tennessee* (Chattanooga: Morrow Chamberlain, 1942) 8.

27. James W. Livingood, "The Tennessee Valley in American History," *The East Tennessee Historical Society's Publications*, No. 21, (1949): 29.

28. Govan and Livingood, The Chattanooga Country, 295-96.

29. RG109: Smith to Grant, October 16, 1867, Smith'sAmnesty Papers.

30. Ibid., Grant to Chase, October 21, 1867, Smith's Amnesty Papers. Smith also commented on his physical condition in a letter to Charles Colcock Jones, Jr. He wrote, "My health has been bad for several months." See Smith to Jones, October 3, 1867, Charles Colcock Jones, Jr., Papers, William R. Perkins Library, Duke University, Durham.

31. Ibid., Chase to Grant, October 21, 1867, Smith's Amnesty Papers.

32. Ibid., Smith to Burns, October 28, 1867, Smith's Amnesty Papers.

33. Ibid., Cooper to Johnson, November 4, 1867, Smith's Amnesty Papers.

34. Lowell H. Harrison, ed., *Kentucky's Governors 1792-1985* (Lexington: University of Kentucky Press, 1985), 81-87.

35. Hambleton Tapp and James C. Klotter, *Kentucky: Decades of Discord, 1865-1900* (Frankfort: Kentucky Historical Society, 1977) 19-22.

36. Roscoe C. Buley, *The American Life Convention 1906-1952: A Study in the History of Life Insurance*, 2 vols. (NewYork: Appleton-Century-Crafts, Inc., 1953) 1: 132-36.

37. Edwin W. Patterson, *The Insurance Commissioner in the United States* (Cambridge: Harvard University Press, 1927) 45.

38. Gustavus W. Smith, *Notes on Life Insurance*, (Frankfort: Kentucky Yeoman Office, 1870; 3rd ed., New York: D. VanNostrand, 1876) 7.

39. See David J. Hartsook to Smith, July 22, 1870, Box 44, Auditor's Office, Kentucky State Archives, Frankfort.

40. Section 39 of the Life Insurance Law, March 12, 1870, Auditor's Office, Kentucky State Archives.

41. S.H. Wolfe, "State Supervision of Insurance Companies," *Annals of the American Academy of Political and Social Science 26* (September 1905): 142.

42. The cash value was the amount of money an insurance company was required to have on hand to cover its policies.

43. Miscellaneous Correspondence, Auditor's Office, Box 70, Kentucky State Archives.

44. Smith, *Notes*, 96.

45. Patterson, *The Insurance Commissioner*, 5.

46. Smith, Notes, 95-96.

47. Kentucky Auditor's Report, January 4, 1871, Kentucky State Archives.

48. Edward B. Smith to Gustavus Woodson Smith, August 27, 1870, Box 44, Auditor's Office.

49. Smith to George B. Church, November 11, 1872, Box 44, Auditor's Office.

50. Smith to Church, November 5, 1872, Box 44, Auditor's Office.

51. Freeman to Smith, October 16, 1872, Box 44, Auditor's Office.

52. Freeman to Smith, October 16, 1872, Box 44, Auditor's Office.

53. Smith to the Board of Trustees, October 19, 1872, Box 44 Auditor's Office.

54. Smith to Church, November 5, 1872, Box 44, Auditor's Office.

55. Smith to Church, November 11, 1872, Box 44, Auditor's Office.

56. *New York Times*, January 14, 1874.

57. George Miller was succeeded as Insurance Superintendent of New York by George B. Church in 1872.

58. *New York Times*, May 30, 1871.

59. The Name of the NCIC was changed to the National Association of Insurance Commissioners at the New York Convention in 1935.

60. *Encyclopedia of Contemporary Biography of New York*, 11 Volume (New York: Atlantic Publishing and Engraving Co., 1882) 2: 64.

61. Smith *Notes*, 5-6.

62. William Alexander, *The Life Insurance Company* (New York and London: D. Appleton and Company, 1905) 170.

# CHAPTER NINE

# Final Engagements and Conclusion

Several years had passed since Smith's departure from New York City in 1861 amidst charges that he was a traitor to the United States. And much had happened in the Kentuckian's life since then. He had fought to create a separate government and had emerged from that war with a shattered reputation as a military leader. Smith had found employment in Chattanooga and Frankfort in the iron industry and the insurance business, respectively. By the late 1870s, time had begun to erase the bitter feelings between the two sections and to heal the wounds that had brought upon the nation the internal conflict of the 1860s.

Smith lived a quiet life after returning to New York. The City Directories listed his occupation as a civil engineer and surveyor. He did not participate in municipal or national politics and had no party affiliation. In fact, Smith's organizational affiliations were limited during the postbellum period. He was a member of the Association of the Graduates of the United States Military Academy but did not attend the annual reunions. Smith was also a Mason who had reached the highest degree in the fraternity, almost certainly a help in advancing in several fields. In addition to Smith, many former Confederates went to New York City to live during the postbellum years. A strong comradeship existed among these veterans of the old Confederacy, which resulted in their establishing an organization there in 1890. The Confederate Veteran Camp was formed with Colonel Andrew G. Dickinson as its first commander.

It not only promoted social interaction but also served a benevolent function as well. The Confederate Veteran Camp was particularly generous in providing financial assistance to comrades who were not eligible to receive government pensions. Smith was among the more prominent members of the group.[1]

It would appear that Smith was motivated to go north in part to be near the publishing houses of New York City. The soldier turned author devoted a substantial amount of time and energy to the writing of articles and full-length books after the war in the hope of publishing them commercially. Smith told General Daniel Harvey Hill that he knew something about publishing companies but his experience with them was very limited. Smith intimated to Hill that his works had been rejected by several publishing houses. A small consolation to Smith was the favorable recommendation by the companies on the historical value of his manuscripts but still they refused to take any commercial risk with them. Smith confided to Hill that all the books he had printed were done at his own expense with borrowed money.[2]

A low point in Smith's later years was the death of his wife in 1881, which left him in a depressed mood. It was a long time before he recovered from the loss of his helpmate and companion to whom he had been married for thirty-seven years. Doubtless, Smith's loneliness was made worse by the fact that no children were born of this union. Through times of torment and triumph, Lucretia Bassett Smith was always at the side of her husband. The couple wandered throughout the Confederacy, unable to call any one place home. The sacrifices of a soldier's wife were often equal to those of her husband. Lucretia was with General Smith or near him during the conflict and had her "full share of privation, hardship, and danger."[3] Lucretia Smith was interred in the Cedar Grove cemetery in New London, Connecticut. At the entrance was a Civil War monument of a Federal soldier.[4] Smith's letter to General Hill at Macon in early 1885 made a poignant reference to the death of his loved one. He wrote, "My wife died four years ago, and with her went out the light of my life on earth."[5]

Three years after her passing, Smith received word of the death of his close friend Mansfield Lovell, who died in New York City after a brief illness in June 1884, at the age of sixty-one. On this occasion, Smith penned a glowing tribute to Lovell for the Fifteenth Annual Reunion of the Association of the Graduates of the United States Military Academy. The friendship between the two former Confederate generals began during their days as aspiring soldiers at West Point. Smith remembered Lovell as a cadet "gifted with fine physical, mental, and social qualities, an independent and manly spirit ...." Both Smith and Lovell were prepared to participate in John A. Quitman's filibustering expedition against Cuba during the early 1850s. Intervention by the Federal government forced the cancellation of the campaign. During the mid-1850s, they had also worked together at the Cooper and Hewitt plant in Trenton. Smith and Lovell were comrades in both the Mexican and Civil Wars.

When Lovell resigned his military commission in 1854, Smith said, "He served more than sixteen years, and when he voluntarily withdrew from the army no officer of his age ... had a higher reputation, or was more esteemed." While serving as Smith's deputy street commissioner, Lovell carried out his duties with fidelity and competence. Lovell was a Democrat and along with Smith was in attendance at the historic Pine Street meeting of New Yorkers for the purpose of trying to avert the impending Civil War. Smith memorialized Lovell as a man whose "memory will ever be cherished by military men who have respect and admiration for manly courage, high capacity for command ... and self-possession in difficult circumstances."[6] In a letter to Hill, Smith wrote, "Lovell's death the 1st of last June, was a staggering blow to me. Our classmates are dropping off."[7] Smith and Lovell had shared many similar experiences including the label of unsuccessful Confederate generals.

Shortly after the publication of Smith's controversial *Confederate War Papers* in 1884,[8] he found himself engaged in an intellectual debate of an historical nature with James B. Fry,[9] reviewer of Smith's book. Fry emphasized that about one-fourth of Smith's volume was devoted to defending Lovell. He considered this excess inappropriate for an historical collection. In response to Fry's commentary, Smith countered, "I desire to say here that no part of the book under review was intended as a defense to anyone. General Lovell was then alive — in good health — and fully capable of defending himself."[10] The reviewer found it somewhat surprising that Smith disagreed with his critique so vehemently. In his defense, Fry conceded that Smith was clearly best qualified to judge what he intended, but not necessarily the best judge of whether the means had achieved the desired end. Fry was an educated officer who was experienced in war, however, Smith concluded that his critique was a poor reflection of this.

To say the least, Fry's critical review of *Confederate War Papers* angered its author. Interestingly, Smith had difficulty accepting criticism both as an officer and a writer. Another point on which Smith strongly disagreed with Fry was the latter's assessment of the conference held at the Fairfax Courthouse in Virginia in October 1861.[11] Fry contended that at the time of the conference, Generals Johnston and Beauregard were already harboring ill feelings for President Davis and Smith was friendly with all of them. According to Smith, Fry was simply inaccurate on this point. He maintained that Johnston was not opposed to Davis' presidential authority and the relationship between Beauregard and the Confederate leader was congenial and good natured. Smith admitted that he had long been on cordial terms with the two generals, but only slightly acquainted at that time with Davis. Smith noted that he remained friendly and hospitable to the Confederate President until his resignation in February 1863.[12]

Following the Fairfax meeting, Smith made a record of the proceedings. No doubt Smith's purpose for writing the memorandum was to fault the Confederate chief for not authorizing the offensive campaign and to deflect criticism from himself and his comrades at the meeting for not taking advantage of a promising opportunity to invade the enemy. On January 31, 1862, approximately four months after the conference, both Johnston and Beauregard signed a statement in which they fully agreed with the contents of the memorandum.[13] In reference to the statement signed by the two named generals, Fry believed that the document was secretly prepared by Davis' detractors and held by Smith to be used against the president should it prove beneficial. Fry was convinced that by January 1862, Smith had no doubt joined forces with Johnston and Beauregard in opposition to the Southern President. Smith asserted that in compliance with the two generals' request, he wrote the memorandum from his recollection of what had occurred at the October meeting. Smith said that the paper was signed in triplicate and each general retained a copy. In arguing that he had not joined with Johnston and Beauregard in January, Smith concluded that the controversy over the Fairfax memorandum would have to await the verdict "by the last court of appeal—the Tribunal of Impartial History."[14] The subsequent publication of the Fairfax conference document years after the war angered Jefferson Davis. The controversial letter placed responsibility for the inaction of the Confederate Army of the Potomac during the latter part of 1861 at the feet of Davis. It was not until 1880, while in the process of gathering information, records, and materials for his memoirs, *The Rise and Fall of the Confederate Government* that the former president learned about the extant minutes of that meeting. Since Davis had not required that notes be taken of the Fairfax conference, he believed the memorandum by Smith was written many years after the war.

Davis strongly disagreed with Smith's version of what had occurred at the council of war meeting in October 1861. According to him, Smith's report was marred by errors and inconsistencies. One of the major criticisms Davis had of the Smith report was the paraphrase of the Johnston letter that was sent to the War Department on September 26, 1861, as claimed by the three signatories. In fact, Davis questioned whether such a letter ever existed. He only wished that Smith had attached Johnston's letter to the memorandum. Another point of controversy was Smith's recommendation that called for "seasoned soldiers". Davis noted that if such a proposal had been made, it would have only served to reveal Smith's absurdity.[15] Davis concluded that Smith's paper was written to enhance the importance of the military in the Confederate government. Writing to Marcus J. Wright in October 1880 at Beauvoir, Mississippi concerning the Smith paper, Davis said, "It does not in some important respects agree with my recollection of what occurred, and is wanting in consistency, that infallible test of truth."[16]

In retrospect, Davis categorized the three generals at the Fairfax council of war as men who lacked both modesty and military experience. Davis argued that an experienced officer would not have recommended transferring troops from one location to another without first knowing how many were there. It was obvious that this not so subliminal criticism was directed toward Smith. The irascible and combative Kentucky general profoundly disagreed with Davis' invidious appraisal of himself and his two friends, all of whom had military experience equal to that of their Commander-in-Chief. Therefore, Smith could not understand why they were relegated by Davis. The three Confederate officers had gained valuable experience in General Winfield Scott's famous march from Vera Cruz to the Mexican capital. Each time Davis criticized the coterie of generals, he was in essence criticizing himself. After all, it was he who had appointed them to high command in the Confederate army and he who had traveled to Fairfax to be in conference with them in the fall of 1861.[17] Smith's *Confederate War Papers* was as much an attempt to exalt his military record as it was to take issue with Davis on several historical and personal events of the Civil War including the council of war meeting at Fairfax, the fiasco at Seven Pines, the question of promotion, and his resignation.

Smith was not the only former Confederate military leader who hurled invectives at Davis. Beauregard also bitterly denounced Davis' attempt to impugn the truthfulness and validity of Smith's memorandum. Beauregard stated that the letter was written while the meeting was fresh in Smith's mind and that at no time was an effort made to conceal the paper from Davis. The Louisiana general reminded Davis that he also had an opportunity to record the meeting for historical purposes. Beauregard maintained that the memorandum was not written for vindictive reasons or to embarrass Davis, but to preserve for posterity an important military event during the Civil War.[18] Of course, Davis saw it differently. Several years after the war, he complained to Wright that as Chief Executive of the Confederacy he should have had an opportunity to review the memorandum to make certain the proceedings of the famous conference were correctly documented. Davis believed the record of the meeting was made up to enhance the future reputations of Johnston, Beauregard, and Smith.[19] He was disappointed when he learned that the Smith memorandum including the endorsement of Johnston and Beauregard would appear in the *Official Records*. Davis lamented, "This settles the question as to the acceptance of that statement for publication." When it became obvious to Davis that his rebuttal to the Smith paper would not be placed among the official records, he concluded, "I am not the less sorry that my answer should not be in juxtaposition with the secret concoction of their laudatory ... production."[20]

Disagreement over the responsibility for the mismanagement at the battle of Seven Pines was the focal point of yet another dispute engaging Smith during the postwar years. The second party in the feud was James Longstreet. In 1891, Smith wrote a book entitled *The Battle of Seven Pines*[21] that restated much of what was documented a few years earlier in his *Confederate War Papers*. This was Smith's classic effort to absolve himself of any responsibility for the Confederate army's failure to achieve victory on the outskirts of Richmond in the spring of 1862. The incompetence of the Confederate generals was no doubt magnified in this the first great battle of the Peninsula campaign. For certain, there was more than enough fault to go around.

Smith placed much of the blame for the blunders at Seven Pines on Longstreet, whom he criticized for either misunderstanding or disobeying orders. Instead of approaching the enemy directly down the Nine-Mile road, Longstreet without explanation advanced down the Williamsburg road. Smith argued that failure to achieve victory was due to the lack of cooperation of the forces on the Williamsburg road. Smith claimed it was his mission to prevent the reinforcement of Union soldiers from the east side of the Chickahominy River. It should be noted that by then Longstreet, who had turned Republican, had become the favorite scapegoat of Confederate postwar writings.

Longstreet was determined to clear his name of the negative implication in the Seven Pines debacle. He accused Smith of failure to assist him and to make use of his artillery. Smith's strategical error was ordering an offensive without committing his entire force. He had placed a portion of it in a defensive position. Smith should have moved in with his whole force in an attempt to finish the battle. It was Longstreet's opinion that Smith had lost his fighting spirit after his bungling encounter with Major General John Sedgwick's division on the afternoon of May 31.[22]

Joseph E. Johnston's *Narrative of Military Operations* published in 1874, was an attempt to defend his war record and also a scurrilous attack on Davis. The book angered not only the former Confederate President but also his friend Smith, who was implicated by Johnston as the leading reason for the Seven Pines debacle.[23] Johnston always believed that had it not been for a stray bullet, he would have been able to lead the Confederate army to a decisive victory at Seven Pines. Smith disagreed with him, arguing that nothing more could have been achieved on the second day even if Johnston had been in charge. Smith noted that the Northern forces were united and their position was defended by strong entrenchments by June 1. General Erasmus D. Keyes who commanded the 4th Corps of McClellan's army at Seven Pines criticized Johnston for not attacking his right flank that was vulnerable throughout the battle. Keyes was certain that had Johnston attacked his right, his entire corps would have been destroyed or captured. Johnston's oversight was the Union army's good fortune.[24] Davis also joined in the polemics concerning the Confederate futility at Seven Pines. He said the battle was a series of blunders and all of the movements were to the last degree faulty.[25] One salient point about which there was no disagreement was that the fight at Seven Pines was hotly contested.

With the passage of time, Smith's delicate health grew progressively worse, so that by 1890 the sixty-eight year old Kentuckian had deteriorated to the point of being unable to perform active physical work. Despite his frailty, Smith found the strength to continue his writing. In 1892, he wrote a brief account of the roles of Generals Johnston and Beauregard at the first battle of Manassas. Smith had become acquainted with the major events of the battle during his stay in the neighborhood of Centreville in the fall of 1861. Smith noted that the historic battle made a lasting impression on him and stated, however, that he was "shocked and surprised" when he read an account of the battle in Johnston's *Narrative*. Drawing heavily from the *Official Records*, particularly the reports of Johnston, Smith concluded that Johnston was far too complimentary to himself in the first important battle of the war. And by exalting his record, Johnston in the process depreciated the well-earned reputation of General Beauregard.[26]

Smith's final piece of historical writing was the publication of *Company "A" Corps of Engineers* in 1896.[27] Because of its lesser known subject matter, this was undoubtedly Smith's greatest contribution. This book detailed the creation, recruitment, and training of the engineering company. It also chronicled the Company's distinguished service during the Mexican campaign for its reconnaissance work. With the death of Captain Alexander J. Swift in 1847, command of Company A devolved to Smith. Although Smith attempted to balance the story by writing equally of the accomplishments of others, he never failed to call attention to himself. One of the problems inherent in writing about oneself is the tendency to exaggerate successes and accomplishments while diminishing weaknesses and failures. Smith was generous with praise for George B. McClellan and appreciated the relationship that developed while McClellan was a student of his at West Point. Smith always admired his abilities as a military officer. Responding to a letter of inquiry about McClellan from M. S. O'Donnell in 1889, Smith wrote, "I would say that Genl McClellan was very highly respected, as a Military Commander, by me, and so far as I know, by the general officers of the Confederate Army."[28] At any rate, Smith did an admirable job of placing Company A within the proper historical context of the Mexican conflict. Favorable endorsements from General Scott and others in their official reports serve as evidence of the success of Smith and his Company during the war. Smith emerged from the Mexican campaign with a creditable reputation and the brevet rank of captain, showing promise of one day becoming an outstanding military leader.

ᘒᕙ

Although Smith's military record was by no means equal to his great promise, he excelled as a writer. Albeit Smith was not a trained historian, he was unquestionably a prolific author. The post-Civil War era witnessed a plethora of soldiers who recorded for posterity their experiences in the form of memoirs, reminiscences, narratives, and articles. Several general officers wrote to defend their records during the late war; others wrote to clear their names from association with a military fiasco. Smith was no exception in that he also fell prey to the temptation of writing to absolve himself of military embarrassment in his account of the battle of Seven Pines.

Smith's ability to combine individual facts and details with anecdotal stories, and his fundamental commitment to truth was perhaps his strongest asset as a writer. Smith was scrupulous in the interpretation of evidence and the application of critical analysis. Smith wrote on various subjects including events in which he had participated. He was blessed with the gift of communication, possessing the ability to express his views with force and clarity in a style that was lucid and persuasive. Though conscientious, Smith's writing was not devoid of biases, and he could be as caustic as he was judicious.

Smith wrote several articles for *Century Magazine*.[29] In some cases as with these articles, the hope of remunerative benefit was a motivating factor for writing. Smith used his connections among Confederate veterans to try to sell his books. Writing to Colonel Charles C. Jones, Jr. at Augusta after the publication of *Confederate War Papers*, Smith asked him to recommend it to his friends.[30] The pedantic Smith also sent two copies of his book, *The Battle of Seven Pines* to General Stephen D. Lee, one for his private use and one for the library of Mississippi State College of which he was president. In making the donation, Smith said, "I hope you will find time to read the book; and that it may interest you."[31] His books were not masterpieces or bestsellers, but they were important for their content and for comparison with contemporary works and future publications. Through comparison, one can gain an appreciation for the writings of Smith and an understanding of the political, social, and economic climate of the author's own time. In some ways, Smith's literary work stands among his greatest achievements.

During Smith's life, he won the respect and admiration of many of the most influential men in politics, business, and military life. A generous man who cherished friendship and cordiality, his loyalty and rectitude were of rare quality. Smith was a strong disciplinarian though not to the point of abusing the rights of others. He was sensitive to the difficulties of those who served under him in both military and civil pursuits. He recognized the potential of people whom he superintended and knew how to prod them to reach it to the benefit of them both. He did not attempt to seize the adulation deserved by others, but gladly bestowed compliments upon his subalterns. Smith's civil record was far more impressive than his military one. Wherever he labored, he left a lasting impression by the work accomplished. The duties of the many important offices held by him were performed honestly, competently, and with a Herculean effort. Smith, who had a strong aversion to corruption and dishonesty was, a man of lofty character.

To the very end, Smith's mind was clear and responsive, but his body showed the signs of physical weakness brought on by years of chronic sickness and heart disease. After an illness of several months, Smith peacefully passed away at his residence of 130 East 115th Street on June 23, 1896.[32] Smith's penurious condition, the death of his wife, and the lack of offspring may help to explain why he died intestate. This was uncharacteristic of a man who had possessed superb administrative talents and had always paid close attention to details. William B. Hawkins of Lexington petitioned the court to be appointed administrator of his deceased uncle's estate. Although Smith was blessed with longevity, he did not accumulate much wealth. He did not own real estate, and his personal property amounted to only $750.00. Smith's estate was divided among his seven nephews and six nieces.[33]

On June 27, Smith was buried in an unmarked grave beside his wife. In fact, the only reference to the Confederate general from Kentucky was on Lucretia's grave marker as her husband.[34] The death of Smith brought a tribute from his friend, C. Seaforth Stewart for the

Twenty-Eighth Annual Reunion of the Association of the Graduates of the United States Military Academy. Stewart remembered the old soldier as a "warm hearted genial friend." He continued:

> At an earlier date, it was my lot to be associated with General Smith for several years on duty, and thus to become much attached to him. His decision, firmness, justice and tact enabled him always to retain the confidence of those under him. The ties by which he held his intimates was very strong. His good deeds, not few in number, were done quietly.[35]

Gustavus Woodson Smith's seventy-four years were filled with a multitude of experiences. The Kentucky native had lived through and participated in some of the most historic and memorable events in the United States during the nineteenth century. Variety is perhaps the most adequate description of Smith's life which spanned almost three-fourths of the century. His influence touched many facets of American life. Few contemporaries left such an indelible imprint on the military and civil fabric of the nineteenth century with so much drama and conviction of purpose as did Smith.

Smith's life demonstrated how a youth from humble circumstances who received an important appointment to West Point could succeed through mathematical ability to become an engineer. And how through the Mexican War service could win a reputation that would bring him near the top of the Confederate high command in 1861. His problems there revealed the ineptitude of the Confederacy's method of making appointments and the weakening effect of petty quarrels over rank. Nonetheless, Smith figured in several significant military operations and in civilian life showed the important influence of military-trained engineers. The proud Kentuckian affected the life of both the North and the South.

# Notes

1. "Ex-Confederate Citizens of New York," *Confederate Veteran* 9 (July 1901): 307. By 1900 the Confederate Veteran Camp had more than 300 members.

2. Smith to Hill, January 14, 1885, Hill Papers, North Carolina Department of Archives and History, Raleigh.

3. *Encylopaedia of Contemporary Biography of New York*, 11 vols. (New York: Atlantic Publishing and Engraving Co., 1882) 2: 64.

4. *Frankfort State Journal*, February 13, 1955.

5. Smith to Hill, January 14, 1885, Hill Papers.

6. *Fifteenth Annual Reunion of the Association of the Graduates of the United States Military Academy at West Point, New York* (Saiginaw: Carrier Printing Co., 1884) 126. For a complete text of Smith's memorial, see pp. 113-26.

7. Smith to Hill, January 14, 1885, Hill Papers.

8. Gustavus Woodson Smith, *Confederate War Papers* (New York: Atlantic Publishing and Engraving Co., 1884). This book contains an appendix of letters from fellow officers and politicians supporting Smith during his many memorable controversial encounters with Davis.

9. Fry of Illinois, was a West Pointer, and a veteran of the Mexican and Civil Wars. In 1872, he resigned his commission in the U.S. army to devote more time to military writing. He died in Rhode Island in July 1894. See Ezra J. Warner, *Generals in Blue: Lives of the Union Commanders* (Baton Rouge: Louisiana State University Press, 1964) 162-63.

10. Gustavus Woodson Smith, "Reply to Fry's Review of Smith's Confederate War Papers," *Journal of the Military Service Institution of the United States* (New York: G. P. Putnam's Sons, 1885) 6: 158. Fry's original review of Smith's book was published in this journal.

11. Smith, *Confederate War Papers*, 13.

12. Smith, "Reply to Fry's Review", 160.

13. Smith, *Confederate War Papers*, 20.

14. Smith, "Reply to Fry's Review", 161.

15. Jefferson Davis, *The Rise and Fall of the Confederate Government*, 2 vols. (New York and London: D. Appleton and Company, 1912) 1: 450.

16. "Some War History Never Published: Famous Conference at Centerville When Question of Invading North was Settled," *Southern Historical Society Papers* 34 (January-December 1906): 136.

17. Smith, *Confederate War Papers*, 37-38.

18. Alfred Roman, *The Military Operations of General Beauregard, In the War Between the States, 1861 to 1865*, 2 vols. (New York: Harper and Brothers, 1884) 1: 140-41.

19. Davis to Marcus J. Wright, October 14, 1880, Jefferson Davis Collection, Western Reserve Historical Society, Cleveland.

20. Davis to Wright, August 6, 1882, Davis Collection. For a complete text of Smith's memorandum, see U.S. War Department, *The War of the Rebellion: A Compilation of the Official Records of the Union and Confederate Armies*, 128 volumes and index (Washington: Government Printing Office, 1880-1901), Series 1, 5: 884-87.

21. Gustavus W. Smith, *The Battle of Seven Pines* (New York: C. G. Crawford, Printer and Stationer, 1891). In a letter to Colonel W. Gordon McCabe after the publication of Seven Pines, Smith informed him of the many complimentary references he had received about his book. Smith was particularly appreciative of McCabe's favorable comments about his volume. Bound in cloth, the book sold for $2.00. See Smith to McCabe, October 23, 1891, Smith Collection, Virginia Historical Society, Richmond.

22. James Longstreet, *From Manassas to Appomattox: Memoirs of the Civil War in America* ( Philadelphia: J.B. Lippincott Company, 1896) 111.

23. Graig L. Symonds, *Joseph E. Johnston: A Civil War Biography* (New York and London: W. W. Norton & Company, 1992) 364-65.

24. Erasmus D. Keyes, "The Battle of Fair Oaks," Autograph Manuscript, 1889, 5. William P. Palmer Collection, Western Reserve Historical Society.

25. Davis to Lucius B. Northrop, April 24, 1879, William P. Palmer Collection.

26. Gustavus W. Smith, *Generals J. E. Johnston and G. T. Beauregard at the Battle of Manassas, July 1861* (New York: C. G. Crawford, Printer and Stationer, 1892) 6.

27. Gustavus W. Smith, *Company "A" Corps of Engineers, U.S.A. 1846-1848 in the Mexican War* (New York: The Batallion Press, 1896).

28. Smith to O'Donnell, May 6, 1889, Smith Collection, Western Reserve Historical Society.

29. The following articles by General Smith appeared in the *Century Magazine*: "Two Days of Battle at Seven Pines"; "The Georgia Militia about Atlanta"; and The Georgia Militia During Sherman's March to the Sea".

30. Smith to Jones, February 22, 1884, Smith Collection, William R. Perkins Library, Duke University, Durham.

31. Smith to Lee, June 6, 1891, Lee Papers, Southern Historical Collection, University of North Carolina, Chapel Hill.

32. *New York Times*, June 26, 1896. See also *Augusta Chronicle*, June 26, 1896.

33. Smith's Estate Records, Surrogate's Court of the City and County of New York, New York.

34. *Frankfort State Journal*, February 13, 1955.

35. *Twenty Eighth Annual Reunion of the Association of the Graduates of the United States Military Academy at West Point, New York* (Saiginaw: Seemann and Peters, Printers and Binders, 1897) 22.

# BIBLIOGRAPHY

## Manuscript Collections

Beauregard, P. G. T. *Papers*. Rare Book and Manuscript Library. Columbia University. New York.

_____. *Papers*. The South Caroliniana Library. University of South Carolina. Columbia, South Carolina.

Clingman, Thomas L. Papers. *The Southern Historical Collection*. University of North Carolina. Chapel Hill, North Carolina.

*Colcock Family Miscellaneous Papers*. William H. Courtenay, "A Tribute to Charles Jones Colcock," 1898. South Carolina Historical Society. Charleston, South Carolina.

*Jefferson Davis Collection*. The Western Reserve Historical Society. Cleveland, Ohio.

_____. *Papers*. Louisiana Historical Association Collection, Manuscripts Department, Tulane University Library. New Orleans, Louisiana.

_____. *Papers*. The William R. Perkins Library. Duke University. Durham, North Carolina.

_____. *Papers*. William L. Clements Library. University of Michigan, Ann Arbor, Michigan.

Hankins Family. *Papers*. The Virginia Historical Society. Richmond, Virginia.

Haskell, John Cheves. *Memoirs*. The William R. Perkins Library. Duke University. Durham, North Carolina.

Hawes, Richard. *Papers*. Special Collection and Archives, Margaret I. King Library, University of Kentucky. Lexington, Kentucky.

*Heth Family Papers*. The Virginia Historical Society. Richmond, Virginia.

Hill, Daniel Harvey. Papers. North Carolina Department of Archives and History. Raleigh, North Carolina.

*Hunter Family*. *Papers*. The Virginia Historical Society. Richmond, Virginia.

Jones, Charles Colcock, Jr. *Papers*. The William R. Perkins Library.

Duke University. Durham, North Carolina.

*Robert E. Lee Letter Book.* The Virginia Historical Society. Richmond, Virginia.

_____. *Papers.* The Southern Historical Collection. University of North Carolina. Chapel Hill, North Carolina.

_____. *Papers.* The Western Reserve Historical Society. Cleveland, Ohio.

_____. Misc. Mss. Wood, F. The New-York Historical Society. New York.

*John Quincy Adams Nadenbousch Papers, 1821-1867.* The William R. Perkins Library, Duke University. Durham, North Carolina.

*William P. Palmer Collection.* The Western Reserve Historical Society. Cleveland, Ohio.

*John A. Quitman Papers.* Box 4, Folder 12, Mississippi Department of Archives and History. Jackson, Mississippi.

*Schoff Civil War Collection.* William L. Clements Library. University of Michigan, Ann Arbor, Michigan.

Smith, Gustavus Woodson. *Amnesty Papers.* Record Group 109. National Archives, Washington, D. C.

_____. *Letters.* Dearborn Collection. The Houghton Library. Harvard University. Cambridge, Massachusetts.

_____. *Collection.* United States Military Academy. West Point, New York.

_____. *Collection.* The William R. Perkins Library. Duke University. Durham, North Carolina.

_____. *Collection.* The Western Reserve Historical Society. Cleveland, Ohio.

_____. *BV War 1861-1865.* The New-York Historical Society. New York.

_____. *Papers.* Ms 848, Hargrett Rare Book and Manuscript Library, University of Georgia Libraries. Athens, Georgia.

*Murray J. Smith Collection.* United States Army Military History Institute, Carlisle Barracks, Pennsylvania.

*James Ewell Brown Stuart Collection.* The Virginia Historical Society. Richmond, Virginia.

*Zebulon B. Vance Papers.* North Carolina Department of Archives and History. Raleigh, North Carolina.

# Archival Material

*Aztec Club Papers.* United States Army Military History Institute, Carlisle Barracks, Pennsylvania.

*Civil War Miscellaneous Collection.* United States Army Military History Institute, Carlisle Barracks, Pennsylvania.

Georgia. Adjutant and Inspector General. "Incoming Correspondence to Henry C. Wayne." Georgia Department of Archives and History. Atlanta, Georgia.

Kentucky Auditor. Kentucky Insurance Bureau. Auditor's Office. Boxes 44 and 70. Kentucky Department for Libraries and Archives. Frankfort, Kentucky.

_____. Report of Howard D. Smith. January 4, 1871. Kentucky Department for Libraries and Archives. Frankfort, Kentucky.

New York. Smith, Gustavus Woodson. Estate Records. Surrogate's Court of the City and County of New York, New York.

U. S. Treasury Department. Office of Construction. "Proofs of Office Letters." Roll 2. Record Group 121. National Archives, Washington, D. C.

_____. War Department. Adjutant General. "Appointment of Gustavus W. Smith to the Engineer Company." Roll 398. Record Group 94. National Archives, Washington, D. C.

_____. "Compiled Service Records of Confederate Generals and Staff Officers, and Nonregimental Enlisted Men." Roll 229. Record Group 109. National Archives, Washington, D. C.

_____. "Merit Roll of the Cadets of the United States Military Academy Showing the Results of the General Examinations in June 1839, June 1840, and June 1842." National Archives, Washington, D. C.

_____. "Monthly Consolidation of the Weekly Class Reports Including the Conduct Roll of the Cadets of the United States Military for September 1838." National Archives, Washington, D. C.

_____. "Qualifications for Admission to the United States Military Academy." Letters Received. Records of the Adjutant General's Office. Record Group 94. National Archives, Washington, D. C.

_____. "Report of Gustavus W. Smith's Company of Engineers in the action at Churubusco in the afternoon of August 2, 1847." Roll 359. Record Group 94. National Archives, Washington, D. C.

_____. "United States Military Academy Cadet Application Papers, 1805-1866." Record Group 688. National Archives, Washington, D. C.

_____. "United States Military Academy Weekly Class Reports, January 1835-December 1841." Records of the Office of the Adjutant General. National Archives, Washington, D. C.


## Government Documents

U. S. Congress, Senate. "Report of Alexander H. Bowman." Executive Doc. No. 2, 34th Congress, 1st session, vol. 12, 1856.

_____. "Report of the Secretary of the Treasury, James B. Guthrie." Executive Doc. No. 2, 33rd Congress, 1st session, vol. 10, 1853.

_____. "Report of General Winfield Scott." Executive Doc. No. 1, 30th Congress, 1st session, 1847.

_____. "Report of Gustavus W. Smith." Appendix. Executive Doc. No. 1, 30th Congress, 1st session, 1847.

_____. "Report of General Persifer F. Smith." Executive Doc. No. 1, 30th Congress, 1st session, 1847.

_____. "Report of Colonel Joseph G. Totten." Executive Doc. No. 1, 30th Congress, 1st session, 1847.

U. S. War Department. Adjutant General. "Confederate Papers Relating to Citizens or Business Firms." Microcopy 346, Roll 287. Record Group 109. National Archives, Washington, D. C.

_____. "War Department Collection of Confederate Records." Record Group 109. National Archives, Washington, D. C.

U. S. War Department. *The War of the Rebellion: A Compilation of the Official Records of the Union and Confederate Armies.* 128 vols. and Index. Washington, D. C. Government Printing Office, 1880-1901.


## Newspapers

*Augusta Chronicle,* 1896.
*Daily Constitutionalist,* (Augusta), 1864.
*Frankfort State Journal,* 1955.
*Georgia Journal and Messenger,* (Macon), 1864.
*The Macon Daily Telegraph,* 1864.
*Mobile Advertiser and Register,* 1862.

*New York Herald*, 1861-62.
*New York Journal of Commerce*, 1860.
*New York Times*, 1858, 1859, 1860, 1863, 1871, 1874, 1881, 1896, 1903, 1905.
*New York Tribune*, 1846, 1858, 1859, 1860, 1861, 1875, 1894.
*Richmond Dispatch*, 1861-62.
*Richmond Examiner*, 1862.
*Savannah Republican*, 1864.
*The Southern Confederacy*, (Atlanta), 1864.
*Sunday News* (Charleston), 1899.
*Weekly Chronicle and Sentinel*, (Augusta), 1864.

## Books and Articles

Abercrombie, John J. "Battle of Honey Hill." *Confederate Veteran* 22 (October 1914): 452-54.

Alexander, William. *The Life Insurance Company*. New York and London: D. Appleton and Company, 1905.

Anderson, Archer. "Campaign and Battle of Chickamauga." *Southern Historical Society Papers* 9 (September 1881): 385-418.

Armistead, Drury L. "The Battle in which General Johnston was Wounded." *Southern Historical Society Papers* 18 (January-December 1890): 185-88.

Avery, Isaac W. *The History of the State of Georgia from 1850 to 1881*. New York: Brown and Derby Publishers, 1881; reprinted. New York: AMS Press Inc., 1972.

Barber, John W. *Connecticut Historical Collections*. New Haven: Durrie, Peck, and Barber, 1836.

Barney, William. *The Road to Secession: A New Perspective on the Old South*. With a Foreword by James P. Shenton. New York: Praeger Publishers, 1972.

Barnwell, Robert W. "The Battle of Seven Pines." *Confederate Veteran* 36 (February 1928): 58-61.

Barrett, John G. *The Civil War in North Carolina*. Chapel Hill: University of North Carolina Press, 1963.

————. *Sherman's March Through the Carolinas*. Chapel Hill: University of North Carolina Press, 1956.

Black, Robert C. *The Railroads of the Confederacy*. Chapel Hill: University of North Carolina Press, 1952.

Boatner, Mark Mayo. *The Civil War Dictionary.* New York: David McKay Company, Inc., 1959.

Booth, Mary L. *History of the City of New York: From Its Earliest Settlement to the Present Time.* New York: W.R.C. Clark and Meeker, 1859.

Bragg, William Harris. *Joe Brown's Army: The Georgia State Line, 1862-1865.* Macon: Mercer University Press, 1987.

_____. "A Little Battle at Griswoldville: A Rough Stop on the March to the Sea." *Civil War Times Illustrated* 19 (November 1980): 44-49.

Brent, Joseph L. *Memoirs of the War Between the States.* New Orleans: Fontana Printing Co., 1940.

Brown, Charles H. *Agents of Manifest Destiny: The Lives and Times of Filibusters.* Chapel Hill: University of North Carolina Press, 1980.

Brummer, Sidney D. *Political History of New York State During the Period of the Civil War.* New York: Longmans, Green and Company, 1911.

Bryan, T. Conn. *Confederate Georgia.* Athens: The University of Georgia Press, 1953.

Buley, Roscoe C. *The American Life Convention 1906-1952: A Study in the History of Life Insurance.* 2 vols. New York: Appleton-Century-Crafts, Inc., 1953.

Burn, Duncan. *The Economic History of Steelmaking, 1867-1939: A Study in Competition.* Cambridge: The University Press, 1940; reprinted 1961.

Carroll, Howard. *Twelve Americans: Their Lives and Times.* New York: Harper and Brothers, 1883.

Caulkins, Frances M. *History of New London, Connecticut.* New London: Published by the Author, 1852.

Castel, Albert. *Decision In The West: The Atlanta Campaign of 1864.* Lawrence: University Press of Kansas, 1992.

Chamberlain, Morrow. *A Brief History of the Pig Iron Industry of East Tennessee.* Chattanooga: Morrow Chamberlain, 1942.

Chapman, Herman H. *The Iron and Steel Industries of the South.* Birmingham: University of Alabama Press, 1953.

Childs, Henry T. "The Battle of Seven Pines." *Confederate Veteran* 25 (January 1917): 19-20.

Cisco, Walter Brian. *States Rights Gist: A South Carolina General of the Civil War.* Shippensburg: White Mane Publishing Co., 1991.

Claiborne, John F. *Life and Correspondence of John A. Quitman.* 2 vols.

New York: Harper and Brothers Publishers, 1860.

Clark, Victor S. *History of Manufacturers in the United States, 1860-1893*. 3 vols. New York: McGraw-Hill Book Company, 1929.

Clark, Walter E. ed. *Histories of the Several Regiments and Battalions from North Carolina in the Great War 1861-65*. 5 vols. Raleigh: Published by the State, 1901.

Courtenay, William A. "The Coast Defense of South Carolina, 1861-5: The Battle of Honey Hill." *Southern Historical Society Papers* 26 (January-December 1898): 62-87.

Cox, Jacob D. *The March to the Sea*. New York. Charles Scribner and Sons, 1906.

Cullen, Joseph P. *The Peninsula Campaign 1862: McClellan and Lee Struggle for Richmond*. Harrisburg: Stackpole Books, 1973.

Cunningham, Horace H. *Doctors in Gray: The Confederate Medical Service*. Baton Rouge: Louisiana State University Press, 1958.

Davis, Burke. *Gray Fox: Robert E. Lee and the Civil War*. New York: Holt, Rinehart and Winston, 1956.

Davis, Jefferson. *The Rise and Fall of the Confederate Government*. 2 vols. New York and London: D. Appleton and Company, 1912.

Davis, William C. *Jefferson Davis: The Man and His Hour*. New York: HarperCollins Publishers, 1991.

Denson, C. B. "William Henry Chase Whiting." *Southern Historical Society Papers* 26 (January-December 1898): 129-81.

Dew, Charles R. *Ironmaker to the Confederacy: Joseph R. Anderson and the Tredegar Iron Works*. New Haven and London: Yale University Press, 1966.

Dinkins, James. "Lieut. Gen. D.H. Hill." *Confederate Veteran* 38 (June 1930): 218-21.

Dorris, Jonathan T. "Pardoning the Leaders of the Confederacy." *Mississippi Valley Historical Review* 15 (June 1928): 3-21.

Dowdey, Clifford, and Manarin, Louis H. eds. *The Wartime Papers of R. E. Lee*. Boston and Toronto: Little, Brown and Company, 1961.

DuBose, John W. "Gen. Joseph Eggleston Johnston, C. S. A." *Confederate Veteran* 22 (April 1914): 176-77.

Easley, D. B. "Experiences at Seven Pines." *Confederate Veteran* 37 (April 1929): 130-31.

Eckenrode, Hamilton J. *Jefferson Davis: President of the South*. New York: The MacMillan Company, 1923.

_____. and Bryan Conrad. *George B. McClellan: The Man Who Saved the Union*. Chapel Hill: University of North Carolina Press, 1941.

Eliot, Ellsworth, Jr. *West Point in the Confederacy*. New York: G.A. Baker and Co., Inc., 1941.

Ellis, Edward Robb. *The Epic of New York City*. New York: Coward-McCann, Inc., 1966.

Emilio, Luis F. *History of the Fifty-Fourth Regiment of Massachusetts Volunteer Infantry, 1863-1865*. Boston: The Boston Book Co., 1894.

*Encyclopaedia of Contemporary Biography of New York*, 11 vols. New York: Atlantic Publishing and Engraving Co., 1882.

Evans, Clement Anselm. *Confederate Military History*. 12 vols. Atlanta: Confederate Publishing Co., 1899.

"Ex-Confederate Citizens of New York." *Confederate Veteran* 9 (July 1901): 307.

Fielder, Herbert. *A Sketch of the Life and Times of Joseph E. Brown*. Springfield: Press of Springfield Printing Co., 1883.

*Fifteenth Annual Reunion of the Association of Graduates of the United States Military Academy at West Point, New York*. Saiginaw: Carrier Printing Co., 1884.

Foner, Philip S. *Business and Slavery: The New York Merchants and the Irrepressible Conflict*. Chapel Hill: University of North Carolina Press, 1941; reprinted, New York: Russell and Russell, 1968.

Forman, Sidney. *West Point: A History of the United States Military Academy*. New York: Columbia University Press, 1950.

Freeman, Douglas Southall. *Lee's Lieutenants: A Study in Command*. 3 vols. New York: Charles Scribner's Sons, 1944.

French, Samuel G. *Two Wars: An Autobiography*. Nashville: Confederate Veteran, 1901.

Furber, George C. *The Twelve Months Volunteer*. Cincinnati: J.A.W.P. James, 1848.

Gaines, B. O. *The B. O. Gaines History of Scott County*. 2 vols. Georgetown: Frye Printing Co., 1957.

Gallagher, Gary W. ed. *Fighting for the Confederacy: The Personal Reflections of General Edward Porter Alexander*. Chapel Hill and London: University of North Carolina Press, 1989.

Gates, Paul W. *The Illinois Central Railroad and its Colonization Work*. Cambridge: Harvard University Press, 1934.

Govan, Gilbert E. and Livingood, James W. *The Chattanooga, Country,*

*1540-1976: From Tomahawks to TVA.* Knoxville: University of Tennessee Press, 1977.

Grabtree, Beth G. *North Carolina Governors, 1585-1958: Brief Sketches.* Raleigh: State Department of Archives and History, 1958.

Grant, Ulysses S. *Personal Memoirs of U.S. Grant.* 2 vols. New York: Charles L. Webster, 1885.

Harrison, Lowell H. *Kentucky's Governors.* Lexington: University of Kentucky Press, 1985.

_____. *The Civil War In Kentucky.* Lexington: University of Kentucky Press, 1975.

Hartje, Robert G. *Van Dorn: The Life and Times of a Confederate General.* Nashville: Vanderbilt University Press, 1967.

Hendrick, Burton J. *Statesmen of the Lost Cause: Jefferson Davis and His Cabinet.* New York: The Literary Guild of America, Inc., 1939.

Henry, Robert Selph. *The Story of the Mexican War.* New York: The Bobbs-Merrill Company, Inc., 1950.

Hess, Earl J. "Civilians at War: The Georgia Milita in the Atlanta Campaign." *The Georgia Historical Quarterly* 66 (Fall 1982): 333-45.

Hogan, William T. *Economic History of the Iron and Steel Industry in the United States.* 5 vols. Lexington, Toronto, and London: D. C. Heath and Company, 1971.

Hood, John B. *Advance and Retreat: Personal Experiences in the United States and Confederate Armies.* New Orleans: For the Blood Orphan Memorial Fund, 1880.

_____. "The Defense of Atlanta." *Battles and Leaders of the Civil War,* 4 vols. Edited by Robert Underwood Johnson and Clarence Clough Buel. New York: The Century Co., 1884; reprint ed. with an introduction by Roy F. Nichols. New York: Thomas Yoseloff Inc., 1956. vol. 4: 336-44.

Howe, Daniel Wait. *Political History of Secession: The Beginning of the American Civil War.* New York: The Knickerbocker Press, 1914.

Hudson, Leonne M. "Gustavus W. Smith and the Battle of Seven Pines." *Confederate Veteran* (March-April 1993): 15-23.

_____. "A Confederate Victory at Grahamville: Fighting at Honey Hill." *South Carolina Historical Magazine* 94 No. 1 (January 1993): 19-33.

Hughes, Nathaniel Cheairs, Jr. *General William J. Hardee: Old Reliable.* Southern Biography Series. Baton Rouge: Louisiana State University

Press, 1965.

Hughes, Robert M. *General Johnston*. New York: D. Appleton and Company, 1897.

"In Memoriam: General Joseph Eggleston Johnston." *Southern Historical Society Papers* 18 (January-December 1890): 158-216.

"Inaugural Address of President Davis at Montgomery Alabama, February, 1861." *Southern Historical Society Papers* 1 January 1876): 19-23.

Johnston, Joseph E. *Narrative of Military Operations, During the Late War Between the States*. New York: D. Appleton and Company, 1874.

————. "Official Report of Seven Pines or Fair Oaks." *Southern Historical Society Papers* 8 (December 1880): 235-38.

Jones, Allen and Malone, Dumas. *Dictionary of American Biography*. 11 vols. New York: Charles Scribner's Sons, 1931-1932.

Jones, Charles C. Jr. *The Battle of Honey Hill*. Augusta: Chronicle Printing Establishment, 1885.

Jones, James Pickett. *Yankee Blitzrieg: Wilson's Raid through Alabama and Georgia*. Athens: University of Georgia Press, 1976.

Jones, John B. *A Rebel War Clerk's Diary, ed. Earl S. Miers*. New York: Sagamore Press, Inc., 1958.

Key, William. *The Battle of Atlanta and the Georgia Campaign*. New York: Twayne Publishers, 1958.

Ladd, Horatio O. *History of the War with Mexico*. New York: Dodd, Mead, and Company, 1883.

Lash, Jeffrey, N. "Joseph E. Johnston and the Virginia Railways, 1861-62." *Civil War History* 35, No. 1 (March 1989): 5-27.

Livingood, James W. "The Tennessee Valley in American History." *The East Tennessee Historical Society's Publications* No. 21. (1949): 19-32.

Longacre, Edward G. *From Union Stars to Top Hat: A Biography of the Extraordinary James Harrison Wilson*. Harrisburg: Stackpole Books, 1972.

Longstreet, James. *From Manassas to Appomattox: Memoirs of the Civil War in America*. Philadelphia: J. B. Lippincott Company, 1896.

Luraghi, Raimondo. "The Civil War and the Modernization of American Society: Social Structure and Industrial Revolution in the Old South Before and during the War." *Civil War History* 18, No. 2 (September 1972): 230-50.

————. *The Rise and Fall of the Plantation South*. New York: New

Viewpoints, 1978.

Lynn, Bushrod W. "In The Battle of Manassas." *Confederate Veteran* 26 (May 1918): 192.

MaCall, George A. *Letters From the Frontiers.* Philadelphia. J.D. Lippincott and Co., 1868; Knoxville: University of Tennessee Microfilms, Reel #339.

Mack, Peter. *Peter Cooper: Citizen of New York.* New York: Duell, Sloan and Pearce, 1949.

Mackay, G. Reid. ed. *Cyclopedia of Insurance in the United States.* New York: The Index Publishing Company, 1949-50.

Maclean, Joseph B. *Introduction to Life Insurance.* 5 vols. New York: Life Office Management Association, 1951.

Mansfield, Edward D. *Life and Services of General Winfield Scott.* New Haven: H. Mansfield, 1852.

Marcuse, Maxwell F. *This was New York: A Nostalgic Picture of Gotham in Gaslight Era.* New York: LIM Press, 1965; reprint ed., 1969.

Marks, James J. *The Peninsula Campaign in Virginia or Incidents and Scenes on the Battle-Fields and in Richmond.* Philadelphia: J. B. Lippincott and Co., 1864.

Martin, David G. *The Peninsula Campaign, March-July 1862.* Conshohocken: Combined Books, Inc., 1992.

Maury, Dabney Herndon. *Recollections of a Virginian in the Mexican, Indian and Civil Wars.* New York: Charles Scribner's Sons, 1895.

May, Robert E. *John A. Quitman: Old South Crusader.* Baton Rouge: Louisiana State University Press, 1985.

_____. "Young American Males and Filibustering in the Age of Manifest Destiny: The United States Army as a Cultural Mirror." *Journal of American History* 78 (December 1991): 857-86.

McClellan, George B. "The Peninsula Campaign." *Battles and Leaders of the Civil War* 4 vols. Edited by Robert Underwood and Clarence Clough Buel. New York: The Century Company, 1884; reprinted with an introduction by Roy F. Nichols. New York: Thomas Yoseloff, Inc. 1956 vol. 2: 160-88.

McDonough, James Lee and James Pickett Jones. *War So Terrible: Sherman and Atlanta.* New York and London: W. W. Norton and Company, 1987.

McGuire, Hunter. "General Thomas J. Jackson." *Southern Historical Society Papers* 19 (January 1891): 298-318.

McIntosh, James T. ed. *The Papers of Jefferson Davis.* 5 vols. Baton Rouge: Louisiana State University Press, 1974.

McMurry, Richard M. *John Bell Hood and the War for Southern Independence.* Lexington: University Press of Kentucky, 1982.

Meade, George. *The Life and Letters of General George Gordon Meade.* 2 vols. New York: Charles Scribner's Sons, 1913.

Michie, Peter. *General McClellan.* New York: D. Appleton and Company, 1901.

Moore, Frank. ed. *The Rebellion Record* 12 vols. New York: D. Van Nostrand, 1868.

Morrison, James L., Jr. *The Best School in the World: West Point, the Pre-Civil War Years, 1833-1866.* Kent: Kent State University Press, 1986.

Mushkat, Jerome. *Fernando Wood: A Political Biography.* Kent: The Kent State University Press, 1990.

Myers, William Starr. *The Mexican War Diary of George B. McClellan.* Princeton: Princeton University Press, 1917.

Nevins, Allan. *Abram S. Hewitt: With Some Account of Peter Cooper.* New York: Octagon Books, Inc., 1935; reprint ed. 1967.

Nye, S. "James H. Wilson—A Profile." *Civil War Times Illustrated* 1 (May 1962): 40-41.

Parks, Joseph H. *Joseph E. Brown.* Southern Biography Series. Baton Rouge: Louisiana State University Press, 1977.

Patrick, Rembert W. *Jefferson Davis and his Cabinet.* Baton Rouge: Louisiana State University Press, 1944.

Patterson, Jerry. *The City of New York: A History.* New York: Harry N. Abrams, Publisher, 1978.

Patterson, Edwin W. *The Insurance Commissioner in the United States.* Cambridge: Harvard University Press, 1927.

Perrin, William Henry. ed. *History of Bourbon, Scott, Harrison, and Nichols Counties of Kentucky.* Chicago: O. L. Baskin and Company, Historical Publishers, 1882.

Peterson, Charles J. *The Military Heroes of the United States: With Narratives of the War of Independence, the War of 1812, and the War With Mexico.* 2 vols. Philadelphia: William A. Leary, 1848.

Pleasants, Samuel Augustus. *Fernando Wood of New York.* New York: Columbia University Press, 1948.

Pressley, John G. "Diary of Lieutenant-Colonel John G. Pressley of the Twenty-Fifth South Carolina Volunteers." *Southern Historical Society*

*Papers.* 14 (January-December, 1886): 35-62.

Ramsdell, Charles W. *Behind the Lines in the Southern Confederacy.* Edited and foreword by Wendell H. Stephenson. Baton Rouge: Louisiana State University Press, 1944.

————. "The Confederate Government and the Railroads." *American Historical Review* 22 (July 1917): 794-810.

Randall, James G. and Donald David. *The Civil War and Reconstruction.* 2nd ed. Lexington: D. C. Heath and Company, 1969.

Redkey, Edwin S. ed. *A Grand Army of the Black Men: Letters from African-American Soldiers in the Union Army, 1861-1865.* New York: Cambridge University Press, 1992.

"Robert E. Lee." *Southern Historical Society Papers* 18 (January-December 1890): 133-58.

Robins, Edward. *William T. Sherman.* American Crisis Biographies. Philadelphia: George W. Jacobs and Company, 1905.

Roller, David C. and Twyman, Robert W., eds. *The Encyclopedia of Southern History.* Baton Rouge: Louisiana State University Press, 1979.

Roman, Alfred. *The Military Operations of General Beauregard in the War Between the States, 1861 to 1865.* 2 vols. New York: Harper and Brothers, 1884.

Rowland, Dunbar. *Jefferson Davis, Constitutionalist: His Letters, Papers and Speeches.* 10 vols. Jackson: Mississippi Department of Archives and History, 1923.

Salley, Alexander S., Jr. "Captain Colcock and Some of His Descendants." *South Carolina Historical and Genealogical Magazine* 3 (October 1903): 217-41.

Sanborn, Alvan F., ed. *Reminiscences of Richard Lathers.* New York: The Grafton Press, 1907.

Sears, Stephen W. *George B. McClellan: The Young Napoleon.* New York: Ticknor & Fields, 1988.

————. *To the Gates of Richmond: The Peninsula Campaign.* New York: Ticknor & Fields, 1992.

Secrist, Philip L. *The Battle of Resaca: Atlanta Campaign, 1864.* Macon: Mercer University Press, 1998.

Sherman, William T. *Memoirs of William T. Sherman.* 2 vols. New York: Charles L. Webster and Co., 1891.

Shunk, William A. "The Services of Graduates in the Mexican War."

The Centennial of the United States Military Academy at West Point, New York 1802-1902. 2 vols. Washington, D. C.: Government Printing Office, 1904.

Slocum, Henry W. "Sherman's March From Savannah to Bentonville." *Battles and Leaders of the Civil War*. 4 vols. Edited by Robert Underwood Johnson and Clarence Clough Buel. New York: The Century Co., 1884; reprint ed. with an introduction by Roy F. Nichols. New York: Thomas Yoseloff Inc., 1956. 14: 681-95.

Smith, Gustavus Woodson. *Battle of Seven Pines or Fair Oaks*. New York: C. G. Crawford, Printer and Stationer, 1891.

_____. *Company "A" Corps of Engineers, U.S.A. 1846-1848 in the Mexican War*. New York: The Batallion Press, 1896.

_____. *Confederate War Papers*. New York: Atlantic Publishing and Engraving Co., 1884.

_____. *Generals J. E. Johnston and G. T. Beauregard at the Battle of Manassas, July 1861*. New York: C. G. Crawford, Printer and Stationer, 1892.

_____. *Notes on Life Insurance*. New York: D. Van Nostrand, 1870; reprint ed. 1876.

_____. "Reply to Fry's Review of Smith's Confederate War Papers." *Journal of the Military Service Institution of the United States*. New York: G. P. Putnam's Sons, 1885.

_____. "The Georgia Militia About Atlanta." *Battles and Leaders of the Civil War*. 4 vols. Edited by Robert Underwood Johnson and Clarence Clough Buel. New York: The Century Co., 1884; reprint ed. with an introduction by Roy F. Nichols. New York: Thomas Yoseloff Inc., 1956. vol. 4: 667-74.

_____. "The Georgia Militia During the Sherman's March to the Sea." *Battles and Leaders of the Civil War*. 4 vols. Edited by Robert Underwood Johnson and Clarence Clough Buel. New York: The Century Co., 1884; reprint ed. with an introduction by Roy F. Nichols. New York: Thomas Yoseloff Inc., 1956. 4: 697-99.

_____. "Two Days of Battle at Seven Pines." *Battles and Leaders of the Civil War*. 4 vols. Edited by Robert Underwood Johnson and Clarence Clough Buel. New York: The Century Co., 1884; reprint ed. with an introduction by Roy F. Nichols. New York: Thomas Yoseloff Inc., 1956. vol. 2: 220-63.

Smith, Justin H. *The War With Mexico*. 2 Vols. New York: The MacMillan

Co., 1919.

"Some War History Never Published: Famous Conference at Centerville When Question of Invading North was Settled." *Southern Historical Society Papers* 34 (January-December 1906): 128-43.

Stampp, Kenneth M. *And the War Came: The North and the Secession Crisis 1860-1861*. Baton Rouge: Louisiana State University Press, 1950.

Stiles, John C. "The Peninsular Campaign." *Confederate Veteran* 28 (June 1920): 212.

Strode, Hudson. *Jefferson Davis: Confederate President*. New York: Harcourt, Brace and Company, 1959.

Strother, D. H. *Illustrated Life of General Winfield Scott Commander-in-Chief of the Army in Mexico*. New York: A. S. Barnes and Company, 1848.

Tapp, Hambleton and Klotter, James C. *Kentucky: Decades of Discord, 1865-1900*. Frankfort: Kentucky Historical Society, 1977.

Taylor, Richard. *Destruction and Reconstruction: Personal Experiences of the Late War*. ed. Richard B. Harwell. New York, London, and Toronto: Longmans, Green, and Company, 1955.

Temin, Peter. *Iron and Steel in Nineteenth-Century America: An Economic Inquiry*. Cambridge: The Massachusetts Institute of Technology Press, 1964.

"The Medical History of the Confederate States." *Southern Historical Society Papers* 20 (January-December 1892): 109-66.

*The National Cyclopaedia of American Biography*. 63 vols. New York. James T. White and Company, 1944.

Thomas, Emory M. *The Confederate Nation 1861-1865*. New York: Harper and Row Publishers, 1979.

Trotter, William R. *The Civil War in North Carolina*. 3 vols. Winston-Salem: John F. Blair Publishing, 1989.

*Twenty-Eighth Annual Reunion of the Association of Graduates of the United States Military Academy at West Point New York*. Saiginaw: Seeman and Peters, Printers and Binders, 1897.

Urban, Chester Stanley. "The Abortive Quitman Filibustering Expedition 1853-1855." *Journal of Mississippi History* 18 (1956): 180-95.

Wakelyn, Jon L. *Biographical Dictionary of the Confederacy*. Westport and London: Greenwood Press, 1977.

Warner, Ezra J. *Generals in Blue, Lives of the Union Commanders*. Baton Rouge: Louisiana State University Press, 1964.

_____. *Generals in Gray, Lives of the Confederate Commanders*. Baton Rouge: Louisiana State University Press, 1959.

Watkins, Sam R. *"Co. Aytch,"* A Side Show of the Big Show. With a new introduction by Roy P. Basler. New York: Collier Books, 1962.

Webb, Alexander S. *The Peninsula: McClellan's Campaign of 1862*. New York: Charles Scribner's Sons, 1908.

Werner, Morris R. *Tammany Hall*. New York: Doubleday, Doran, and Company, Inc., 1928.

Wilcox, Cadmus M. *History of the Mexican War*. Washington, D. C.: The Church News Publishing Co., 1892.

Williams, T. Harry. *P. G. T. Beauregard: Napolean in Gray*. Baton Rouge: Louisiana State University Press, 1955.

_____. ed. *With Beauregard in Mexico: The Mexican War Reminiscences of P. G. T. Beauregard*. Baton Rouge: Louisiana State University Press, 1956.

Wilson, Harold F. *Outline History of New Jersey*. New Brunswick: Rutgers University Press, 1950.

Wilson, James Grant. *The Memorial History of the City of New York: From Its First Settlement to the Year 1892*. 3 vols. New York: New York History Company, 1893.

Wilson, James Harrison. *Under the Old Flag*. 2 vols. New York and London: D. Appleton and Company, 1912.

Wilson, R. S. "The Battle of Jenkins Ferry." *Confederate Veteran* 22 (October 1910): 468.

Wolfe, S. H. "State Supervision of Insurance Companies." *Annals of the American Academy of Political and Social Science* 26 (September 1905): 137-52.

Woodson, Henry Morton. *Historical Genealogy of the Woodsons and Their Connections*. Columbia: E. W. Stephens Publishing Co., 1915.

Woodward, C. Vann, ed. *Mary Chestnut's Civil War*. New Haven and London: Yale University Press, 1981.

Wright, William C. *The Secession Movement in the Middle Atlantic States*. Rutherford, Madison, and Teaneck: Fairleigh Dickinson University Press, 1973.

Wright, Marcus J. *General Officers of the Confederate Army*. New York: The Neale Publishing Company, 1911.

Yates, Richard. *The Confederacy and Zeb Vance. Confederate Centennial Studies Number Eight*. Tuscalosa: Confederate Publishing Company,

Inc., 1958.

Yearns, Buck., ed. *The Confederate Governors*. Athens: University of Georgia Press, 1985.

Younger, Edward, ed. *Inside the Confederate Government: The Diary of Robert Garlick Hill Kean*. New York: Oxford University Press, 1957.

# INDEX